5

Grammar Connection

CONTENT

SERIES EDITORS

Marianne Celce-Murcia

M. E. Sokolik

Cathleen D. Cake

HEINLE
CENGAGE Learning™

Australia • Brazil • Japan • Korea • Mexico • Singapore • Spain • United Kingdom • United States

Grammar Connection 5:
  Structure Through Content
Cathleen D. Cake

Series Editors: Marianne Celce-Murcia, M. E. Sokolik

Publisher: Sherrise Roehr

Consulting Editor: James W. Brown

Acquisitions Editor, Academic ESL: Tom Jefferies

Senior Development Editor: Michael Ryall

Editorial Assistant: Cécile Bruso

Director of Product Marketing: Amy Mabley

Product Marketing Manager: Katie Kelley

Senior Content Project Manager:
  Maryellen Eschmann-Killeen

Manufacturing Buyer: Betsy Donaghey

Production Project Manager: Chrystie Hopkins

Production Services: InContext Publishing Partners

Index: Alexandra Nickerson

Cover and Interior Design: Linda Beaupre

Cover Image: © Cristiano Mascaro/SambaPhoto/
  Getty Images

Credits appear on page 352, which constitutes a continuation of the copyright page.

Library of Congress Control Number: 2008920431

ISBN 13: 978-1-4240-0034-0

ISBN 10: 1-4240-0034-3

International Student Edition
ISBN 13: 978-1-4240-0037-1
ISBN 10: 1-4240-0037-8

Heinle
25 Thomson Place
Boston, MA 02210
USA

Cengage Learning is a leading provider of customized learning solutions with office locations around the globe, including Singapore, the United Kingdom, Australia, Mexico, Brazil, and Japan. Locate our local office at: **international.cengage.com/region**

Cengage Learning products are represented in Canada by Nelson Education, Ltd.

Visit Heinle online at **elt.heinle.com**

Visit our corporate website at **cengage.com**

Printed in the United States of America.
1 2 3 4 5 6 7 8 9 10 — 12 11 10 09 08

Contents

Using language grammatically and being able to communicate authentically are important goals for students. My grammar research suggests that students' mastery of grammar improves when they interpret and produce grammar in meaningful contexts at the discourse level. *Grammar Connection* connects learners to academic success, allowing them to reach their goals and master the grammar.

— Marianne Celce-Murcia

"Connections" is probably the most useful concept in any instructor's vocabulary. To help students connect what they are learning to the rest of their lives is the most important task I fulfill as an instructor. *Grammar Connection* lets instructors and students find those connections. The series connects grammar to reading, writing, and speaking. It also connects students with the ability to function academically, to use the Internet for interesting research, and to collaborate with others on projects and presentations.   — M. E. Sokolik

Dear Instructor,

With experience in language teaching, teacher training, and research, we created *Grammar Connection* to be uniquely relevant for academically and professionally oriented courses and students. Every lesson in the series deals with academic content to help students become familiar with the language of college and the university and to feel more comfortable in all of their courses, not just English.

While academic content provides the context for this series, our goal is for the learner to go well beyond sentence-level exercises in order to use grammar as a resource for comprehending and producing academic discourse. Students move from shorter, more controlled exercises to longer, more self-directed, authentic ones. Taking a multi-skills approach, *Grammar Connection* includes essential grammar that students need to know at each level. Concise lessons allow instructors to use the material easily in any classroom situation.

We hope that you and your students find our approach to the teaching and learning of grammar for academic and professional purposes in *Grammar Connection* effective and innovative.

Marianne Celce-Murcia
Series Editor

M. E. Sokolik
Series Editor

Welcome to Grammar Connection

■ What is *Grammar Connection*?

Grammar Connection is a five-level grammar series that integrates content with grammar instruction in an engaging format to prepare students for future academic and professional success.

■ What is the content?

The content in *Grammar Connection* is drawn from various academic disciplines: sociology, psychology, medical sciences, computer science, communications, biology, engineering, business, and the social sciences.

■ Why does *Grammar Connection* incorporate content into the lessons?

The content is used to provide high-interest contexts for exploring the grammar. The charts and exercises are contextualized with the content in each lesson. Learning content is not the focus of *Grammar Connection*—it sets the scene for learning grammar.

■ Is *Grammar Connection* "discourse-based"?

Yes. With *Grammar Connection,* learners go beyond sentence-level exercises in order to use grammar as a resource for comprehending and producing academic discourse. These discourses include conversations, narratives, and exposition.

■ Does *Grammar Connection* include communicative practice?

Yes. *Grammar Connection* takes a multi-skills approach. The series includes listening activities as well as texts for reading, and the production tasks elicit both spoken and written output via pair or group work tasks.

■ Why are the lessons shorter than in other books?

Concise lessons allow instructors to use the material easily in any classroom situation. For example, one part of a lesson could be covered in a 50-minute period, allowing instructors with shorter class times to feel a sense of completion. Alternatively, a single lesson could fit into a longer, multi-skills class period. For longer, grammar-focused classes, more than one lesson could be covered.

■ Does *Grammar Connection* include opportunities for students to review the grammar?

Yes. A Review section is included after every five lessons. These tests can also be used by instructors to measure student understanding of the grammar taught. In addition, there are practice exercises in the Workbook and on the website (elt.thomson.com/grammarconnection).

■ Does *Grammar Connection* assist students in learning new vocabulary?

Yes. The Content Vocabulary section in each lesson of *Grammar Connection* incorporates academic vocabulary building and journaling. In Book 1 this takes a picture dictionary approach. In later books words from the Academic Word List are used. This, along with the content focus, ensures that students expand their vocabulary along with their grammatical capability.

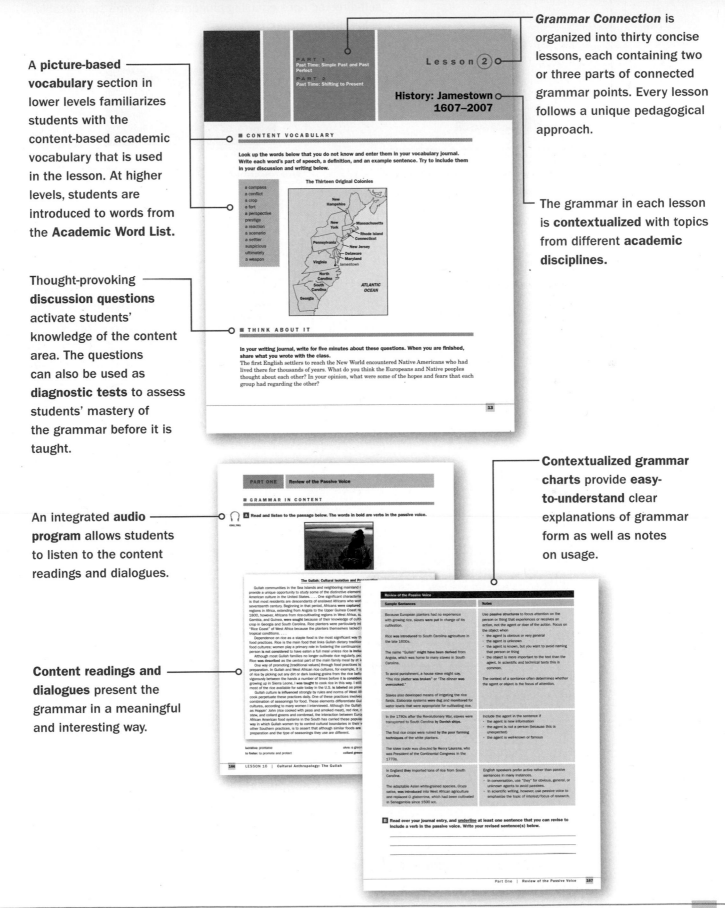

A **picture-based vocabulary** section in lower levels familiarizes students with the content-based academic vocabulary that is used in the lesson. At higher levels, students are introduced to words from the **Academic Word List.**

Thought-provoking **discussion questions** activate students' knowledge of the content area. The questions can also be used as **diagnostic tests** to assess students' mastery of the grammar before it is taught.

An integrated **audio program** allows students to listen to the content readings and dialogues.

Content readings and dialogues present the grammar in a meaningful and interesting way.

Grammar Connection is organized into thirty concise lessons, each containing two or three parts of connected grammar points. Every lesson follows a unique pedagogical approach.

The grammar in each lesson is **contextualized** with topics from different **academic disciplines.**

Contextualized grammar charts provide **easy-to-understand** clear explanations of grammar form as well as notes on usage.

B Change the sentences below to reported speech or thought, disregarding the source of the idea. Use the passive voice, begin each sentence with *It*, and choose the main verb according to the level of certainty of the information.

1. According to experts, animals in European cave art from the Paleolithic Age (32,000 to 11,000 years ago) may have lived in that area.

   It has been suggested that animals in European cave art lived in that area.

2. Researchers are fairly sure that the art also includes imaginary animals like unicorns.

3. There has been some discussion as to whether ambiguous symbols in the caves also represent animals.

4. According to one theory in the 1950s, the large number of paintings of horses and bison must have meant that these animals represented the duality of male and female.

5. According to anthropologists, the red pigment found in Paleolithic cave art has been found in art from the same period around the world.

6. According to one article, cave artists often redrew pictures on top of the old ones in order to guarantee that the animals returned the next year.

7. One researcher wondered if cave artists used red pigment in the paintings because it is aesthetically pleasing.

Guernica symbolizes the chaos and terror of the Spanish Civil War.

C Edit one of the sentences in each of the texts below, focusing on the information rather than the source of the information. Select main verbs that express the level of certainty of the information.

1. In addition to images, colors have various connotations. In all cultures people have words for at least three colors: black, white, and red. ~~The assumption of researchers is~~ *Humans are thought to have* ~~that all humans have~~ an emotional reaction to red since it is the color of blood. It may represent life, or as the color of sunrise and sunset it may connote the East or the West.

2. Images of imaginary or mythological creatures can be found in art throughout the world. Although a creature may be frightening to people in one culture, it may be very positive in another cultural context. For example, people interpret the bat as a sign of happiness in China whereas in the European tradition it is connected with darkness and black magic.

3. Groups of images and figures in some works of art may be allegories, or representations of abstract ideas. For instance, artists have often depicted "the four seasons" with four different flowers or other types of plants. Likewise, viewers realized that human or mythological figures represented the four seasons when they were shown doing seasonal tasks.

4. Pablo Picasso's black and white painting *Guernica* (1937) is a modern allegory protesting war. One can see that the work expresses Picasso's outrage at the Nazi's destruction of this Spanish town in 1937. As in a nightmare, the scene contains many images of panic and claustrophobia.

C Listen to each conversation, and then (circle) the letter of the correct interpretation.

CD2,TR4

1. a. Sam persuaded Kirk to photograph the team.
   (b.) Kirk persuaded Sam to be photographed.
2. a. The coach allowed Kirk to interview Jeff.
   b. Jeff was allowed to be interviewed.
3. a. Kirk encouraged Sam to help Jeff with his equipment.
   b. Kirk was encouraged to help Jeff.
4. a. The coach prompted Sam to introduce Jeff to the others.
   b. Sam was prompted to be introduced to Jeff.
5. a. Sam expected Kirk to pass him the first ball of the game.
   b. Sam was expected to pass Kirk the first ball of the game.
6. a. Sam doesn't permit Kirk to check his wheelchair.
   b. Sam isn't permitted to check Kirk's wheelchair.
7. a. Only the coach is authorized to load the wheelchairs in the van.
   b. The coach has authorized only one person to load the wheelchairs in the van.
8. a. This season the coach made Kirk captain of the team.
   b. Next season Sam will be made captain.

■ COMMUNICATE

D **GROUP WORK** What devices have been invented or refined to increase our mobility? Discuss the design, purpose, and benefits of these inventions. Use gerunds and infinitives with passive constructions whenever possible.

Elevators **were invented** to help people get to the top of a high building.

What about escalators? They **are used** for going up just one or two levels.

Nowadays there are even moving sidewalks, especially at airports. They **might have been invented** for people who can't walk, but lots of people use them because they're tired or want to move more quickly.

At the end of each lesson, students are encouraged to put together the **grammar and vocabulary** from the lesson in a productive way.

Interesting projects allow students to put newly learned grammatical forms and vocabulary to use in ways that encourage additional independent reading, **research**, and/or communication. Many of these activities are group activities, further requiring students to put their language skills to work.

Internet activities encourage students to connect the grammar with online resources.

A **Review** section after every five lessons helps assess and reinforce language learning.

A **Learner Log** encourages students to reflect on what they have learned and enhances learner independence.

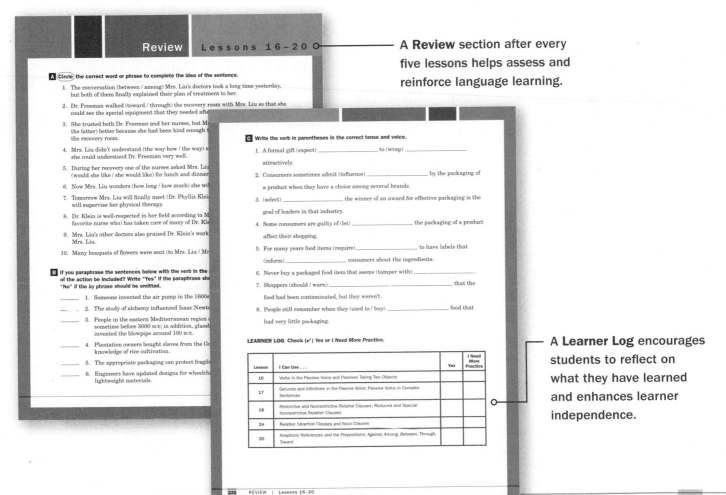

Connection Putting It Together

GRAMMAR AND VOCABULARY Write a composition on one of the topics below. Use as many words as possible from the Content Vocabulary on page 187, and (circle) them in your composition. Use sentences with nonrestrictive and restrictive relative clauses to express some of your ideas, and underline those sentences.

Topic 1: Throughout the centuries scientists have made discoveries that contradict people's perceptions of the world and religious teachings. This happened during the Scientific Revolution, and it is happening today. What is the responsibility of the scientists when their work goes against society's ethical, religious, or moral values? Use concrete examples in your writing.

Topic 2: Do people respect scientists and their work? What is the perception of scientists in popular culture, for example, in movies and on TV? How do the media treat scientists in your culture? Use concrete examples in your writing.

PROJECT Interview at least one student on your campus about his or her knowledge about prominent individuals from the history of science. Find out the following information, and report on it at your next class meeting.

1. Ask your interviewee about four to five of the scientists mentioned in this lesson. Report on how much information your interviewee knew about each one.
2. Ask how important it is to know about the scientists who made significant discoveries. If your interviewee thinks that it is important, find out why.

INTERNET Go online and use the search phrase "science quizzes" to find a website that has quizzes on various branches of science. Select at least one quiz, and take it. Report orally on your quiz results at your next class meeting.

Review   Lessons 16–20

A (Circle) the correct word or phrase to complete the idea of the sentence.

1. The conversation (between / among) Mrs. Liu's doctors took a long time yesterday, but both of them finally explained their plan of treatment to her.

2. Dr. Freeman walked (toward / through) the recovery room with Mrs. Liu so that she could see the special equipment that they needed aft...

3. She trusted both Dr. Freeman and her nurses, but Mi... the latter) better because she had been kind enough t... the recovery room.

4. Mrs. Liu didn't understand (the way how / the way) s... she could understand Dr. Freeman very well.

5. During her recovery one of the nurses asked Mrs. Liu... (would she like / she would like) for lunch and dinner...

6. Now Mrs. Liu wonders (how long / how much) she wil...

7. Tomorrow Mrs. Liu will finally meet (Dr. Phyllis Klei... will supervise her physical therapy.

8. Dr. Klein is well-respected in her field according to M... favorite nurse who) has taken care of many of Dr. Kle...

9. Mrs. Liu's other doctors also praised Dr. Klein's work... Mrs. Liu.

10. Many bouquets of flowers were sent (to Mrs. Liu / Mr...

B If you paraphrase the sentences below with the verb in the ... of the action be included? Write "Yes" if the paraphrase sh... "No" if the by phrase should be omitted.

_____ 1. Someone invented the air pump in the 1600s...

_____ 2. The study of alchemy influenced Isaac Newto...

_____ 3. People in the eastern Mediterranean region ... sometime before 3000 BCE; in addition, glassb... invented the blowpipe around 100 BCE.

_____ 4. Plantation owners bought slaves from the Gu... knowledge of rice cultivation.

_____ 5. The appropriate packaging can protect fragile...

_____ 6. Engineers have updated designs for wheelcha... lightweight materials.

C Write the verb in parentheses in the correct tense and voice.

1. A formal gift (expect) _____ to (wrap) _____ attractively.

2. Consumers sometimes admit (influence) _____ by the packaging of a product when they have a choice among several brands.

3. (select) _____ the winner of an award for effective packaging is the goal of leaders in that industry.

4. Some consumers are guilty of (let) _____ the packaging of a product affect their shopping.

5. For many years food items (require) _____ to have labels that (inform) _____ consumers about the ingredients.

6. Never buy a packaged food item that seems (tamper with) _____

7. Shoppers (should / warn) _____ _____ that the food had been contaminated, but they weren't.

8. People still remember when they (used to / buy) _____ food that had very little packaging.

LEARNER LOG Check (✔) Yes or I Need More Practice.

Lesson	I Can Use . . .	Yes	I Need More Practice
16	Verbs in the Passive Voice and Passives Taking Two Objects		
17	Gerunds and Infinitives in the Passive Voice; Passive Voice in Complex Sentences		
18	Restrictive and Nonrestrictive Relative Clauses; Reduced and Special Nonrestrictive Relative Clauses		
19	Relative Adverbial Clauses and Noun Clauses		
20	Anaphoric References and the Prepositions: Against, Among, Between, Through, Toward		

■ Audio Program

Audio CDs and Audio Tapes allow students to listen to every reading in the book to build listening skills and fluency.

■ Workbook

The Workbooks review and practice all the grammar points in the Student Book. In addition each workbook includes six Writing Tutorials and vocabulary expansion exercises.

■ Website

Features additional grammar practice activities, vocabulary test items, and other resources: elt.heinle.com/grammarconnection.

■ Annotated Teacher's Edition with Presentation Tool CD-ROM

Offers comprehensive lesson planning advice and teaching tips, as well as a full answer key. The Presentation Tool CD-ROM includes a PowerPoint presentation for selected lessons and includes all the grammar charts from the book.

■ Assessment CD-ROM with *ExamView®* Test Generator

The customizable generator features lesson, review, mid-term, and term-end assessment items to monitor student progress.

ExamView®
Test Generator

Grammar Connection is based on scientific research on the most effective means of teaching grammar to adult learners of English.

■ Discourse-based Grammar

Research by Celce-Murcia and Olshtain (2000) suggests that learners should go beyond sentence-level exercises in order to use grammar as a resource for comprehending and producing academic discourse. *Grammar Connection* lets students move from controlled exercises to more self-expressive and self-directed ones.

■ Communicative Grammar

Research shows that communicative exercises should complement traditional exercises (Comeau, 1987; Herschensohn, 1988). *Grammar Connection* balances effective controlled activities, such as fill-in-the-blanks, with meaningful interactive exercises.

■ Learner-centered Content

Van Duzer (1999) emphasizes that research on adult English language learners shows that "learners should read texts that meet their needs and are interesting." In *Grammar Connection* the content readings are carefully selected and adapted to be both high-interest and relevant to the needs of learners.

■ Vocabulary Development

A number of recent studies have shown the effectiveness of helping English language learners develop independent skills in vocabulary development (Nation, 1990, 2001; Nist & Simpson, 2001; Schmitt, 2000). In *Grammar Connection,* care has been taken to introduce useful academic vocabulary, based in part on Coxhead's (2000) work.

■ Using Background Knowledge

Because research shows that background knowledge facilitates comprehension (Eskey, 1997), each lesson of *Grammar Connection* opens with a "Think About It" section related to the lesson theme.

■ Student Interaction

Learning is enhanced when students work with each other to co-construct knowledge (Grennon-Brooks & Brooks, 1993; Sutherland & Bonwell, 1996). *Grammar Connection* includes many pair and group work exercises as well as interactive projects.

■ References

Celce-Murcia, M., & Olshtain, E. (2000). *Discourse and Context in Language Teaching.* New York: Cambridge University Press.

Comeau, R. Interactive Oral Grammar Exercises. In W. M. Rivers (Ed.), *Interactive Language Teaching* (57–69). Cambridge: Cambridge University Press, 1987.

Coxhead, A. (2000). "A New Academic Word List." *TESOL Quarterly,* 34 (2), 213–238.

Eskey, D. (1997). "Models of Reading and the ESOL Student." *Focus on Basics 1 (B),* 9–11.

Grennon Brooks, J., & Brooks, M. G. (1993). *In Search of Understanding: The Case for Constructivist Classrooms.* Alexandria, VA: Association for Supervision and Curriculum Development.

Herschensohn, J. (1988). "Linguistic Accuracy of Textbook Grammar." *Modern Language Journal 72(4),* 409–414.

Nation, I. S. P. (2001). *Learning Vocabulary in Another Language.* New York: Cambridge University Press.

Nation, I. S. P. (1990). *Teaching and Learning Vocabulary.* Boston: Thomson Heinle.

Nist, S. L., & Simpson, M. L. (2001). *Developing Vocabulary for College Thinking.* Boston: Allyn & Bacon.

Schmitt, N. (2000). *Vocabulary in Language Teaching.* New York: Cambridge University Press.

Sutherland, T. E., & Bonwell, C. C. (Eds.). (1996). "Using Active Learning in College Classes: A Range of Options for Faculty." *New Directions for Teaching and Learning, Number 67,* Fall 1996. San Francisco, CA: Jossey-Bass Publishers.

VanDuzer, C. (1999). "Reading and the Adult Language Learner." *ERIC Digest.* Washington, D.C.: National Center for ESL Literacy Education.

Acknowledgments

Special thanks to my family, friends, and colleagues who made it possible for me to devote my time to writing this book in the aftermath of Hurricane Katrina.

— *Cathleen D. Cake*

The author, series editors, and publisher wish to thank the following people for their contributions:

Susan Alexandre
Trimble Technical High School
Fort Worth, TX

Joan Amore
Triton College
River Grove, IL

Cally Andriotis-Williams
Newcomers High School
Long Island City, NY

Ana Maria Cepero
Miami Dade College
Miami, FL

Jacqueline Cunningham
Harold Washington College
Chicago, IL

Kathleen Flynn
Glendale Community College
Glendale, CA

Sally Gearhart
Santa Rosa Junior College
Santa Rosa, CA

Janet Harclerode
Santa Monica College
Santa Monica, CA

Carolyn Ho
North Harris College
Houston, TX

Eugenia Krimmel
Lititz, PA

Dana Liebowitz
Palm Beach Central High School
Wellington, FL

Shirley Lundblade
Mt. San Antonio College
Walnut, CA

Craig Machado
Norwalk Community College
Norwalk, CT

Myo Myint
Mission College
Santa Clara, CA

Myra Redman
Miami Dade College
Miami, FL

Eric Rosenbaum
BEGIN Managed Programs
New York, NY

Marilyn Santos
Valencia Community College
Valencia, FL

Laura Sicola
University of Pennsylvania
Philadelphia, PA

Barbara Smith-Palinkas
University of South Florida
Tampa, FL

Kathy Sucher
Santa Monica College
Santa Monica, CA

Patricia Turner
San Diego City College
San Diego, CA

America Vasquez
Miami Dade College, Inter-American Campus
Miami, FL

Tracy von Mulaski
El Paso Community College
El Paso, TX

Jane Wang
Mt. San Antonio College
Walnut, CA

Lucy Watel
City College of Chicago - Harry S. Truman College
Chicago, IL

Donald Weasenforth
Collin County Community College
Plano, TX

XV

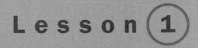

Lesson ①

Business Administration: Developing a Business Plan

■ CONTENT VOCABULARY

Look up any words below that you do not know and enter them in your vocabulary journal. Write each word's part of speech, a definition, and an example sentence. Try to include them in your discussion and writing below.

bankrupt	an entrepreneur	initiative	to persevere	to undermine
a commitment	a franchise	innovative	to signal	to undertake
crucial	inadequate	a line of credit		

■ THINK ABOUT IT

More and more people are starting small businesses. What ideas do you have for starting a new business? What type of business appeals to you? Do you see yourself as an owner of a small business? Discuss your ideas with a classmate.

In your writing journal, write for five minutes about the questions below. When you are finished, share what you wrote with the class.

What kinds of small businesses are there in your community? Which ones succeed and which don't? What is the key to running a successful small business?

■ GRAMMAR IN CONTENT

A Read and listen to the passage below. The words in bold in the text are present perfect verb forms.

CD1,TR1

Plan Your Work—And Then Work Your Plan!

Every year, thousands of Americans decide to go into business for themselves. Every year, thousands of small firms go out of business. Why? The reasons range from too much debt to too much stress. How do some entrepreneurs persevere and become successful? According to many business experts, the answer lies with a business plan.

Experts see the business plan as a crucial tool. On the basis of a well-prepared plan, an entrepreneur can convince a bank or other source of investment funds that he or she is the right person to undertake the hard work of starting up a new business. Also, the plan provides the prospective owner with a road map for assembling the key pieces of the business, including financing, personnel, and marketing.

Take Pat Newton, for example. She **has joined** more than 10 million women who run their own businesses in the United States. Until 2004, she worked for a large corporation in the wireless technology sector. Although she earned a lot, her private life suffered, so she decided to start her own consulting business. After many months of research, she put together a business plan for herself and quit her job. Since 2005, she **has developed** a list of clients and **has struggled** to make her business profitable. In the next year or two, she hopes to double or even triple her income.

Pat Newton's business plan **has played** an important part in her growing success. First, she has a clear idea of her business service since she **has worked** in the field for many years. Naturally, she **has had** business dealings with her competition, so she knows their strengths and weaknesses as well as her own. As a result, she **has found** a special niche for herself within the wireless industry. Second, as a self-employed person, she depends completely on her own skills and talents. She **has been** able to get advice and some financial assistance based on her track record with her previous employer. Third, her target market is essentially the same as the market she served before she quit her former job. Her previous clients **have continued** to give her projects or **have referred** her to potential clients in the field.

Will Pat Newton still be in business four years from now? According to statistics from the U.S. Small Business Administration, more than 50% of new small businesses fail within that amount of time. If Pat is going to be successful, she will need to pursue her dream with passion and persistence. Not everyone is willing to take such risks. Only those who thoroughly analyze their product or service, their management team, their target market, and their financial resources stand a fighting chance.

a niche: a special area or division of a market for a particular product or service

a track record: a record of successes or accomplishments

a target market: a specific market or group of consumers for a product

persistence: pursuing a goal in spite of difficulties and disappointments

a fighting chance: a possibility of succeeding

Sample Sentences	Notes
Experts **recommend** a detailed business plan for new business owners. Many promising small businesses **have gone** bankrupt as a result of poor planning. The owners of such firms **have believed** in their own effort, but **have not anticipated** unexpected circumstances that can seriously undermine a new business.	Use the **simple present** and the **present perfect** to express an idea or an action that has relevance in the present.
The U.S. Small Business Administration **has encouraged** an increase in the number of small businesses for years. It **offers** special loans at lower interest rates. Experts from this office also **advise** potential owners on strategies for growth.	Use the **present perfect** to express a time contrast within the present time. This choice of tense signals that the action or idea is still important to you or to the current situation. In the sample sentence, the **present perfect** introduces the topic, and the **present** gives more detailed information about that topic.
Mr. Peters: Advertising costs a lot at the beginning. You need to contact the bank for a line of credit to cover your advertising costs. **Have you had** any experience with that? **Ms. Owens:** I**'ve taken** out loans before but **I've never applied** for a line of credit. How does it work?	Use the present perfect in conversational questions. It "softens" the impact of personal questions while emphasizing the relevance of the topic to the present time. The answers to such questions are usually in the present perfect as well.
A business plan that includes a home office benefits stay-at-home mothers. **A few decades ago,** such a plan was quite unusual. **Now,** however, many people have realized the advantages of working from their homes.	Use an **explicit time expression** to signal a change from the present to past completed actions that are not relevant to the present situation. Also, use an explicit time expression to signal a switch from past time to present time.

B Read the text on page 2 again, and <u>underline</u> sentences in the past tense. (Circle) the time expressions that signal a change from the present to the past time. Then, compare your answers with a partner's.

C Using the present perfect, write five sentences about past experiences that have been relevant to your success in a job or business. If you do not have such work experience, write about another person you know.

1. _I have always been good in math, so I've done well in my summer jobs as a cashier._

2. _____

3. _____

4. _____

5. _____

6. _____

D Jim Kerr plans to start a smoothie franchise next year. (Note: A smoothie is a cold beverage made of different ingredients mixed in a blender.) Read Jim's résumé, and then, in the space provided, write the section of his business plan that describes his management and work experience. Share your first draft with a partner, then work together to create a final version.

Education
1998   B.A., University of Arizona, Majors: Political Science, Spanish
2005–   Student, Evening M.B.A. Program, Arizona State University

Work Experience
2006–   Assistant Director, Marketing Dept., Ideal Printing Company, Tempe, AZ
2001–06   Project Coordinator, Marketing Dept., Ideal Printing Company, Tempe, AZ
2000–04   Evening Manager, Stop-N-Go Convenience Store, Tempe, AZ
1998–2001 Assistant Manager, Barnes & Noble Books, Tempe, AZ
1995–98   Part-time Manager, Coffee Stop, University of Arizona

Volunteer Experience
1996–98   tutored children of Spanish-speaking migrant workers

I have gained the pertinent education and supervisory experience needed to manage my
own Slush-E-Treat franchise in Tempe.

_____

_____

_____

_____

_____

_____

_____

E Read each conversation below, and <u>underline</u> the verbs that show time changes. Then, look at the verbs you underlined and select the reason for the time change from the choices below. Follow the examples.

A = a time contrast within the present time. The action is still relevant.
B = a time contrast. The action is no longer relevant to the present time.
C = the introduction of a different topic relevant to the present time.
D = a question to confirm that the listener is following the conversation.

1.   **Jim:**   Thanks for meeting with me. I appreciate your time.

    Loan Officer: No problem. I have your loan application papers right here. <u>Have</u> you <u>applied</u> for a business loan with our bank before?   **A**

    Jim: No, I've only had a car loan. I <u>paid</u> that off about 2 years ago.   **B**

    Loan Officer: I see that in your records. How about a line of credit?

    Jim: I don't think so. I don't own a house and <u>have</u> always <u>worked</u> for someone else. I've never needed a large amount of money.   **A**

2.   **Jim:**   I need to decide on the site for my business. What do you think of the building down on Fifth Street?

    Rita: It's OK, but the neighborhood isn't too great. I like the one over on Howard Street better. Have you seen that one?

    Jim: No, I haven't.

3.   **Jim:**   Ms. Roberts, I'd like to make an appointment to see the shop on Howard Street. I drove by it yesterday, and I want to take a closer look.

    Ms. Roberts: What time is convenient for you? I haven't made any other appointments for tomorrow, so I'm flexible.

    Jim: Let's say 10 o'clock tomorrow morning.

    Ms. Roberts: Sounds good. The owner is eager to rent. He hasn't had a tenant in there for over a year.

    Jim: At this point I have to wait until the bank approves my loan. I haven't heard from them in a few weeks, but I guess that everything is OK.

F Respond to the questionnaire below, (circling) "Yes" or "No" to show which traits apply to you. Then, elaborate on each response, writing one or two sentences. Use the past, present, and present perfect in your responses. When you are finished, share your examples with classmates.

Are you a budding entrepreneur?
How many personality traits do you share with successful business owners?

Yes	No	possessing a strong desire to achieve
Yes	No	creativity
Yes	No	having strong personal initiative
Yes	No	having a demanding nature
Yes	No	adaptability
Yes	No	trustworthiness

1. _I have always had a strong desire to achieve. I've always tried my best, and I usually reach the goals I set for myself._

OR: _I have never cared if my work was perfect. I'm satisfied with a passing grade._

2. _____

3. _____

4. _____

5. _____

6. _____

G **PAIR WORK** Look at the pie chart below. Explain the data to your partner. Use the past, present, and present perfect as appropriate.

Ownership of Companies by Race and Ethnicity

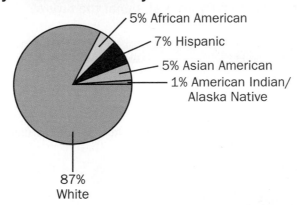

5% African American

7% Hispanic

5% Asian American

1% American Indian/ Alaska Native

87% White

According to the pie chart, Asian Americans and African Americans own the same percentage of small businesses.

Self–Employment by Gender, 1979–2003

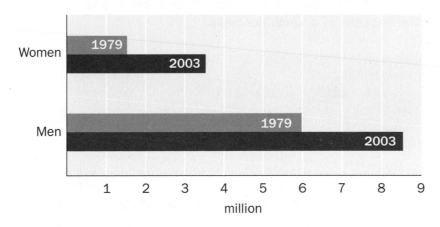

Women — 1979, 2003

Men — 1979, 2003

1 2 3 4 5 6 7 8 9

million

H **PAIR WORK** With a partner, discuss how graduates from your college or university get jobs. As you discuss the system, ask your partner some questions to be sure that he or she understands what you're saying.

We usually register with an employment agency that specializes in jobs for recent graduates. **Have you heard** of this kind of agency?

Yes, I have. We've got the same kind of agencies at my school, too.

■ GRAMMAR IN CONTENT

A Reread the text at the beginning of this lesson, and put an "X" by every sentence that expresses future time. Which verb form(s) signal the future?

Future	
Sample Sentences	**Notes**
Mr. Lewis has almost completed his marketing program and **is going to meet** with his advisor next week. Once the advisor gives his approval, Lewis **will present** the plan to his investors.	Use an **explicit time expression** to signal a change from the present time to the future.
According to the latest issue of *Business Quarterly,* the website MySpace has experienced double-digit growth since January and **will continue** at this rate well into the next quarter.	Use *will* in more formal contexts.

B Select seven characteristics of successful entrepreneurs from the box below. For each characteristic, write 2–3 connected sentences explaining why that characteristic is important for the success of a small business.

persistence	curiosity	~~high energy level~~
self-confidence	vision	reliability
tolerance for failure	problem-solving skills	independence
commitment	competitiveness	innovation

1. _Small business owners need a high energy level because they will handle all of the problems and complaints in their businesses as well as the daily routine. They will have to work from morning to night and maybe on the weekends, too._

2. _____

_____

3. _____

_____

4. _____

_____

5. _____

_____

6. _____

_____

7. _____

_____

8. _____

_____

C **Read while you listen to Jim Kerr's conversation with Helen, a new part-time employee at the Slush-E-Treat shop. Jim needs to plan Helen's training at his shop, so he has to find out her job skills. In the chart on the next page, take notes on Helen's skills.**

Jim: OK, Helen, we need to figure out your training plan. I'm going to give the information to Sara and she'll actually do the training in the next few days.

Helen: OK.

Jim: I remember from your interview that you used a cash register in your last job. How often did you ring up sales?

Helen: Not very often—only when the other salespeople were on lunch break.

Jim: You know that you will have to do it all the time for us, right?

Helen: No problem.

Jim: How about processing credit card payments?

Helen: Not many customers paid by credit card, and I never had to do that. They showed me how, but I never practiced.

Jim: OK, then Sara will work with you on that. Another important part of the job here is making sure that the customers have a positive impression, not just a good Slush-E-Treat. Whether they call or come into the store, I want each person to receive great service.

Helen: I think that I'm pretty good at that. I love to talk on the phone, so that part's no problem.

Jim: As long as you don't talk on the phone too much!

Helen: Don't worry. You know, I think I'm pretty good at talking with customers. My previous boss always complimented me. All of my friends say that I'm easy to talk to. I think that I can handle it.

Jim: But what about people who complain? How do you handle those customers?

Helen: I don't. I just call the manager, or I ask one of the other workers.

Jim: Around here, you might be alone sometimes. I don't want you to ask other people to handle your problems. I want to be sure that you know what to say. OK, last thing—the equipment. I don't expect you to know how to operate the machines now, but I need to know how comfortable you are with equipment like this.

Helen: As far as I can see, they don't look too complicated. If Sara shows me, I'll take notes on how to do it.

Jim: Sounds good. I'll have Sara contact you after we decide on the training schedule.

Helen: Thank you.

Skills	OK → Good	Inadequate
cash register		*training, but didn't use much*
phone etiquette		
credit card payments		
customer relations		
operating equipment		
teamwork		

D Now write a memo from Jim to Sara, the employee who will train Helen. In the memo tell Sara about areas where Helen's skills are inadequate and Jim's instructions for her training. The first sentence has already been written.

TO: Sara
FROM: Jim
DATE: June 10
RE: Training plan for Helen

Helen has had some retail experience with customer contact, so you will spend most of your time on the more technical aspects of her job.

_____

_____

_____

_____

_____

_____

_____

_____

E There are five errors in the e-mail message below. The first error has been corrected. Find and correct the remaining four errors.

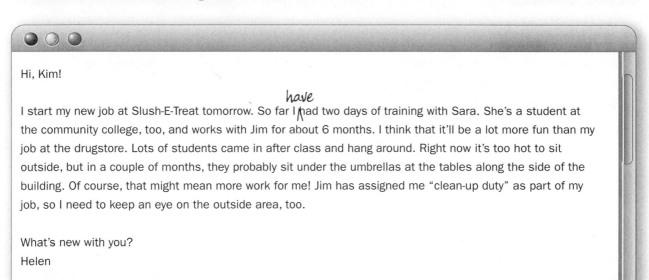

Hi, Kim!

I start my new job at Slush-E-Treat tomorrow. So far I ~~had~~ *have* two days of training with Sara. She's a student at the community college, too, and works with Jim for about 6 months. I think that it'll be a lot more fun than my job at the drugstore. Lots of students came in after class and hang around. Right now it's too hot to sit outside, but in a couple of months, they probably sit under the umbrellas at the tables along the side of the building. Of course, that might mean more work for me! Jim has assigned me "clean-up duty" as part of my job, so I need to keep an eye on the outside area, too.

What's new with you?
Helen

■ **COMMUNICATE**

F **PAIR WORK** Choose a business from the list below, and then compile a list of 6–8 questions to ask applicants for a job in that field. Role-play interviews for the job with a classmate.

Types of Businesses:
- retail
- hotel/restaurant
- medical/dental
- security
- publishing
- teaching
- computer programming

Have you operated a cash register before?

Yes, I used a cash register at my last job.

G **SMALL GROUP** Discuss customer service with your group and include the topics below in your discussion. Be ready to share your group's ideas with the class.

- In the U.S., there is the saying: "The customer is always right." Do you know any other proverbs related to business?
- What are some examples of good customer service? What do companies and employees do to provide their clients and customers with excellent service?
- Have you noticed good customer service in the shops and businesses in the town or city where you live? Have you been satisfied with the employees' behavior in the places where you shop? Why or why not?

GRAMMAR AND VOCABULARY Write a composition on one of the topics below. Use as many words as possible from the Content Vocabulary on page 1. Use verbs in the present time to express your ideas, and <u>underline</u> those verbs.

Topic 1: Every community has particular types of small businesses. What kind of business do you think is missing from your campus or in the place where you live now? Describe that business, and explain why it is a good idea to have that type of business where you are now.

Topic 2: Some business owners make a lot of money, but many self-employed people don't. In fact, many people start their businesses to gain independence and respect or to use their creativity, not to become rich. How have you balanced the need for money with your values, talents, and skills in thinking about your career choices?

PROJECT Interview at least one student who has a part-time job off-campus. Find out the following information and report on it at your next class meeting:

a. What kind of business? How many employees work there? How does the business treat the employees?
b. What is the target market for the business? How does the business advertise?
c. Has the student met the owner? What kind of business person is he/she? Does he/she manage the business effectively?

 INTERNET Go online, and use the search phrase "sample business plans" to find examples of business plans and executive summaries. Go to one of the websites and choose a business plan that interests you. In class, present an oral report on the product or service.

History: Jamestown 1607–2007

■ CONTENT VOCABULARY

Look up the words below that you do not know and enter them in your vocabulary journal. Write each word's part of speech, a definition, and an example sentence. Try to include them in your discussion and writing below.

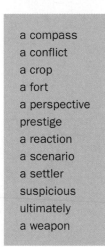

a compass
a conflict
a crop
a fort
a perspective
prestige
a reaction
a scenario
a settler
suspicious
ultimately
a weapon

The Thirteen Original Colonies

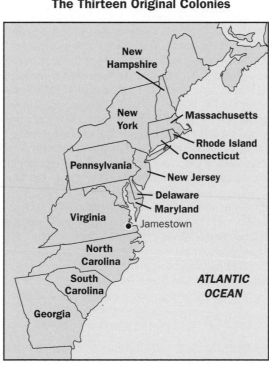

New Hampshire
New York
Massachusetts
Rhode Island
Connecticut
Pennsylvania
New Jersey
Delaware
Maryland
Virginia
Jamestown
North Carolina
South Carolina
Georgia
ATLANTIC OCEAN

■ THINK ABOUT IT

In your writing journal, write for five minutes about these questions. When you are finished, share what you wrote with the class.

The first English settlers to reach the New World encountered Native Americans who had lived there for thousands of years. What do you think the Europeans and Native peoples thought about each other? In your opinion, what were some of the hopes and fears that each group had regarding the other?

PART ONE | Past Time: Simple Past and Past Perfect

■ GRAMMAR IN CONTENT

A Read and listen to the passage below. The words in bold signal a time contrast.

John Rolfe

Pocahontas

Survival in Virginia

From the very outset, the officers of the Virginia Company intended that the settlers in their proposed colony should produce their own food, trade with the natives, and send back home a variety of vendible commodities, some exotic, others of their own manufacture. Virginia was a country where fruits, berries, game, and fish existed in profusion, and to the organizers of the colony their expectations did not seem unreasonable . . .

The first colonist to succeed in growing marketable West Indian tobacco was John Rolfe, formerly of Norfolk in East Anglia, who **had reached** Virginia from the Bermudas in 1610. His ship, *Sea Venture,* was blown aground there in a storm on the voyage out to Virginia, and several months passed before the survivors could build two pinnaces from the timbers of the wrecked vessel and proceed to the Chesapeake. During this delay, Mrs. Rolfe gave birth to a daughter, christened Bermuda, who soon died; the mother died shortly after they reached the colony. No man among the early English colonists of Virginia, not even Captain John Smith, contributed more, ultimately, to making the plantation a going concern or was so influential in giving direction to its destiny than the young widower.

On April 13, 1613, at the very time John Rolfe was raising his first good crop of tobacco, Captain Samuel Argall brought Pocahontas, the favorite daughter of Powhatan and niece of Opechancanough, to Jamestown as a prisoner and hostage. This "well featured but wanton [lively]" friend of Captain John Smith, called Matoaka by her own people, **had not visited** her English acquaintance since she saved the soldier's life five years before. Now she **had matured** and **blossomed** into an attractive young woman of eighteen or nineteen years of age. According to a report written two years before her death by Ralph Hamor, an intimate of Rolfe, the young planter **had fallen** in love with Pocahontas within a few months of her arrival in the English village, "and she with him."

Jamestown 1544-1699 © 1980, Carl Bridenbaugh, pg 34-35. By permission of Oxford University Press, Inc.

the Virginia Company: the British company that financed the Virginia colony

vendible: marketable, capable of being sold

aground: onto the shore

a vessel: a ship

a pinnace: a small sailing ship

christened: named

Captain John Smith: leader of the Virginia Colony from 1607–1609

a widower: a man whose wife has died

profusion: abundance

an intimate: a close friend

a going concern: a successful business

Sample Sentences	Notes
When English colonists **landed** at Jamestown, Virginia, they **built** a fort and **prepared** to plant corn. The Pasbehay Indians **had lived** in that area for centuries, and a major village of theirs was located nearby. Like other Native American tribes in this area, they **spoke** the Algonquian language and **had accepted** the Powhatans as chiefs years before the English arrived.	Use the **simple past** to tell about past events, situations, and conditions that are completed and remote to you now. Use the **past perfect** to tell about a situation or event that happened at an even earlier point in the past.
In the first year of the Jamestown settlement, the Powhatans and other tribes **cooperated** with the Englishmen. The settlers **learned** about native crops from them, and everyone **shared** local hunting and fishing grounds. The first permanent British colony **had finally taken** root in 1607, thanks to the efforts of these native people.	Use the **past perfect** in informal writing to express the purpose or climax of an event or situation in the **past**. In this context, past perfect does not express a time contrast. It signals the result or resolution of a situation.

B Read over your journal entry on page 13, and <u>underline</u> at least one sentence that you can revise to include a time contrast in the past. Write your revised sentence(s) below.

_____

_____

C Imagine you are a colonist in Jamestown, and that you have to write a report to the Virginia Company in England. Use the words in parentheses to describe what happened, including time shifts whenever possible.

1. (row ashore; return from trip up James River)

   May 14: <u>About noon the first group of men began to row ashore. We had returned earlier from our trip up the James River and decided that this area looked the best.</u>

2. (gather wood for campfires; shoot some rabbits and birds)

   May 14: _____

   _____

3. (cut down trees for fort; bring tools and supplies from the ships)

   May 15: _____

   _____

4. (see a group of Indians in canoes; prepare gifts for the Indians)

   May 15: _____

   _____

5. (unload other supplies from the ships; hunt for deer and other larger game)

   May 16: _____

   _____

6. (meet with Powhatan chiefs; travel to nearby Indian village)

   May 17: _____

   _____

D **Complete the final sentence in the passages below to express the results or resolution of the situation. The first exercise has been completed as an example.**

1. The English settled Roanoke Island in 1585, but all of those colonists died sometime between 1587 and 1590. They didn't have enough food, clothing, or tools. When the ships left England in 1607, *the colonists had planned better and had loaded the necessary supplies and equipment.*

2. The crews of the *Discovery,* the *Susan Constant,* and the *Godspeed* rowed ashore on May 14, 1607, with their weapons and basic tools. Each of the colonists was responsible for getting his personal items from the ship. By the night of May 17,

   _____

   _____

3. When the Powhatans saw the three English ships on the Powhatan River, they became worried. When the Englishmen started to build a fort, the Indians suspected that the Englishmen planned to stay in the Powhatans' territory. Within a month,

   _____

   _____

4. Opechancanough, who was the older brother of the Powhatan chief, went to Spain in 1561 with a group of Spanish sailors who were returning home from Cuba. There the young Indian man learned Spanish and had lessons about Christianity. By the time he returned to America in 1570, _____

   _____

E (Circle) the correct paraphrase of the sentences. The first one has been done as an example.

1. Indians in Virginia met the English with feelings of suspicion. They had already learned about European ways from the Spanish.

   (a.) Their suspicion of the English was based on their previous experiences with the Spanish.
   b. They felt suspicious of the English, so they felt that way about the Spanish, too.

2. When the Powhatan chief first met the English settlers, many Indians hid nearby with bows and arrows. They had observed that some of the Europeans carried guns.

   a. The Indians saw the Europeans' guns and then hid near the village.
   b. The Indians hid nearby, and as a result they saw the guns.

3. During the winter of 1609–1610, the settlers didn't have enough to eat because they hadn't grown enough food. Many of them lived with the Indians, who shared their food.

   a. Many of the settlers had lived with the Indians so they didn't grow enough food for the winter.
   b. Many of the settlers did not grow enough food to prepare for the winter, so they lived with the Indians who had enough food.

4. The bad relationship between the English settlers and Indians got worse, especially after the English had kidnapped Pocahontas.

   a. The relationship worsened, so the Englishmen kidnapped Pocahontas.
   b. The Englishmen kidnapped Pocahontas, and then the relationship worsened.

5. John Rolfe and Pocahontas had fallen in love, and then they married in 1614. The relationship between the Indians and the English improved after that.

   a. The relationship between the Indians and the English improved, so Rolfe married Pocahontas.
   b. Rolfe married Pocahontas, and then the relationship between the Indians and the English improved.

6. Tobacco from Virginia became very popular after Rolfe had sent his first crop to England. By 1617, tobacco was the only crop that people raised in the area.

   a. Rolfe's tobacco had grown very popular in England, so everyone planted this crop.
   b. Because Virginia tobacco had become popular in England, Rolfe planted this crop.

F **PAIR WORK** Talk about a time you first met someone from a different culture. What assumptions did you have about that person's country or culture? Were those assumptions confirmed, or did you change them as a result of getting to know that person? Use the simple past and past perfect as appropriate.

My friend Amos is from Nigeria. Before I **met** him, I **had never known** anybody else from Africa. Amos **told** me that the British **had colonized** Nigeria, and that's why English is an official language there.

| PART TWO | Past Time: Shifting to Present |

■ GRAMMAR IN CONTENT

CD1,TR4

A Listen as a Virginia Indian tells about his experience as a member of the 54-member delegation that went to England during the week of July 12, 2006. <u>Underline</u> the verbs that show a tense shift. Why do you think the speaker chose to shift tenses?

The Gravesend Festival

"After we arrived in Gravesend—you know it's a few miles southeast of London—we met all of the local officials in the town hall. It was incredible. They were wearing these long robes—just like in the movies. I guess that you can say the same about us with all of our feather headbands, leather clothes, and moccasins. Anyway, we presented our gifts, and the chiefs of the eight tribes danced the welcome dance and sprinkled tobacco on the ground according to our custom. After all of these centuries, it's amazing to think that we can meet together with the descendants of the men who changed the lives of all the native people of Virginia.

The next day we were all guests at the Gravesend annual multicultural festival. Some of the Virginians played music and others performed ceremonial dances for the crowds. This was the first time that any Native Americans had participated in their festival. It was a great event, but later in the day, they took us to see Pocahontas's grave at St. George's Church. We get out of the bus and walk around the church to the little cemetery—and there it is. Everyone just stands around the tomb silently. It was quite a spiritual moment.

On our last day we went to a seminar at the University of Kent. The professors there had organized a program for all of us to discuss the history and culture of the Virginia Native Americans in the last 400 years. A lot of people don't even know that there are any native people left in Virginia! We appreciated their interest and tried our best to present our perspective on colonial times and our opinions about the issues that face Native Americans who live in Virginia today."

Sample Sentences	Notes
"We **started** rowing down the James River, but at the bend we **saw** a Powhatan canoe. John **takes** his oars out of the water and **gets** his gun. Meanwhile, Joseph and I **turn** the boat toward the tall grass along the south shore."	English-speakers often start a story in the **past** tense, but then switch to the **present** when telling the main part of the story. In such contexts, speakers do not tend to use explicit time expressions to signal a shift in verb tense.
"After they **shot** Joseph with an arrow, John and I **hid** behind the trees and **waited** for them to come ashore. **It's** amazing what **flashes** through your mind at a time like that. It **seems** like time stands still."	Switching from the **past** to the **present** can make a story more vivid or lively. It also provides a way to comment on the situation or to give background information.
The Powhatans **were** suspicious of the settlers' expansion along the James River. By 1609, many families **had arrived** in Virginia, and the colonists **pushed** the Indians farther inland. The same scenario **repeats** itself throughout U.S. history as Europeans **take** possession of land that the Native Americans **view** as open for all to use.	In some academic writing, authors use a combination of **present** and **past** tenses. Typically, the past tense is used for real-life examples, and the present tense is used for comments or generalizations about the example.

B (Circle) the choice that tells why the speaker changes from the past tense to the present tense in each conversation. The first one has been done for you.

1. A: How was your trip to Hong Kong?
   B: I had never been to Asia before, so it was really interesting. It's the most interesting trip I have ever taken. I met so many friendly people who showed me around.

   a. shift from an example to a generalization
   b. shift from the story to a comment about the story
   c. shift to a lively style of telling the story

2. A: I had read about a church on the top of the mountain above Hong Kong, so I went to the tram stop at the bottom of the mountain. I'm standing there, looking at the ticket machine. An older Chinese gentleman comes up to me and helps me buy the ticket that I need. Then, he shows me where to get on the right tram. He actually ended up going with me and showed me the church and the other sights at the top of the mountain.

   a. shift from an example to a generalization
   b. shift from the story to a comment about the story
   c. shift to a lively style of telling the story

3. A: How did you like the food in Hong Kong?

   B: Luckily, one of the people that I'd met took me to a local restaurant. The food was great, but it was the first time that I'd ever eaten with chopsticks. It's a lot harder to eat with them than you might expect. It took me much longer to eat than it usually does.

   a. shift from an example to a generalization
   b. shift from the story to a comment about the story
   c. shift to a lively style of telling the story

4. A: Pocahontas went to London with John Rolfe and lived there for only one year. She died, probably of tuberculosis, in 1618. She is a famous example of how diseases that are common in one region can affect people who have had no contact with them before.

   a. shift from an example to a generalization
   b. shift from the story to a comment about the story
   c. shift to a lively style of telling the story

5. A: The colonists in Jamestown had few supplies from England, so they depended on hunting and gathering local fruits and vegetables until they could grow their own food. The Indians showed them how to plant native vegetables and gave them gifts of food so that they were able to survive. Regardless of language or culture, this kind of hospitality often saves the lives of newcomers.

   a. shift from an example to a generalization
   b. shift from the story to a comment about the story
   c. shift to a lively style of telling the story

6. A: My men and I were out hunting deer when a group of Indians captured us and took us to the Powhatan village. The chief himself comes out to see what's happening. I'm thinking that we're in very bad trouble when I remember that I have my compass in my pocket. I take it out and show it to the chief.

   a. shift from an example to a generalization
   b. shift from the story to a comment about the story
   c. shift to a lively style of telling the story

7. A: How did you escape from there alive?

   B: I thought that the compass was probably something new for the Indians. The chief looked at it and passed it around so that everyone could take a look at it. Thank goodness, I can speak some of their language. I told the chief how it worked and showed them how to use it. After that, he decided to let us go.

   a. shift from an example to a generalization
   b. shift from the story to a comment about the story
   c. shift to a lively style of telling the story

C Write the beginning of a story about one of the topics below. After you set the stage for your story, continue in a livelier style. Write only the beginning of the story (4–5 sentences) and stop at a suspenseful moment.

Topics:
- your arrival in a new place
- your first day at a new school or job
- the first time you ate something very strange

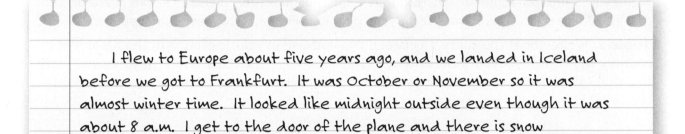

I flew to Europe about five years ago, and we landed in Iceland before we got to Frankfurt. It was October or November so it was almost winter time. It looked like midnight outside even though it was about 8 a.m. I get to the door of the plane and there is snow everywhere and the wind is blowing really hard. As I start walking

D There are five errors in the e-mail below. The first error has already been corrected. Find and correct the four errors that remain.

We landed in Prague at 9:30 last night but didn't get to the dorm till midnight. The baggage handlers ~~haven't~~ *hadn't* loaded the suitcases in the airport in Washington, so the luggage didn't arrive with us. (Hopefully, tomorrow!) When we got to the dorm, we had been so tired and hungry. The person there spoke only Czech, had given us the wrong room keys, and then had disappeared. Some people got pretty irritated and decided to go to a hotel. I guess that this is typical for an overseas experience, but it is hard for our first day.

■ **C O M M U N I C A T E**

E **PAIR WORK** Choose one of the statements below. Brainstorm some real-life examples of the statement and choose one. Prepare your example with as much detail as you can. Then, present it to your classmates. They will then decide which of the statements below is the appropriate generalization for your example.

a. Different beliefs or values can create misunderstandings or cause conflict between people of different cultures.
b. People who know the language of the other group gain power or prestige.
c. Body language can cause serious misunderstandings between people of different cultures.
d. People from different cultures may avoid contact with each other as a result of cultural misunderstandings.

GRAMMAR AND VOCABULARY Write a composition on one of the topics below, using specific examples. Use as many words as possible from the Content Vocabulary on page 13. Use verbs in the past time to express your ideas where appropriate, and <u>underline</u> those verbs.

Topic 1: Mark Twain, an American humorist and writer, said, "Travel is fatal to prejudice, bigotry and narrow-mindedness." Explain what this quotation means. Do you agree or disagree? Use specific examples from your past experience to support your opinion.

Topic 2: Write about the contact between two cultural or ethnic groups in the history of a country that interests you. How or why did they make contact? How did they live and work together? Were there conflicts between the groups? What caused misunderstandings and conflicts? Use specific examples.

PROJECT Interview a student on your campus who has studied abroad.

Find out:

   a. the student's first impressions of the place where he/she stayed
   b. the student's experience with local people in the market or supermarket
   c. an example of the student's opinion about the local people's customs or behavior

Be prepared to report on your interview at your next class meeting.

 INTERNET Go online, and use the search term "Powhatan clothing." Find and read information about clothing that Powhatan Indians wore at the time that the English arrived in Virginia. Are you surprised by this information? What were your assumptions before reading this information? How had you learned about Native American clothing and lifestyle before you looked at this material? Be prepared to talk about your expectations and your reactions in class.

Food Sciences: Biotech Crops

■ CONTENT VOCABULARY

Look up the words below that you do not know and enter them in your vocabulary journal.
Write each word's part of speech, a definition, and an example sentence. Try to include them
in your discussion and writing below.

an acid/a base	ethical	to germinate	to reap
an allergic reaction	to field test	manipulation	resistant
aware	genetic engineering	ongoing	unforeseen

■ THINK ABOUT IT

How are organic products different from conventional food products? What are the advantages
of organic food? Can you think of any disadvantages?

In your writing journal, write for five minutes about the questions below. When you are
finished, share what you wrote with the class.

Does your local grocery store sell organic products? What does "organic" mean in this
context? Do you ever buy organic food products? Why or why not? Discuss your ideas with a
classmate.

■ GRAMMAR IN CONTENT

A **Read and listen to the passage below. The words in bold are verb forms expressing future time.**

CD1,TR5

Food Options in Our Future

McDonald's, Starbucks, and similar companies are rising to meet the demand for food that is quick and convenient. Could there be any negative consequences of this trend? The world's population is becoming more urban, and experts worry that our eating habits **won't match** the availability of the food that farmers produce. What solutions **will** researchers **find** in order to deal with the demand for more nutritious food for more people on Earth?

Predictions about population growth are rather gloomy. According to the United Nations Population Division, the world's population **will continue** to grow until about 2050 when it **will reach** 10.5 billion. By that point, experts predict that life expectancy rates around the world **will have improved** and fertility rates **will have declined.** If those expectations bear out, the world's population **will have achieved** a replacement level; in other words, there **will be** no more net growth. What **will happen** to the percentage of Earth's land used for crops and pastureland as the population grows and then levels off?

Specialists in the fields of biotech engineering and agriculture are working on ways to increase the productivity of the land available for raising food. Researchers have observed that as people move into urban areas, their diets change to include a larger variety of fruit and vegetables and more protein from meat. Currently, farmers cultivate approximately 300 plants for human and animal consumption, but only 24 of those plants provide us with nearly all of our food. Farmers are changing their crops to match the demand for animal feed and are devoting more acreage to pasture. Given the increased land resources needed to support such food preferences, scientists are hoping that genetic engineering **will prove** to be a powerful tool to solve this global problem.

Researchers and advocates of genetic engineering **will persevere** in their efforts to increase agricultural productivity. So far, genetically engineered crops have developed many desirable characteristics. These transgenic plants **will yield** more crops per acre because they are resistant to disease, tolerant of extreme weather and of various soil conditions, and uniform in size and shape and, therefore, easier to harvest. Despite these improvements, many consumers and consumer organizations are highly critical of "genetically manipulated" food. They fear that such products **will have** unpredictable, long-term harmful effects on the environment and on people.

an acre: a measure of land (one hectare = 2.47 acres)

to bear out: to confirm

fertility rates: rate of births in a population

life expectancy: the average age of death according to population statistics

a pasture: grassland for domestic animals

Sample Sentences	Notes
Fewer people **will go** hungry in the next decades. **I'm going to contribute** to UNICEF to help feed children around the world.	Use *will* or *be going to* + verb to tell about an action, event, or situation in the future.
Researchers **will have field-tested** the new tomato crop for better texture by the time government officials review the research for approval next year.	Like the present perfect in a present context and the past perfect in a past context, use the future perfect (*will* + *have* + past participle) to express a prior time within a future context.
According to the United Nations, the percentage of hungry people in developing countries **will have fallen** to 10% by 2015.	Use the preposition *by* with the future perfect to express a deadline or point of completion for a future action.
Our Biology Department **is going to offer** a lecture series about ethics in biotech research. They'll **invite** some researchers from other universities. A representative from Greenpeace **will be included** in the series, too. I'll save you a seat at the lecture tomorrow. This lecture series **will be** extremely interesting. **I'm going to attend** all of the sessions—they're already on my calendar. The campus newspaper **is going to announce** each lecture two days in advance. Our speaker **arrives** around 10:00 A.M., so someone will have to pick her up at the airport and bring her to the meeting. At 11:00 A.M. **she's speaking** about biotech projects across our state.	Like the present perfect tense, the future form (*be going to* + verb) is often used to introduce a topic or to set the scene. In a narrative about the future, English speakers may use *will* or its contracted form ('ll) in the rest of the narrative in the future context. *Will* is used to make offers and promises and to make predictions about formal occasions in the future. *Be going to* shows more personal involvement or interaction. Use it for • predictions • plans • scheduled events The present and present progressive verb forms can sometimes express the future time. Use the **present** for scheduled events and the **present progressive** for scheduled activities that are a bit longer in duration.

B Read over your journal entry, and <u>underline</u> at least one sentence that you can revise to include a verb in future time. Write your revised sentence(s) below.

_____

_____

_____

C Imagine you write for your campus or local newspaper. Prepare a short article for the newspaper about an upcoming conference on biotech ethics. Use the information below.

Date/Time: Tuesday, 9:00 a.m.–12:00 noon
Location: Williamson Auditorium
Admission: Free with student ID card
Sessions/Topics:
9:00 Professor James Leonard, "The Dangers of Biotech Crops in the Third World"
10:00 Professor Michael Barnes, "Appropriate Labels on Genetically Engineered Foods in the Grocery Store"
11:00 Professor Julie Reagan, "Proper Testing of Genetically Engineered Crops"

D Complete the sentences below, predicting the outcomes of various types of transgenic food items.

1. When farmers raise tomatoes that all become ripe at the same time, _they won't need to hire tomato-pickers more than once._

2. When Hawaiian farmers plant papaya seeds that are virus-resistant, _____

3. When cotton farmers decide to plant varieties of cotton that produce their own natural pest-killing proteins, _____

4. When farmers plant soybeans with a higher protein content, _____

5. When farmers in developing countries raise crops of "golden rice" that should meet daily vitamin A requirements for rice-based diets, _____

6. When Mexican farmers raise drought-resistant maize, _____

7. When Colombian farmers plant maize that has been adapted to acidic soils, _____

E Select 3–4 criticisms of genetically modified (GM) crops in the notes below. Complete the paragraph below about future predictions.

GM plants
= herbicide-tolerant → undesirable plants (= weeds) may get
genes from nearby GM plants or seeds and
become harder to control = "Superweeds"

= genetically manipulated → organ damage in people or animals due to
toxic chemicals produced in plants,
unexpected allergic reactions to chemicals
in plants
– danger to local native plants
they may die out
– unforeseen danger to local animals and insects
their habitat may change

= insecticide-resistant → insects adapt easily to environmental
changes and may become resistant

According to critics of genetically modified foods, our world will probably change in many unforeseen ways if farmers continue to plant GM crops.

_____

_____

_____

_____

■ COMMUNICATE

F **GROUP WORK** Discuss the typical grocery store that you imagine you might find ten years from now. In this age of the global economy and world travel, what kinds of food items will we see in a typical grocery store? What will consumers expect? Will an urban store be considerably different from a rural one?

I think consumers are going to expect more choices.

They already have lots of choices. In the future, I think they'll expect more quality.

■ GRAMMAR IN CONTENT

A Reread the text at the beginning of this lesson, and (circle) the examples of verbs in the progressive aspect. Compare your results with a partner.

Review of Progressive Aspect

Examples	Notes
Farmers have been testing tomato seeds that should produce tomatoes of a uniform size. Local farmers are raising the transgenic tomatoes in fields next to their regular crops. Volunteers have been tasting the new crops of transgenic tomatoes to be sure that the tomatoes haven't lost any flavor.	Choose a progressive form of the verb to emphasize that an action is not yet complete or can still change. Progressive forms signal an activity still in progress or a temporary situation. Remember, stative verbs are rarely used in progressive aspect.
A good tomato tastes tangy and slightly sweet. Some gardeners raise tomatoes in big pots.	Use simple verb tenses to tell about a generalization, habit, fact, or situation that will not change or is complete.
My father was forever tending his tomatoes. He's always looking at seed catalogs and ordering new seeds for his big flowerpots.	In conversation, use present or past progressive to comment on behavior or actions.

B Read the statements below and label each with the correct interpretation of the verb in progressive aspect:

a. the action or activity is happening right now or was happening right then
b. the action extends over a period of time
c. the situation is temporary and can change

1. ___a___ Dr. Cho is checking some rice seedlings while Mark takes notes.

2. _____ Mark has been working in Dr. Cho's lab since he started graduate school.

3. _____ The seeds that Mark planted last week are starting to germinate.

4. _____ Dr. Cho has been researching several varieties of rice.

5. _____ She is now conducting a study on the effects of quicker germination in rice.

6. _____ When she came into the lab earlier, Mark was monitoring the seedlings.

7. _____ Since then, she has been supervising Mark's work but has to leave soon.

8. _____ Mark is working as a lab assistant to earn money during his studies.

C Complete each sentence with a verb from the box below. More than one correct form of the verb may be possible.

mention	~~practice~~	perform	examine
test	maintain	determine	develop

Since she hasn't done lab work in a long time, Dr. Petersen's new lab assistant Pat Furey _has been practicing_ (1) her lab techniques so that she doesn't skew the results of Dr. Petersen's new experiments on maize. Last week she _____ (2) the equipment in the lab and the notes on various ongoing experiments while Mark was preparing some new maize seeds for the experiments. She _____ (3) some new equipment when Mark knocked it over with a seed tray and broke it. Tomorrow when she meets with Dr. Petersen, she _____ (4) the incident because she is afraid that she'll be blamed for Mark's carelessness.

At Pat's meeting with Dr. Petersen, they discussed the new maize research at great length. In the course of the research, they _____ (5) a series of experiments to identify a gene that will make the maize more tolerant of poor soil conditions. Dr. Petersen _____ (6) a new hypothesis, and she needs to have meticulous records of each experiment. Pat _____ (7) records for each set of maize seeds. On the basis of Pat's records, Dr. Petersen _____ (8) the seeds that have low tolerance and will proceed with new experiments on the seeds with higher tolerance.

D Listen to an interview with two students at Yale who support their university's efforts to provide sustainable food in the campus cafeteria. As you listen, take notes on the various campus activities they describe. Then, summarize the ongoing activities by continuing the summary that starts below.

CD1,TR6

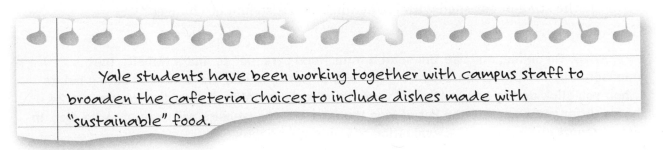

Yale students have been working together with campus staff to broaden the cafeteria choices to include dishes made with "sustainable" food.

E **PAIR WORK** Make a list of things that your school or community is doing to encourage sustainability. Sustainability includes not only food, but also all other actions to conserve Earth's resources and to act responsibly toward our environment. When you are finished, compare your list with the lists of your classmates.

Connection | Putting It Together

GRAMMAR AND VOCABULARY Write a composition on one of the topics below. Use as many words as possible from the Content Vocabulary on page 23. Use verbs in the future time where appropriate to express your ideas.

Topic 1: Many people fear a future in which scientists will manipulate genetic material in all kinds of organisms and thereby change our lives in unforeseen ways. How will we protect ourselves and our planet while also reaping the benefits of such groundbreaking research? Give concrete examples.

Topic 2: Many supporters of genetically engineered plants consider the natural world to be imperfect. Consequently, they see this kind of technology as a way to use their creativity to overcome problems and make the world better for future generations. Critics of transgenic plants often see nature quite differently—as a complete system that works perfectly well without human interference. How will we resolve these differences as we secure the food supply for the future? Give concrete reasons to support your position.

PROJECT Interview at least one student on your campus about the food available in the cafeterias or dining halls. Find out the following information and report on it at your next class meeting:

1. Does the student think that the campus food service offers enough healthy foods?
2. Is there any organic food available in campus cafeterias?
3. What does the student know about sustainable food?
4. Does your school offer advice on smart food choices and a balanced diet?
5. Is the student satisfied with his/her diet? What should be changed?

 INTERNET Go online, and use the search term "food pyramid" to find a website that is sponsored by the U.S. Department of Agriculture. Here you can evaluate your eating habits when you click on the box to "track" your diet. Create a profile of your diet for the last 24 hours. After you complete the list of food that you ate, the website will evaluate your diet. In class, report on the website's evaluation of your eating habits.

PART 1
Verb Review: Transitive,
Intransitive, and Middle Voice

PART 2
Verbs with Indirect Objects

Lesson 4

Journalism:
Sources of the News

■ CONTENT VOCABULARY

Look up the words below that you do not know and enter them in your vocabulary journal.
Write each word's part of speech, a definition, and an example sentence. Try to include them
in your discussion and writing below.

a briefing	to decline	to fare	an overview
to broadcast	to detach	a figure	a shelter
a deal	an evacuee	a news anchor	vis-à-vis

■ THINK ABOUT IT

How are news broadcasts on TV different from news broadcasts on the radio? How do they
differ from newspapers? In your writing journal, write for five minutes about the questions
below. When you are finished, share what you wrote with the class.

What sources of news do people use regularly? What is your favorite source of news? What
kinds of reports do you read or listen to? What are the advantages and disadvantages of
each source?

■ GRAMMAR IN CONTENT

CD1,TR7

A Read and listen to the panel discussion among journalists. The words in bold are verbs used intransitively.

Getting the Latest News

Moderator: Last week the Pew Research Center released its survey on the audience for Internet news and trends in newspaper readership. Richard, can you give us an overview?

R. Cotter: I think that most journalists were pleasantly surprised to learn that the amount of time Americans spend on the news **hasn't decreased** since 1996. The report indicates that Internet news has taken some of the audience away from traditional sources of the news—newspapers, TV, and radio. Americans over 25 still spend about 1 hour per day on the news.

Moderator: Henry Atkins, let's examine that demographic in more detail.

H. Atkins: Mike, Internet use among adults in the 25–64 age group **has grown** substantially in the last 10 years, vis-à-vis getting the news. It used to be that 18–25-year-olds made up a major part of the audience of Internet news sites. Now many more people over 25 appreciate the convenience of online news sites and log on to the Internet for business and international news in particular.

Moderator: How **have** news blogs **fared?**

H. Atkins: The percentage of young people who read news blogs **has risen,** but most online news consumers have never even read a news blog. Older Americans still prefer radio programs or the editorial page for opinions or commentary on the news.

Moderator: Richard, according to the report, fewer people get their news from newspapers and news broadcasts. How much **have** the numbers actually **declined?**

R. Cotter: The country's major newspapers and broadcast news outlets **have stabilized.** As you may **recall,** in the 90s the market for all of the traditional news outlets **dropped** alarmingly. Now, for example, newspaper readership has **leveled off.** This is primarily due to online newspapers. Most major newspapers offer readers an online version, hoping to attract new customers.

Moderator: So the figures for newspaper readership include online readers, too?

R. Cotter: That's right. And, I need to point out that the people who read online newspapers are a much smaller number than those who check the headlines out at CNN or MSNBC.

Moderator: Thank you, gentlemen. For those of you who want to read over the full report, you can go to our website.

a demographic: a portion of a population

substantially: to a great extent, significantly

an editorial page: the page of a newspaper with articles that express opinions

to level off: to become stable; to no longer change

Sample Sentences	Notes
A good editor **demands** accuracy from every reporter.	Transitive verbs are verbs with direct objects (*demand, cause, get, need, think through, look up, create*).
When a serious traffic accident **occurs**, a local TV reporter usually broadcasts from the scene. When TV reporters **set out** from the studio, they never know what might happen.	Intransitive verbs are verbs without direct objects (*seem, die, happen, set out, come back, stand out*).
The news anchor usually **opens** the broadcast with an overview of the stories. Our local TV news **opened** with a story about a local case of arson. Some vandals **burned down** an old barn. The weather has been so hot and dry that the barn **burned down** in 30 minutes.	Some verbs can be both transitive and intransitive (*end, change, drop, close; burn down, blow up, light up*). When intransitive, these verbs express a **middle voice** between active and passive structures. In such sentences, grammatical subjects do not take the role of the agent or "doer" despite the active form of the verb.
1. Porter **brought the weapon up** because he was curious about the lack of evidence in the case. 2. During the news conference, the reporter Ned Porter **brought up the missing weapon.** 3. The police chief was angry that Porter **had brought it up.** Porter **ran into** Chief Walker later and asked him again.	Many transitive phrasal verbs follow special rules for the order of the particle and direct object. If the direct object is a noun, use: 1. verb + noun + particle **OR** 2. verb + particle + noun But if the direct object is a pronoun, use: 3. verb + pronoun + particle NOTE: A small group of transitive phrasal verbs are not separable, such as *come across, get over, run into*.

Useful Transitive Phrasal Verbs That Are Separable

bring up	figure out	put/set forth	sum up
carry out	get/put across	read up on	work out
clear up	point out	rule out	write up

B Read over your journal entry, and <u>underline</u> at least one sentence that you can revise to include a verb that is used intransitively. Write your revised sentence(s) below.

_____

_____

_____

C Write "X" by each sentence with at least one verb that can be used both transitively and intransitively. Circle the verb. Follow the example.

___X___ 1. My Jetta (drives) really well, but I rarely drive it any more.

_____ 2. Fifty journalists were waiting when Air Force One landed at the Air Force base in Nebraska.

_____ 3. All of the journalists rose when the President entered the briefing room.

_____ 4. The news conference finished early.

_____ 5. Several of the reporters left even earlier.

_____ 6. Air Force One refuels after every flight as a security precaution.

_____ 7. After the news conference, the President immediately turned and walked out.

_____ 8. Back at the Air Force base, he boarded the plane and waved to the crowd.

_____ 9. Air Force One taxied down the runway and took off.

D Underline the verbs used intransitively in the news item below. Then, circle the verbs that can also be used transitively.

Houston—According to NASA scientists, communications with a Mars probe broke down late last week. Earlier an antenna had detached, and the signal from the probe weakened considerably. The probe was operating on energy from its solar packs, which have also partially shut down. Researchers had anticipated such problems if any part of the probe deteriorated or fell off.

E Edit the following article. Change the focus in each sentence from the agent of the action to the objects. Use intransitive verbs from the list below. You will not use all of the verbs.

| start | increase | burn | burn down |
| die | light up | end | ~~survive~~ |

Fifty houses survived

Griffin, OR—~~Firefighters saved 50 houses~~ in the eastern part of Griffin, Oregon, as fires burned another

500 acres of grassland outside town. In the past 2 weeks, fires have destroyed 25 homes in the area.

According to local fire officials, careless campers may have started the fires in a campground about 5

miles from Griffin. So far the fires have not killed anyone.

F **SMALL GROUP WORK** Imagine you work at a newspaper. Explain to your editor why you need an extension for your group project. Use all the phrasal verbs in the box for each excuse. An example has been provided.

| turn in | back up | hand out | plan out |

1. I'm sorry, but we won't be able to (turn our article in) tomorrow. When you (handed out) the assignment, our team met right away and (planned it out) very carefully. Unfortunately, Suzie's computer crashed, and she forgot to (back her interviews up.)

| figure out | leave out | read over | write up |

2. _____
_____
_____

| narrow down | check out | get through | come up with |

3. _____
_____
_____

| try out | read up on | work out | look up |

4. _____
_____
_____

G **PAIR WORK** Using as many phrasal verbs as possible, make a short, informal presentation on tips for a successful news conference.

At the beginning of a news conference, start by clearing up any confusion from the previous briefing.

■ GRAMMAR IN CONTENT

A Reread the text of the panel discussion on page 32, and <u>underline</u> examples of indirect objects. Compare your answers with a classmate's.

Verbs with Direct and Indirect Objects

Sample Sentences	Notes
Diana and her friends Irene and Owen follow the news, and Diana often sends Owen[I.O.] e-mail messages with commentaries from news blogs.[D.O.] She sent one [D.O.] to Owen[I.O.] last night. She e-mailed some other people[I.O.] the same information,[D.O.] but they didn't respond. She doesn't e-mail the blogs [D.O.] to other friends[I.O.] because they don't care very much about bloggers' opinions.	Some transitive verbs have two objects: a direct and an indirect object. For many verbs, for example *give, send, lend, bring, pay,* the order of objects depends on the information the speaker wants to highlight. 1. **Verb + Indirect Object (I.O.) + Direct Object (D.O.)** shows that: 　• the indirect object is already known or of less importance to the context. 　• the direct object is the focus of attention in the context. 2. **Verb + Direct Object + *to* + Indirect Object** shows that: 　• the direct object is already known or of less importance. 　• the indirect object is the highlight of the communication.
She promised him[I.O.] a list of her favorite blogs.[D.O.] She'll probably send it [D.O.] to anyone who is interested.[I.O.] She'll send it [D.O.] to us[I.O.] if you ask for a copy, too.	If either object is a pronoun, put the pronoun after the verb. Then, follow the rules above.
She explained her interest in the blogs [D.O.] to her friends,[I.O.] but they weren't interested. Did she mention the purpose of the blog [D.O.] to them?[I.O.]	For other verbs, such as *explain, mention, describe, say, announce,* only pattern 2. above is correct.
A friend of Diana's had found her[I.O.] a whole list of news blogs,[D.O.] so Diana made a copy of the list [D.O.] for Owen.[I.O.] She left it [D.O.] for him[I.O.] with a note on it. She saved it [D.O.] for some other friends,[I.O.] too.	Some verbs with two objects express an action done for somebody's benefit. (See the list of verbs below.) Use one of these two patterns: 3. **Verb + Indirect Object + Direct Object** 4. (Verbs that use *for* include *buy, cook, draw, find, get, leave, make, order, save, sew, spare.*) **Verb + Direct Object + *for* + Indirect Object**

B Each of these editorials has three errors in usage. Edit the awkward phrases, rewriting them to correct or improve the usage of indirect objects. Follow the example.

. . . according to recent reports, the Prime Minister approved the purchase of ten fighter planes. He shouldn't

order them for the military
~~order the military them~~ just as peace negotiations are beginning among the countries in that region. It sends the

wrong message to their allies. Instead the Prime Minister should promise a postponement of the airplane deal

---

…announced the creation of a new national monument around a chain of Hawaiian islands. We applaud this

decision, which sets aside 1,200 nautical miles of the Pacific Ocean to protect the fragile coral reef there. The

law saves the extensive reef to the native fish and sea mammals. Since the area is so remote, only a limited

number of tour operators will offer to visitors access to the monument. We urge all citizens to contact their

representatives and give positive feedback on the measure to them….

C Listen to each statement and (circle) the letter of the correct interpretation. The first one has been done as an example.

CD1,TR8

1. a. Jay didn't mention his children.
   b. Jay didn't mention his daughter.

2. a. The bookstore placed a textbook order for us.
   b. The bookstore told us that we had to buy copies of the textbook.

3. a. His supervisor found the mistake for him.
   b. His supervisor pointed at the mistake with her finger.

4. a. George took the newspaper out of the mailbox when he came in the house.
   b. George bought a newspaper for me when he came home from work.

5. a. I'll e-mail him about the new deadline.
   b. I'll e-mail her about the new deadline.

6. a. My editor read over the article and then approved it.
   b. My editor read the articles over and then approved them.

7. a. A colleague left the office and now I can't find his message.
   b. A colleague wrote a message to me and put it in my office, but it's lost.

8. a. I need to ask them more questions to finish the interview.
   b. I need to ask him more questions to finish the interview.

D On a separate piece of paper, write a 5–6 sentence report about relief efforts for evacuees of a recent typhoon on the island of Macao (off China). Focus on the efforts of local volunteers to assist the evacuees, who arrived with few possessions and must live in shelters for at least 2–3 weeks.

E Use the notes below to prepare a briefing for the press about the President's agenda for an upcoming trip. Complete the script for the briefing below, using verbs in the box.

promise	give	teach	show
~~offer~~	grant	assign	award

Monday:

10:00 meeting with Gov. Ortiz:	$15 million in federal funds for school construction
	$300 million increase in scholarships for minority students
12:00 Lunch Gov. & mayors:	"Most Improved School System" prize to Mayor Scott of Springfield
2:30 Central H.S.:	donation of 500 books to school library
	meeting with junior class and demonstration of software for scholarship applications

Ladies and gentlemen, on Monday, President Ryan will offer $15 million to Governor Ortiz for school construction.

F Use the notes and the verbs in the box to prepare another briefing for the press about the President's trip. Look at the example to see how one student got started.

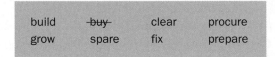

build	~~buy~~	clear	procure
grow	spare	fix	prepare

Tuesday:

Meeting with Mayor Nguyen about emergency planning

· promise to purchase emergency supplies for shelters at schools

· up to $200 million in federal funds available for school safety/construction

· models of "safe school" available from Corps of Engineers

· 10-year program: $10 million available annually for school infrastructure

The government will buy supplies for schools that operate as emergency shelters.

G Find and correct the four errors in the informal e-mail message below.

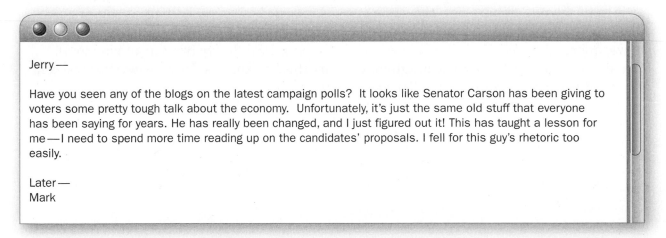

Jerry —

Have you seen any of the blogs on the latest campaign polls? It looks like Senator Carson has been giving to voters some pretty tough talk about the economy. Unfortunately, it's just the same old stuff that everyone has been saying for years. He has really been changed, and I just figured out it! This has taught a lesson for me — I need to spend more time reading up on the candidates' proposals. I fell for this guy's rhetoric too easily.

Later —
Mark

■ COMMUNICATE

H **SMALL GROUP/CLASS WORK** Write a story to be included in a newsletter about the people in your English class. Before you begin, decide about the items for the newsletter with your classmates, and choose a topic with your partner. Together, draft a short article (5–7 sentences) about the latest news in your class. Once you have finished your draft, give it to another team so that they can edit it. After all of the articles have been edited, compile them as a newsletter.

GRAMMAR AND VOCABULARY Write a composition on one of the topics below. Use as many words as possible from the Content Vocabulary on page 31. Use structures that you practiced in this lesson to express your ideas.

Topic 1: Does recent news have any personal relevance or importance for you? Explain why or why not and give concrete examples.

Topic 2: Statistics show that local news is especially popular among people who read newspapers and watch or listen to TV and radio news broadcasts. Why do people take an interest in this kind of news and pay less attention to national or international news stories? Explain and give concrete examples.

PROJECT Interview a student.

Interview at least one student on your campus and find out the following information:

1. Does the student follow the news?
2. How much time does the student spend every day on the news?
3. What is the main source of the news for that person?
4. Does the student talk about the news with friends or classmates?

Then, report on the student's responses in your class.

 INTERNET Compare Sources

Go online or look at the print version of major newspapers available on your campus or in your town. Compare how the same story is reported in several different sources and report to your class on 2–3 similarities and/or differences. Choose one of these newspapers: *The New York Times* (www.nytimes.com), *USA Today* (www.usatoday.com), *The Washington Post* (www.washingtonpost.com), the *Los Angeles Times* (www.latimes.com), *The Wall Street Journal* (www.wallstreetjournal.com).

PART 1
Articles to Express a Generic
Reference

PART 2
The for Unique Reference:
Definite Reference

Lesson ⑤

**History and
Musicology:
The Silk Road**

■ CONTENT VOCABULARY

Look up the words below that you do not know and enter them in your vocabulary journal.
Write each word's part of speech, a definition, and an example sentence. Try to include them
in your discussion and writing below.

cast iron	a fabric	a repertoire	to originate
a commodity	a fiddle	a route	unique
a device	goods	a technique	widespread

■ THINK ABOUT IT

Look at the map on the following page of the trade route known as the Silk Road. With a
partner, brainstorm a list of the modern countries that are located along the Silk Road. What
goods did merchants probably transport over this route? Discuss your ideas with a classmate.

In your writing journal, write for five minutes about the questions below. When you are
finished, share what you wrote with the class.

In ancient times, what countries were trading partners with your country? Did any trade
routes cross through your country or include your harbors? Do you know what goods
merchants transported over this route? What kinds of goods did people in your country
consider precious in those times?

■ GRAMMAR IN CONTENT

CD1,TR9

A Read and listen to the passage below. The words in bold express generic references.

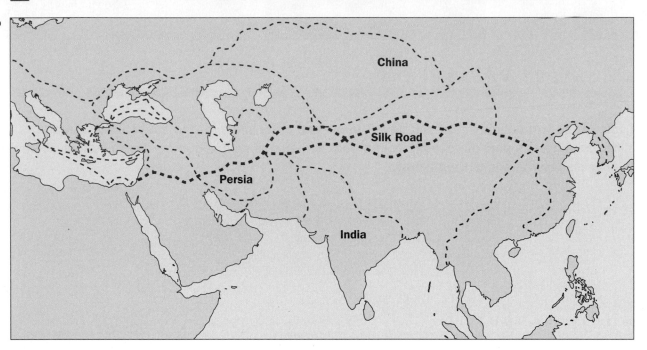

The Mystery and Romance of the Silk Road

Centuries before the Silk Road got its name in 1877 from German explorer Ferdinand von Richthofen, the trade in **jade** between **the Chinese** and the people in oasis towns of Central Asia was quite active. In this area **the jade-carvers** were famous, and their carvings were transported from China along the southern Silk Road for centuries. In contrast to the sale of jade, which stayed primarily within Asia, Chinese silk became the East's first important export to the West, specifically to **the Romans**. By the second century BCE, **silk** had reached the Mediterranean, but the people there had no clear idea of the source of this highly prized fabric.

Those who moved along the Silk Road generally traveled only part of the total distance, except for the great explorers like Marco Polo. **Traders** and **pilgrims** went from oasis to oasis, avoiding the harsh central desert. **The two-humped camel** was especially well suited to this environment, and stories of caravans of camels piled with exotic fabrics and jewels fueled the West's romantic view of the arduous trek toward China. However, other travelers went by foot or on horseback. **The Buddhists**, for example, usually walked between their holy sites and monasteries in China and India.

Today, **anthropologists**, ethnomusicologists, art historians, and even engineers in materials science have become interested in tracing the consequences of cultural contacts along the Silk Road. For example, **extra-long sleeves** are still seen today in Chinese opera and in some traditional Asian clothing, but that style of sleeve came from Western Asia, near modern-day Ukraine. In the eighth-century Shosoin collection of stringed musical instruments in Japan, the design on one lute (*biwa* in Japanese or *pipa* in Chinese) shows camels and another has an elephant. Clearly, these instruments did not originate in Japan, but somewhere else along the Silk Road. Chinese industrial texts from the seventeenth century include illustrations of **blast furnaces** and describe techniques that didn't become widespread until several centuries later in the West. Over time, as traders moved their goods from region to region, **ideas**, **philosophies**, **arts**, **religions**, and **technologies** accompanied them, found new homes, and developed in new directions.

a lute: a stringed instrument with a pear-shaped body   **jade:** a green gemstone that is often carved for decorations or jewelry

Articles to Express a Generic Reference

Sample Sentences	Notes
Without **the camel**, transportation was very difficult along much of the Silk Road.	Some articles can signal generic meanings of the nouns they modify. In other words, an article and noun refer to **something general or abstract**, not concrete or specific. The choice of article depends on the formality of the context and the meaning of the noun.
The best filaments for making silk are produced by **the moth** *Bombyx mori*. **The mechanical clock** was in use in China by the eleventh century. **The mulberry tree** provides nourishment for caterpillars of the *Bombyx mori*.	In a formal context, you can use *the* and **a singular countable noun** from the following categories: • animate objects (animals, plants, body parts/organs). • musical instruments. • human inventions and devices (*the iPod, the engine*), but not everyday items that developed through history (*tables, pencils*).
Among the travelers, there were **pilgrims, traders,** and **adventurers.** A trader on the Silk Road might have transported **silk** toward the West and **furniture** toward the East to satisfy his customers.	Using Ø (no article) and **a plural noun** is common in informal contexts. You can also use Ø with **noncount nouns.**
A caravan was the most economical way to transport precious goods because **a trader** needed to carry enough merchandise to make the long trip profitable.	Use *a* or *an* and **a singular countable noun** when giving an example of a group, type, or category.
In contrast to **the Chinese, the Europeans** didn't have clocks until the fourteenth century.	Use *the* and **a plural noun** when referring to human groups for people of the same religion, nationality, language, social, or professional background.
Nowadays you can take **the plane** to Xi'an, which was the beginning of the Silk Road in China. In rural areas people use **the Internet** to sell their goods to the outside world. In central Asian towns and villages, most locally produced goods are available at **the bazaar.**	Use *the* and **a singular noun** when you mention the following in daily routine activities: • Public transportation: the bus, the train, the plane. • Mass communications: the phone, the radio, the Internet. • Common institutions and businesses: the store, the bank, the movies/cinema, the hairdresser, the dentist.

B Read over your journal entry, and <u>underline</u> at least one sentence that you can revise to include an article with a generic reference. Write your revised sentence(s) below.

_____

_____

_____

C Does the underlined noun phrase express a generic reference? Write "Yes" or "No" in the space provided. Follow the example.

1. _Yes_ Many explorers wrote about a huge wild sheep in remote areas along the Silk Road.

2. _____ The zoo in Samarkand has a huge wild sheep in one of the exhibits.

3. _____ Buddhists were among the pilgrims that traveled on the Silk Road.

4. _____ Travelers on the Silk Road watched for palm trees in some regions because they knew that water was available nearby.

5. _____ The palm tree is native to this region.

6. _____ In one traveler's diary, he mentioned a Buddhist among the other travelers in the caravan.

7. _____ At the end of each day, Samir took the saddles off his camels after he unloaded his goods.

8. _____ A saddle lay by the side of the road, and members of the caravan wondered what had happened.

9. _____ Later, the caravan passed a Buddhist and a camel.

10. _____ At night one of the travelers entertained his fellow travelers by playing a flute.

11. _____ Musicologists have found the flute or a similar instrument in most cultures.

12. _____ The silk weaver was a valued member of Chinese society.

D Read the texts below, looking closely at the underlined articles and nouns. If the noun is used generically, write "G." If the noun is definite, write "D."

1. _G_ Several types of animals were brought to China from western regions. Tibetans, for example, introduced the yak to China.

2. _____ The Chinese used dogs from Persia and Tibet as hunting dogs. The dog in Castiglione's painting of the Chinese court was known as a "Roman dog."

3. _____ Most eastern houses and palaces were designed for people to sit on mats, rugs, or cushions on the floor. When traders brought the chair to China, Chinese court architecture changed.

4. _____ Although Indians produced both silk and cotton, the cotton was more famous.

5. _____ The Chinese learned techniques to make iron from metal-workers in West Asia, but Chinese artisans were able to improve the techniques.

6. _____ By 1100 the Chinese were able to mold cast iron objects. The Europeans did not produce the cast iron cooking pot for another 300 years.

7. _____ Buddhism had a strong influence on Chinese culture over the centuries. This influence is even visible in silk designs, which included the elephant.

E **GROUP WORK** Choose five things (animate or inanimate) that visitors to your country may notice or want to see as they travel across your land. Give some background or an explanation about those five things in 1–2 sentences. Then, share the information with a group.

> Visitors may see buffaloes in many western states. Settlers nearly killed off the buffalo in the 1800s, but now there are big herds of them in reserves and other protected areas.

PART TWO	*The* for Unique Reference: Definite Reference

■ GRAMMAR IN CONTENT

A Reread the text about the Silk Road, and <u>underline</u> every example of *"the + noun"* that is not in bold print. Which phrases express something that is unique, not to be confused with anything else? Which phrases are definite or specific because of information that comes *after* the noun? Compare your answers with a classmate's.

The for Unique Reference

Sample Sentences	Notes
(at rehearsal) Could I move **the stand** a little closer, please? (at rehearsal) I saw your violin case in **the rehearsal room** before rehearsal started. (at the theater) Is **the ticket office** near **the stage door?** **The moon** rose directly over **the stage** at their first outdoor concert.	Use *the* to signal information is shared with your listener or reader and can be inferred from: • environment • context • general knowledge
The first selection on tonight's program is considered **the best** song in their repertoire. **The remaining** music will be performed by **the same** string players with a guest singer.	Use *the* before adjectives that uniquely identify nouns: *the first, second, third . . . last/final* *the same/identical* *the only/single* superlative forms: *the best, the highest . . .*

Sample Sentences	Notes
Our host played a folk song for us, and then his family sang <u>the song</u> again later.	Use *the* when previous information in the sentence or text identifies the noun.
I had never heard **the music of Azerbaijan** before. I have a DVD of **the performance that introduces several musicians from the Silk Road Project.** One segment of it was filmed in **the town square where the musicians often play.** The DVD included interviews with **the people there.**	Use *the* when a noun is followed by identifying information in: • prepositional phrases • relative clauses • adverbials

B For each of the contexts below, write five things that you expect to find there.

1. a concert hall: *the stage, the orchestra pit, the balcony, the coat room, the restrooms*

2. an airport: _____

3. a sports center: _____

4. a hospital: _____

5. a college campus: _____

6. a typical house in your country or region: _____

C Edit the text below, inserting the definite article wherever necessary.

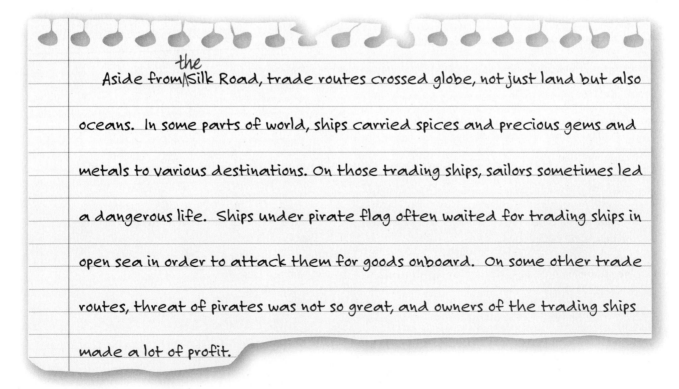

Aside from ^the Silk Road, trade routes crossed globe, not just land but also oceans. In some parts of world, ships carried spices and precious gems and metals to various destinations. On those trading ships, sailors sometimes led a dangerous life. Ships under pirate flag often waited for trading ships in open sea in order to attack them for goods onboard. On some other trade routes, threat of pirates was not so great, and owners of the trading ships made a lot of profit.

D On a separate piece of paper, write a comparison/contrast of three types of fiddles found in countries along the Silk Road. Use *the* as appropriate.

Name of fiddle	*erhu* "foreign string instrument"	*kemancheh*	*morin khuur* "horse fiddle"
Countries	China	Iran, Azerbaijan	Mongolia
Strings	2		3, horsehair
Bow	horsehair on bamboo		horsehair
Body	wood: round, hexagonal, octagonal, or tubular	wood: small, round w/spike from the base	wood, or wood frame with camel, goat, or sheepskin covering
Face of body	snakeskin	animal skin	
Neck	long	cone-shaped	peg box in shape of horse's head; tuning pegs = "horse's ears"
Playing position	supported on left thigh with left hand	on player's knee or on ground; turned on spike	sound box on lap or between player's knees
Sound	fine, lyrical	elegant, warm, like human voice	like a horse neighing or a breeze
Use	solo instrument	solo or small groups	with folk singers
Cultural note		used in tradition of improvised music	horses are important to national identity

CD1,TR10

E Listen to part of Professor Taylor's musicology class. (Circle) your interpretation of each part of his presentation.

1. a. He is defining the *kemancheh*.
   b. He is talking about a particular *kemancheh*.

2. a. He is defining the *ney*.
   b. He is talking about a particular *ney*.

3. a. He is describing the general technique for playing the *ney*.
   b. He is describing how a particular musician plays the *ney*.

4. a. He is talking about the material used to make a particular *ney*.
   b. He is talking about the general construction of all *neys*.

5. a. He is describing the general techniques of playing the *shakuhachi*.
   b. He is describing the way that a particular player performed on the *shakuhachi*.

6. a. He compares the general use of the *ney* and the *shakuhachi* in meditation.
   b. He compares the use of both instruments in particular types of meditation.

F **GROUP WORK** Ask classmates about the cuisine, traffic, music, fashion, or celebrations in a country that they have visited.

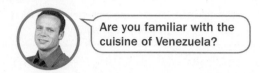

Are you familiar with the cuisine of Venezuela?

Connection | Putting It Together

GRAMMAR AND VOCABULARY Write a composition on one of the topics below. Use as many words as possible from the Content Vocabulary on page 41. Use the appropriate articles to express your ideas, and <u>underline</u> the articles.

Topic 1: Around the world individuals learn and perform traditional songs and dances, often in costumes based on traditional clothing from their culture. These individuals may also learn the folk songs and dances of other cultures and perform them at festivals or ceremonies. In our high-tech world, why do these "old-fashioned" arts survive?

Topic 2: Since ancient times countries have had both cultural and economic connections. China was a "major player" in the world of the Silk Road, and the impact of Chinese culture and technology has been found in different corners of the world. Choose one cultural connection with the United States that has affected another country that you are familiar with in the last 50 years—either positively or negatively. Explain that connection or influence, and give examples.

PROJECT Interview at least one student on your campus about traditional North American music. Find out the following information, and report on it at your next class meeting.

1. Which musical instruments do Americans typically use for playing folk songs or other traditional music?
2. What kinds of music do most people consider typical traditional American music?
3. Does the student enjoy folk music? Why, or why not?

INTERNET Go online, and use the search phrase "musical instruments from Middle East" or "musical instruments from Asia." Find an instrument that is similar to a traditional musical instrument in your culture. Then, prepare a comparison of the two instruments for class, and, if possible, print out pictures of the instruments for your classmates to see. (If you search for the name of your instrument, you will find many websites with pictures of musical instruments from around the world.)

A Complete each sentence, using a verb from the box in the appropriate verb tense and aspect. When appropriate, put an article (including Ø) or indirect object that completes the ideas.

observe	exceed	harvest	send	build	appear	strike
plant	germinate	burn down	develop	return	grow	

TO: Partners of the Virginia Company
FROM: John Rolfe
DATE: July 15, 1613
RE: Update on Tobacco Cultivation in Jamestown, Virginia

_____ tobacco crop this year _____
        (1)   (2)

our expectations. After we _____ 20 more acres in early
                                         (3)

spring, _____ seeds _____ and
                   (4)   (5)

quickly matured. For the past three weeks my men _____ the
                                                              (6)

tobacco leaves. _____ tobacco _____
                     (7)   (8)

well-suited to _____ climate and soil in Virginia. While
                        (9)

visiting Indian settlements last summer, I _____ that
                                           (10)

_____ corn, _____ beans, and other
            (11)   (12)

vegetables also _____ well in this region.
                       (13)

    This winter I _____ a 5-year plan for my plantation,
                          (14)

which I _____ on _____ ship which
              (15)   (16)

is scheduled to leave here in April. Aside from agricultural products, I intend to raise

_____ livestock. _____ first structure
            (17)   (18)

on my property for our few cattle _____ after lightning
                                   (19)

_____ it a few weeks ago. We _____ a barn
         (20)   (21)

after the next ship _____ from England.
                   (22)

B (Circle) the correct word(s) or phrase(s) in the second sentence of the text or conversation.

1. Many farmers are interested in transgenic crops because such crops can offer an alternative to herbicides and pesticides. These chemicals (had posed / **have posed**) potential health problems to farm workers and to consumers.

2. For several years farmers in the United States have been experimenting with drought-resistant corn. They (**plant** / planted) this type of corn in small quantities in isolated parts of their property.

3. **Fred Porter:** "What do you think of the insect-resistant plants that you've planted this year?"
   Luke Walker: "They seem to be doing well, but (the cotton / **cotton**) grows well this time of year anyway."

4. Some genetically manipulated crops are very nutritious. For example, biotech researchers have been able to raise the protein content of (**a soybean** / the soybean.)

5. **Wilt Owens:** ". . . I was checking out the corn field yesterday afternoon and heard a strange buzzing sound. I (walk / **walked**) over to the section with the biotech corn and see this giant grasshopper, and then it flies . . ."

6. In order to survive, farmers in Jamestown had to increase their agricultural knowledge. They planted seeds that they (brought / **had brought**) from England and learned to harvest fruits and vegetables that (grew / **had grown**) wild in Virginia.

7. **Mary Carter:** "I wasn't familiar with some vegetables in Virginia, so at the beginning I followed the Powhatans' style of preparing them. Later, I cooked them (**for us** / to us) with different spices."

8. **Ned Baker:** "I have to be careful with the biotech crops because I want to keep them separate from everything else that I harvest. I store all of the biotech crops in (a barn / **the barn**) since I have space in there."

9. Many people fear the long-term effects of eating genetically engineered food. By 2020 researchers (will complete / **will have completed**) several studies that track the effects of such food on humans and animals.

10. Agricultural entrepreneurs pay attention to the research on biotech crops and to public response to such crops. Before they plan their planting schedule for the year, they (have considered / **considered**) the potential market for their products.

LEARNER LOG Check (✔) *Yes* or *I Need More Practice.*

Lesson	I Can Use . . .	Yes	I Need More Practice
1	Verbs in the Present, Past, and Future		
2	Verbs in Simple Past and Past Perfect; Shifts to the Present		
3	Verbs in the Future Time; Verbs in the Progressive Aspect		
4	Transitive Verbs, Intransitive Verbs, and Verbs in Middle Voice; Verbs with Indirect Objects		
5	Articles for Generic, Unique, and Definite Reference		

Linguistics: Spelling, Codes, and Alphabets

■ CONTENT VOCABULARY

Look up the words below that you do not know and enter them in your vocabulary journal. Write each word's part of speech, a definition, and an example sentence. Try to include them in your discussion and writing below.

a correspondence	literacy	a shortcut	to encode
cursive script	presumably	a syllable	to digitize
cyberspace	reasonable	to condone	to reform

■ THINK ABOUT IT

How much experience have you had with learning a different alphabet or another writing system? How long did it take you to become comfortable writing in a new way? What was the hardest part of learning to write the new language? Discuss your ideas with a classmate.

In your writing journal, write for five minutes about these questions. When you are finished, share your opinions with the class.

In your opinion, should students use the language and spelling of text messaging in school assignments and tests? Is it appropriate to e-mail your instructor with the same special e-mail symbols and spellings that you use with your friends and family? Why or why not?

■ GRAMMAR IN CONTENT

CD1,TR11

A Read and listen to the passage below. The words in bold are phrasal modals or modal-like verbs.

If u thnk txt-spk is the deth o nglsh, thnk agin

As a new academic semester begins, educators around the country are haunted by New Zealand's decision to allow text-speak—those shortcuts and abbreviations used in text messaging—on national exams.

What does the New Zealand Qualifications Authority's policy say about the future of our language? **Are we to condone** Suzi who cant use apostrophes? and what about chad, a student I know whos given up on capitals? Worse yet, what do we do about Johnny (u wont believe this 1) who drops vowels and uses acronyms?

Given the prevalence of such language abuses, why would New Zealand officially allow students to use abbreviations that most of us would like to see confined to the world of IM and text messaging? Surely, if we **are to believe** the media hype, those New Zealanders must have kiwi-size brains to degrade our language in such a deliberate manner.

The hype, however, is not the reality.

The real threat to the English language comes from bad writing and questionable literacy. Most of us can think of a U.S. president who abuses our language more than the average teenage blogger.

Text-speak does, of course, have significant limitations. The most commonly used acronyms are just that—common—and we**'re not going to win** any Pulitzer Prizes writing either "GMTA" or "great minds think alike." An acronym of a cliché is still a cliché.

Rather than view text-speak as a Hurricane Katrina of language, educators should recognize its appearance as that most valuable of pedagogical tools, the "teachable moment." Text-speak provides us with an opportunity to introduce students to some basics of English composition: tone, audience, style, and clarity.

Our mode of writing is always context-specific. A biology lab report might be written entirely in the passive voice, but a passive style will make that paper on *Great Expectations* a dud. Contractions might be acceptable in an editorial, but not a formal history essay. The first-person voice works in an opinion piece or job letter, but we**'d better** use the third-person when writing a biography of Harriet Tubman.

Text-speak requires similar rules. Only a fool would try to write in full Standard English using a cell-phone keypad. At the same time, we should recommend a cranial CAT scan for the student who writes a term paper using text-speak. The guidelines of the New Zealand Qualifications Authority make such distinctions clear—students will be penalized for using abbreviations in an exam that requires them to demonstrate language use.

In many academic contexts, text-speak will never be appropriate. Formal essays, which presumably always require a demonstration of sound language use, are not the place for shortcuts. Exams represent a different scenario. Students need to consider the subject matter and exam issues. In a timed psychology test, abbreviations such as "b/c" and "M/F ratio" should pose no problem. In a literature exam with tight time constraints, a student might be wise, after the first usage, to save time by abbreviating "point of view" and "Fyodor Dostoevsky" with POV and FD.

Whatever the exam guidelines, students need to show clearly their understanding of the subject. The student who writes "drng t g8 dprsn, pvrty wz, ttbomk, a bg prblm" (during the Great Depression, poverty was, to the best of my knowledge, a big problem) is being neither clear nor insightful, whether in the United States or New Zealand.

Two centuries ago, Jane Austen's Henry Tilney mocked female letter writers for having a "general deficiency of subject, a total inattention to stops, and a very frequent ignorance of grammar." Then, as now, language was in flux. However, if we approach current changes thoughtfully, as Austen did, language need not be in a state of decline.

IM: instant messaging, a form of interpersonal communication on the Internet

media hype: excessive media attention and publicity

a Pulitzer Prize: an annual American prize for journalism and literature

a cliché: a superficial or overused expression or saying

M/F ratio: the proportion of males to females

a dud: something that is unsuccessful or disappointing

a CAT scan: a 3-dimensional, computerized scan

Jane Austen: a British novelist (1775–1817)

Henry Tilney: a character in Austen's novel *Northanger Abbey*

to mock: to ridicule, to make fun of

in flux: in the process of changing

Sample Sentences	Notes
Bill **was about to** text his friends when his teacher walked in the door.	*Be about to* signals that an action will occur in the near future, even immediately.
If you **are to** master English spelling, you need to learn all of the exceptional spellings.	*Be to* signals a future plan or intention. It represents formal usage.
Any ESL student **has to** spend a lot of time on spelling.	*Have to* signals both personal and external necessity. Americans prefer *have to* for this meaning and use *must* for inferences (see Part Two).
I've **got to** study this list of terms before class tomorrow.	*Have got to* expresses an urgent necessity, mostly in informal contexts.
Homework assignments **ought to** have correct spelling and punctuation.	*Ought to* signals an obligation to follow external social or moral rules.
Students **shouldn't** hand in assignments with spelling errors.	Use *should* instead of *ought to* in questions and negative sentences.
We're **supposed to** have a spelling test next week. The teacher **wasn't supposed to** tell us the words on the next test (but she did). The test **was only supposed to** take 10 minutes (but it took 30 minutes).	*Be supposed to* expresses the obligation to follow rules imposed by an impersonal outside authority or by a plan or schedule. In the past tense, the affirmative implies the action didn't happen, and the negative implies that the action did happen.
Were we to memorize all of the irregular spelling words for the /f/ sound? My advisor said I **am to** complete all my required courses by the end of the year.	*Be to* expresses an arrangement that implies external supervision or authority.

B Read over your journal entry, and <u>underline</u> at least one sentence that you can revise to include a phrasal modal. Write your revised sentence(s) below.

_____

_____

_____

_____

C (Circle) **the letter of the appropriate paraphrase for each statement below.**

1. The Simplified Spelling Society (SSS) is to meet next Friday to elect its next president.
   - a. The Simplified Spelling Society has a meeting scheduled for next Friday.
   - b. The president of the Simplified Spelling Society has required that the members meet next Friday.

2. According to the SSS, English speakers have to reform English spelling.
   - a. The SSS thinks that it is necessary for English speakers to reform the spelling of English words.
   - b. The SSS thinks that English speakers have an obligation to reform the spelling of English words.

3. English spelling has got to change to make worldwide communication easier.
   - a. Worldwide communication will only improve after certain spelling changes have been made.
   - b. Certain changes have to happen before spelling can be improved.

4. For example, they say that extra, or surplus, letters like the final *-e* in the words *little, terrible,* or *resemble* ought to disappear from English spelling.
   - a. The SSS recommends omitting surplus letters.
   - b. The SSS claims that surplus letters have disappeared from English spelling.

5. Teachers aren't supposed to use any of the SSS's spelling reforms.
   - a. People generally assume that teachers don't use the spelling reforms.
   - b. Teachers shouldn't use the spelling reforms.

6. During their past meetings, SSS members were supposed to recommend five reforms for future application in computer software.
   - a. The members recommended five reforms.
   - b. The members didn't recommend five reforms.

7. During the last meeting, they were about to discuss using the letter *f* for all /f/ sounds when the president had to end the session.
   - a. The members were ready to discuss the letter *f* just before the end of the meeting.
   - b. The members discussed the letter *f* before the end of the meeting.

D What are the students' questions in each situation? Work with a partner and make questions, using different modals. Follow the example.

1. Mr. Atkins assigns his class a research paper on the history of English spelling.

   a. team work? _____Do we have to work together? Who should we work with?_____

   b. due date? _____

2. Mr. Atkins gives his students a spelling exercise that introduces some new spelling rules of the Simplified Spelling Society.

   a. omit surplus letters? _____

   b. write by hand? _____

3. Mr. Atkins returns homework papers with his feedback on them.

   a. correct mistakes? _____

   b. the way to find correct answers? _____

E Look at each question. Write an appropriate answer to each one, using the same phrasal verb in the question. Follow the example.

1. Do I have to dot the letter *j*?
   _____ You don't have to, but it may be easier to read that way. _____

2. Were they to use text-speak on this test?

   _____

3. Should I write my class notes in text-speak?

   _____

4. Aren't you supposed to omit all capital letters in text-speak?

   _____

5. Did we have to use text-speak on the test?

   _____

6. Were we to finish this lesson by Friday?

   _____

F Use the class notes from Mr. Atkins's presentation about spelling reform to answer the questions. Use phrasal modals in your answers. Follow the example.

> Some Principles for International English Spelling
>
> Purpose: to make learning to read easier for children and for non-native speakers
>
> #1: Don't change irregular words that are very common (= 31 words of 100 most frequent words!!)
>
> examples: are, come, should, half, know, of, one, other, pull, what
>
> #2: Use vowel letters a, e, i, o, u for both long and short vowels with a grave accent for long vowels. In other words, omit final silent -e.
>
> examples: mat (= mat) / màt (= mate); bit (= bit) / bìt = bite)
>
> #3: Make consonant letters match the sounds in words:
>
> scent and cent → sent; pleasure → plezhur, little → litl

1. Why does the SSS propose various spelling reforms?

   So people who learn how to read don't have to struggle with spelling.

2. How does this system handle the most frequent words in English?

   _____

3. How will the grave accent help learners of English?

   _____

4. How can someone tell the difference between a long and short vowel in a text?

   _____

5. According to these principles, what are better spellings of *numb, leisure, gauge, leave,* and *enough?*

   _____

   _____

■ COMMUNICATE

G **PAIR WORK** Develop a secret code substituting letters with other letters, numbers, or symbols. (If the number 5 represents *h*, for example, and 2 represents *i*, then 52 spells "hi.") Then, convert this sentence into your code: *Some codes are easy to crack.* Exchange your encoded sentence with another pair. Can you figure out the other pair's code? When you finish, check each other's work.

■ GRAMMAR IN CONTENT

A Reread the text at the beginning of the lesson, and <u>underline</u> all of the other modals. (Circle) the modals that express an inference, deduction, or prediction, and compare your answers with a partner.

Modals: Troubleshooting

Sample Sentences	Notes
Before alphabetic writing, people **used to** keep records in other kinds of writing systems. In Mesopotamia they **would** preserve information in signs, or pictographs. Later, the Egyptians **would** take this form of writing and develop it further into their hieroglyphics. Did the Egyptians **used to** write in a cursive script, too? Children **used to** have fountain pens that they used for penmanship lessons.	The following phrasal modals express past habitual actions: • *Used to* signals a past action or condition, including location and ownership. • *Would* signals past actions or events, often ones that happened regularly. NOTE: A story or text is often introduced with *used to* and continued with *would* or its contraction *'d*.
It **must** be hard to learn a totally new script. Our teacher **has got to** be kidding! We can't learn 25 new Chinese characters by tomorrow! You **must not** understand the way to connect Arabic letters because you wrote the words all wrong. We **should** finish learning the Russian alphabet soon because we've finished all of the consonants already. It **shouldn't** take long to learn to read Russian because most of the letters are the same as the Latin alphabet.	To express a very strong logical inference or logical necessity, use *must* or (especially to express an emotional reaction) *have got to*. Express a negative inference with *must not.* Do not use *must* with references to the future. Use *should* instead: **Incorrect:** We ~~must~~ have a spelling quiz soon. **Correct:** We *should* have a spelling quiz soon. **Should** expresses an inference of reasonable certainty or a prediction.

B Using modals of past habitual actions, answer the questions about the history of literacy. You can write about the history of English or the history of your first language. The first item provides a sample answer.

1. In previous centuries, what kinds of people were able to read?

   Religious leaders and people in the upper class would learn to read.

2. In the old days, where did people learn to read and write?

   _____

3. In those days, how did illiterate people conduct business or learn about things?

   _____

4. In the old days, what other languages did people in your country learn? Why?

   _____

5. When you were a child, how did you learn the writing system for your language?

   _____

6. How did your teacher motivate you to write clearly and legibly?

   _____

C (Circle) the appropriate modal(s) for each sentence. If more than one modal is possible, explain why on a separate piece of paper.

1. When you learn Arabic, you ___ train yourself to write from right to left.
   (a.) have to   b. must   (c.) have got to
   Reason: a & c mean necessity, and c is OK if the speaker is emphasizing the idea in an informal conversation.

2. Students of the Japanese or Chinese language ___ learn the proper order of brush strokes or pen strokes for each character.
   a. have to   b. must   c. have got to

3. Since Arabic letters have different forms at the beginning, in the middle, and at the end of a word, beginning students ___ have a hard time learning the forms.
   a. have to   b. must   c. have got to

4. Japanese and Chinese schoolchildren ___ take years to learn how to read their languages because there are so many characters.
   a. have to   b. must   c. have got to

5. It ___ be easier for a Korean student to learn English than for a Japanese student because the Korean writing system is partly alphabetic.
   a. has to   b. must   c. should

6. Students who first learn to write using an alphabet ___ have some difficulty when they begin to study a language with a system based on syllables as in Japanese.
   a. have to   b. must   c. should

7. When you write Arabic words, you ___ connect the letters.
   a. must   b. should   c. are supposed to

8. It ___ be easy for children to learn two different writing systems at the same time.
   a. doesn't have to   b. must not   c. shouldn't

D Make at least one inference and one prediction about each of the situations.

1. Twenty students enrolled in Hindi 101 this semester. It's the first time that the university has offered a course in Hindi.

   INFERENCE: The instructor must be happy that so many students want to learn Hindi.

   PREDICTION: They should offer another Hindi course next semester because the students will need two semesters of Hindi to fulfill their language requirements.

2. Alice Drake, a student in Hitoshi Sakakibara's Japanese 201 course, won the statewide Public Speaking contest. She will receive a plane ticket to Japan as her prize.

   INFERENCE: _____

   PREDICTION: _____

3. This summer Dan Kowalski is spending a month in Honduras, where he will help on a construction project with local workers.

   INFERENCE: _____

   PREDICTION: _____

4. Richford College is developing a summer study abroad program with a university in Lebanon.

   INFERENCE: _____

   PREDICTION: _____

5. Jeannie Wu and her cousin Cindy Li have decided to spend one month at a language school in Taiwan and then go sightseeing there for another month this summer.

   INFERENCE: _____

   PREDICTION: _____

6. LeMar Peters is a business major, and he hopes to spend one semester in Turkey during his junior year.

   INFERENCE: _____

   PREDICTION: _____

CD1,TR12

E Listen to Professor Wilkes and his class discuss a homework reading. Answer the questions below, using modals of inference.

Let's turn to the article by Dr. Bosworth about globalization and technology. What is the link to our class topic today?

1. What do you think the topic of today's class is?

_____

2. What is the background of Bosworth, the author of their homework assignment?

_____

3. Why do they refer to Chinese characters as ideograms?

_____

4. If ideograms really stimulate the right side of the brain, what does Bosworth predict?

_____

5. How could this new operating system impact other Asian countries?

_____

6. How is the growth of the Arabic immigrant population relevant to digitized Arabic in media technology?

_____

7. What does Zhihua imply about the preference of Arabic-speaking readers?

_____

8. What does Bosworth seem to imply about the direction of globalization?

_____

F Find and correct the four errors in the following letter.

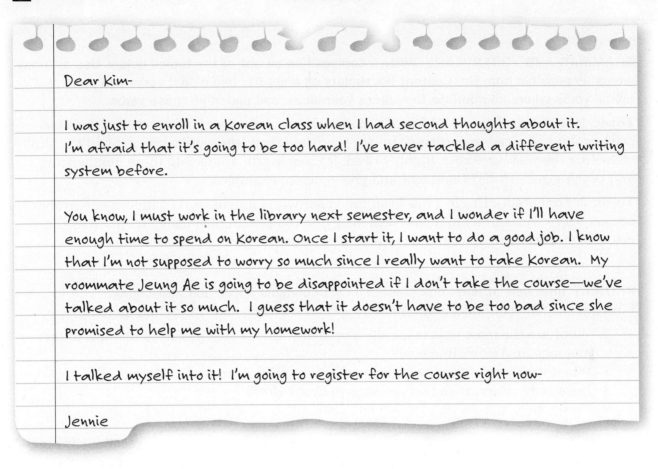

Dear Kim—

I was just to enroll in a Korean class when I had second thoughts about it. I'm afraid that it's going to be too hard! I've never tackled a different writing system before.

You know, I must work in the library next semester, and I wonder if I'll have enough time to spend on Korean. Once I start it, I want to do a good job. I know that I'm not supposed to worry so much since I really want to take Korean. My roommate Jeung Ae is going to be disappointed if I don't take the course—we've talked about it so much. I guess that it doesn't have to be too bad since she promised to help me with my homework!

I talked myself into it! I'm going to register for the course right now—

Jennie

■ **C O M M U N I C A T E**

G **PAIR WORK** Talk with your partner about your most effective methods of studying English (and any other language) before you entered this program.

When I first started learning English, I would make flash cards of new vocabulary.

I used to do that, too. But I'd also learn a lot of words by taking notes in class. I would look up any words I didn't know in the dictionary.

H **GROUP WORK** Design either (a) an English program or (b) a program for students of your native language. Write a short description, giving the basic philosophy or rationale for the course.

The students in our class are supposed to attend class five hours per day.

Yes, they are to spend most of their day speaking Russian.

GRAMMAR AND VOCABULARY Write a composition on one of the topics below. Use as many words as possible from the Content Vocabulary on page 51. Use modal verbs and phrasal modal verbs where appropriate to express your ideas, and <u>underline</u> those verbs.

Topic 1: In our modern world full of e-mails and text messages, is there still a place for calligraphy and nice handwriting? In many cultures, both the words of a text and the skill of writing the text have been highly prized. Do people still appreciate these handwriting and brush-stroke skills? Comment and give concrete examples.

Topic 2: For decades English has been the major world language. As Chinese and Arabic become more widespread in media technology, do you see English losing its place as the medium of international communication? Comment and give concrete examples.

PROJECT Interview at least one student on your campus about text messaging. Find out the following information and report on it during your next class meeting:

1. What are the most important signs or abbreviations that you need to know to text message an American friend?
2. When does your interviewee use text-speak (aside from text messaging)?
3. Does your interviewee text message in class? How?

 INTERNET Go online, and use the search term "writing systems" to find a website with information about writing systems from around the world. Select one group, for example "syllabic alphabets," and then click on one of the languages to get more information. Report to the class on either one alphabet that is no longer used or one that is currently in use. Include brief information on

- who used to use it, or where the alphabet is in use today.
- how it is supposed to be written.

Social Psychology: Experiments

■ CONTENT VOCABULARY

Look up the words below that you do not know and enter them in your vocabulary journal. Write each word's part of speech, a definition, and an example sentence. Try to include them in your discussion and writing below.

to administer	deceptive	guidelines	to subject to
a bystander	an electric shock	a maze	a test subject
to conduct	groundbreaking	to postulate	willingness

■ THINK ABOUT IT

Have you ever been a test subject in an experiment? What kind of experiment was it? What did you have to do? How did you feel about participating as a test subject? Discuss your ideas with a classmate.

In your writing journal, write for five minutes about the questions below. When you are finished, share what you wrote with the class.

Have you ever read or heard about an experiment in which the participants had to do something that they didn't expect? Describe the experiment and then imagine how the participants felt about their experience. If you haven't read about such an experiment, think about a TV show or other type of entertainment in which members of the audience have to do something unexpected.

■ GRAMMAR IN CONTENT

CD1, TR13

A Read and listen to the passage below. The words in bold are perfect modals.

A Lesson in Obedience

The famous Milgram experiment brought important information about human behavior to light, but the design of the experiment raises questions about ethical research methods. For his first experiments in 1963, Stanley Milgram recruited volunteers for a psychological experiment, but his advertisements did not give any specific information about the participants' role in the experiment. On arrival, each vounteer was introduced to another participant who was actually a paid actor that Milgram had hired. The volunteer was not told about this arrangement. The volunteer then played the role of "the teacher" in an experiment on memorization while the actor played "the student." The student sat in a separate room, and the two were able to communicate only by voice.

While the teachers were helping the students with the memorization task, they also had the job of punishing the students if they made mistakes. The teachers gave electric shocks to the students as punishment. The first shocks were at a very low intensity, but the intensity increased as the students continued to make mistakes. The actor/students made many mistakes on purpose, and the teachers gave shocks with higher and higher voltage. Meanwhile, the actors began complaining about the shocks and then screamed in pain after each shock. Milgram and his research team encouraged the teachers to continue with the punishment and told them that they had no choice. The teachers then continued, and their students received shocks until they became completely silent.

At the end of each experiment, Milgram met with the volunteer and explained the experiment. A full 65% of the participants, who were both men and women, had obeyed the experimenters and had administered electric shocks at the highest voltage. At this point, Milgram told them about the "learner's" true identity. Also, they learned that they hadn't actually given any electric shocks at all. Many of the participants had asked the researchers about the procedures during the experiment, but few had actually disobeyed. They could have stopped the shocks at any time and quit the experiment.

When people first hear about this experiment, they have similar responses. Most people think that a large majority of participants **must have disobeyed.** When they hear the statistics, they imagine that Milgram **must have been surprised,** too. People ask themselves how those volunteers could ignore the screams of the learners. Of course, the next step is the question "**Might I have done** the same thing?" The data shows that the answer to that question is probably "Yes." Finally, there are questions about the ethics of such an experiment and about the reactions of the participants. Many critics think that Milgram shouldn't have subjected the volunteers to such a stressful situation. There was concern that the volunteers **may have reacted** very negatively to their own willingness to cause severe pain to another person. However, according to Milgram, most of the volunteers felt that they had learned something valuable about themselves.

In response to the Milgram experiment and others, professional organizations and universities now monitor research designs. Modern guidelines for ethical research place a high value on the safety of participants—both mental and physical—regardless of the knowledge that could be gained from experiments.

to bring to light: to make public, to draw to public attention

an arrangement: an agreement, a plan

on purpose: intentionally

a professional organization: an association of people in a particular profession

Sample Sentences	Notes
The participants **might have reacted** negatively to the experimental results. Milgram **may not have expected** such results.	Use modals in their perfect form (**modal** + *have* + **past participle**) to express your interpretation of a past action or situation. Place *not* after the modal for negation: **modal** + *not have* + **past participle**
Some participants **must have regretted** their actions. Milgram **should have been** surprised by the results. Some of the actors **may have reacted** more strongly than others. The stressful experience **could have caused** psychological problems for the volunteers. The actors **might have screamed** more convincingly with practice.	Choose the modal below that expresses your opinion or feeling about the likeliness of a past event. Your choice signals your inference, expectation, or deduction about an action or situation that occurred previously. *must* *should* high probability *may* *could* low probability *might* NOTE: *Can* is not used at all for affirmative inferences or predictions.
The volunteers **might not have felt** comfortable about their actions. Milgram **may not have anticipated** the future criticisms of his experiments. The volunteers **must not have realized** that the experiment depended completely on their actions. Milgram **couldn't have predicted** the high rate of obedience among the volunteers. He **can't have known** the level of a regular person's obedience before he started the experiments.	The negative forms of perfect modals that express inferences and predictions do not all express the same levels of probability as the affirmative forms above. *might not* high negative probability *may not* *must not* *can't/couldn't* low negative probability You can use the contracted forms *can't* and *couldn't* in these cases, but don't contract *must/may/might* + *not*.

B Read over your journal entry, and <u>underline</u> at least one sentence that you can revise to include a perfect modal. Write your revised sentence(s) below.

_____

_____

_____

C Complete each sentence using a verb from the box and a perfect modal. Follow the example.

question	assume	~~approve~~	understand
misunderstand	respond	explain	cooperate

1. **Dr. Kern:** Your experimental design is excellent, so the ethics committee _____ *should have approved* _____ it by tomorrow afternoon when they meet.

2. **Prof. Walker:** The subjects _____ your directions because few of them filled out the questionnaire properly.

3. **Prof. Aikens:** Milgram _____ that some of his volunteers would obey an authority figure without question.

4. **Prof. Erwin:** Participants _____ the purpose of our research, and so there will be a margin of error in the results.

5. **Dr. Gunther:** The volunteers _____ in the same way without Milgram's deceptive experimental design.

6. **Prof. Nichol:** Don't worry about the experiment. Your research subject _____ the conditions because he signed a consent form.

7. **Prof. Rollin:** Participants _____ the researcher's authority. That's the only explanation for their submissive behavior.

8. **Dr. Clark:** My assistant _____ the purpose of our experiment because the subjects were asking me about it before we started.

D Select the better modal for the situation and (circle) it. Be ready to explain your choice.

1. During an experiment on participant motivation, a researcher gave volunteers 2,000 sheets of paper. On each sheet there were 24 addition problems, which the volunteers were supposed to work on. The researcher said that he would return later and left the room. The volunteers were still working on the problems when he returned 5 hours later.

   a. The volunteers ((must) / may) have thought that the research was important.

      REASON: _The volunteers worked for a long time, so they thought it was important._

   b. The researcher (couldn't / may not) have expected them to work for 5 hours.

      REASON: _____

2. The researcher who designed the experiment in #1 wanted to give the volunteers a task that they would refuse.

   a. The experimenter (can't / may not) have started his research with this task.

      REASON: _____

   b. The volunteers (could / must) have been angry about the purpose of his research.

      REASON: _____

3. The same researcher designed another experiment. He handed out the same sheets. This time the participants had to complete a sheet, tear it into at least 32 pieces, and then continue with the next sheet. Again, the volunteers worked on this task for many hours.

   a. The volunteers (may / must) have wondered about the purpose of this task.

      REASON: _____

   b. Some volunteers (may / might) have torn the sheets into fewer pieces.

      REASON: _____

E Make one negative and one affirmative comment on each experiment below. Use different modals of the logical scale. Follow the example.

1. The subjects in the motivation experiments above spent many hours doing an extremely boring task.

   a. _They might not have wanted to ruin the researcher's experiment by quitting._

   b. _The experiment may have seemed silly to them._

2. People who volunteered for both deceptive and nondeceptive experiments have said that they liked the deceptive experiments better.

   a. _____

   b. _____

3. In one study, researchers stared at certain drivers who had stopped at an intersection. Those drivers left the intersection more quickly than other drivers.

   a. _____

   b. _____

4. In a series of experiments, bystanders who were alone in a situation helped a stranger in an emergency; however, the same bystanders were much less likely to help a stranger if there were other people standing or sitting nearby.

   a. _____

   b. _____

5. A researcher asked a group of 10 participants to identify lines of the same length on two sheets of paper. Participants gave their answers orally. Only one participant was a true volunteer, and the others were paid to give wrong answers. Only 25% of the real volunteers gave the correct answer, and the other 75% gave the same wrong answer as the paid actor/participants.

   a. _____

   b. _____

6. Researchers investigated the effect of noise on the willingness of subjects to help another person. A paid assistant dropped some books in front of a subject in two settings: a quiet one and a noisy one. The test subject helped to pick up the books more frequently in the quiet setting than in the noisy one. The results were the same in a laboratory situation or on the street.

   a. _____

   b. _____

F **PAIR WORK** Discuss and comment on the experiment that Stanley Milgram conducted.

A lot of people don't question authority. I bet the majority of volunteers **must have done** exactly what they were told.

But a few people **might have refused**—at least I hope so!

| PART TWO | Modal Verbs: Other Perfect Meanings |

■ GRAMMAR IN CONTENT

A Reread the text at the beginning of the lesson, and <u>underline</u> other examples of perfect modals. Compare your answers with a partner and discuss the meaning of the modals that you found.

Modal Verbs: Other Perfect Meanings	
Sample Sentences	**Notes**
The researcher should **have gotten** a written consent form (but he didn't). The researcher **shouldn't have lied** to the participants (but he did).	Use the perfect form of *should* to express an obligation or piece of advice that someone did *not* fulfill or follow.
He **could have recruited** many more participants (but he didn't).	Use the perfect form of *could* to express an opportunity that someone missed.
"**Could** you explain the procedure again?" "**Can** I try again?" "**May** I leave now?" He **couldn't** see the participant in the other room during the experiment. They **could** communicate via the intercom system during the experiment.	Do not use modals in perfect form to express • permission or requests • physical ability • possibility/potentiality

B Comment on the mistakes that students made in their experiments, expressing a criticism or telling about a missed opportunity. Use the notes from your psychology lecture about ethical experiments below.

Characteristics of Ethical Experimental Design:

Goal = balance the right to do research / the rights of participants
(= no abuse)

- identify physical risks: check equipment & medical procedures; age & health
- identify psychological risks: anxiety? depression? invading privacy? anger?
- keep information confidential = reduces participants' anxiety
- consult Human Subjects Review Committee = advice about ethical treatment of subjects
- obtain "informed consent" =
  describe general purpose and procedure of the experiment
  warn subjects of risks
  inform subjects that they can quit at any time
  get signatures
- debrief subjects after experiment =
  tell them about deception
  help subjects with emotional reactions to experiment

1. Team One did not tell subjects anything about the experiment.

   They shouldn't have hidden the procedures of the experiment from the subjects.

2. Team Two conducted the Milgram experiment again with college students.

   _____

3. Team Three investigated subjects' willingness to help a stranger. Before the experiment, the participants answered questions about their personal lives.

   _____

4. The test subjects for Team Four left the laboratory as soon as they had finished the experiment on visual perception.

   _____

5. Team Five investigated the relationship between anger and high temperatures. An older subject became so upset that he fainted in the laboratory.

   _____

C Rewrite each sentence, paraphrasing it to show the meaning of the sentence with the modal. Follow the example.

1. Many experimenters should have treated test animals more humanely.

   Many experimenters didn't treat animals humanely.

2. The test subjects could have refused to give electroshocks in the Milgram experiment.

   _____

3. Participants in the experiment should have felt upset when they learned the truth.

   _____

4. Milgram could have felt uncomfortable about the behavior of the participants.

   _____

5. Milgram should have realized that his experiments were groundbreaking.

   _____

6. Some of the participants could have been very angry at Milgram.

   _____

CD1, TR14

D Listen to the classroom discussion of a psychology experiment that a teacher conducted with her students. Then, answer the questions with your inferences.

1. Why did Elliott decide to do this exercise on that particular day?

   The death of Martin Luther King Jr. must/could have affected her.

2. Why did she think that children in Iowa needed a lesson on discrimination?

   _____

3. What kind of special classroom rules did Elliott make for the blue-eyed children?

   _____

4. How did the brown-eyed children probably feel on the first day of the lesson?

   _____

5. How did the parents probably react when they heard about Elliott's lesson?

   _____

6. Why did people in Riceville feel so negatively about the media's attention to Elliott?

   _____

E **SMALL GROUP WORK** Discuss Elliott's experiment from the viewpoint of a Human Subjects Review Committee. Did her exercise meet your ethical standards? What should she have done? What shouldn't she have done? What could she have done differently? Report your findings to the class.

Connection | Putting It Together

GRAMMAR AND VOCABULARY Write a composition on one of the topics below. Use as many words as possible from the Content Vocabulary on page 63. Use modal verb forms from this lesson where appropriate to express your ideas, and <u>underline</u> those verb forms.

Topic 1: People today criticize some researchers from previous decades for a lack of concern about the risks of their experiments to people or to animals. How can we justify the use of animals or people in research projects, especially if there is some physical or psychological danger to the test subjects? Give examples.

Topic 2: Given the lessons of the Milgram experiment, explain the following quotation from Oscar Wilde: "Disobedience, in the eyes of anyone who has read history, is man's main virtue. It is through disobedience that progress has been made, through disobedience and through rebellion." Give concrete historical examples.

PROJECT Interview at least two students on your campus about ethical research.

Find out the following information and report on it at your next class meeting.

   a. Do your interviewees think that research with animals is ethical?
   b. What kind of research is done with animals nowadays?

 INTERNET Go online to the website www.bbc.co.uk/science/humanbody. This website has several surveys that you can take. Choose and complete at least one psychological survey, which will take approximately 10 minutes. At the end of the survey, you will see your results and some explanations. Report on your experience and the survey results at your next class meeting.

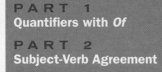
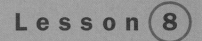

Lesson ⑧

Economics: Microfinance

■ CONTENT VOCABULARY

Look up the words below that you do not know and enter them in your vocabulary journal. Write each word's part of speech, a definition, and an example sentence. Try to include them in your discussion and writing below.

to be liable for	considerable	to encounter	to guarantee
collateral	to default	an entrepreneur	to pay off
to comprise	eligible	funds	a stimulus

■ THINK ABOUT IT

What do you know about small businesses in developing countries? What kinds of businesses exist in a village? How do people start a business in this type of environment?

In your writing journal, write for five minutes about these questions. When you are finished, share what you wrote with the class.

In your opinion, should all adults have credit available to them? What qualifications are important for a person to receive credit, either for a credit card or for a bank loan?

■ GRAMMAR IN CONTENT

CD1,TR15

A Read and listen to the passage below. The words in bold are phrases with quantifiers.

An Entrepreneurial Opportunity

Since 1976 the Grameen Bank has enabled **millions of poor people** to borrow money to pursue their own entrepreneurial projects. This bank started in villages in Bangladesh when Dr. Muhammed Yunus made credit available to the rural poor, a segment of the population that had never been considered "bankable" before. According to Dr. Yunus, providing bank services to such men and women results in the growth of small businesses, which can reduce unemployment in developing countries and serve as a stimulus for economic development.

The sort of loans that the Grameen Bank offers poor people differ from traditional bank loans. Typical bank loans require some kind of collateral; however, borrowers are eligible for these special loans if they apply as a group of five people. Each of the members has to have her own viable business project that the bank officials approve. Then, **two members of the group** receive loans, usually less than $200 each. The group supports those two members as they begin or expand a small business. If either borrower encounters difficulty, bankers supervise and give advice, and the group members may even assist in the business. However, **none of the group members** is liable for the loan payments of the others. Once the loans have been repaid, two more members of the group can borrow money, and then finally the fifth person. The bank pays 5% of the loans into a special group fund so that the five borrowers will also have earned some savings by the time the fifth person has repaid her loan. **The remainder of the loan repayments** (including interest) is used for loans to other groups of five entrepreneurs.

According to data from UNESCO, a considerable number of borrowers have already overcome extreme poverty. This system of credit has especially benefited rural women, who had never been eligible for their own loans before the Grameen Bank offered them. In fact, the vast majority of borrowers are women, who have repaid their loans at a rate above 90%. **Many of their businesses** involve simple processes related to agriculture like selling eggs or traditional skills such as pottery, weaving, and sewing. Research shows that **most of these women entrepreneurs** also reinvest their money in their business projects and in their families. Aside from **all the personal benefits** of this access to credit, women gain recognition for contributing to their communities.

---

viable: workable, capable of being successful

a fund: an amount of money that is reserved for a specific purpose

interest: a fee for a loan that is a percentage of the loan

UNESCO: United Nations Educational, Scientific, and Cultural Organization

to overcome: to succeed in spite of great obstacles

Sample Sentences	Notes
Grameen Bank makes many loans to women. **Few borrowers** default on their loans. (= nonspecific borrowers)	The two following patterns change the meaning of a noun phrase from **general** to more specific:
	1. Quantifier + *of the* + Plural Count Noun
	2. Quantifier + *of the* + Noncount Noun
Few of the borrowers need assistance from their groups. (= a small number of a specific group of borrowers)	· Apply this rule to numbers as well as to other quantifiers. Large numbers used in general estimates require only the word *of*.
In **a few villages** both men and women applied for loans. In **one of them,** the women received **much of the money,** but the men only got **a little of it.**	· Use a plural pronoun in place of a plural count noun.
	· Use a singular pronoun in place of a noncount noun.
	In this pattern, *no* becomes *none*
Millions of women receive loans annually, and **hundreds of them** may hire other women in their villages.	(e.g., *no people* → *none of the people*).
All of the members repaid their loans early because they were able to sell **half of the** merchandise within three months.	Choose either of the following patterns to express a specific noun phrase with *all, both,* and *half*:
	3. *all/both/half of the* + noun
	4. *all/both/half the* + noun
She sold **both of her** goats and **most of those** eggs on Saturday.	Use a possessive determiner or a demonstrative instead of the word *the* to add more specific information.
The Grameen Bank works with **groups of** borrowers. **A team of** bankers advises each group.	Some patterns (e.g., count noun + *of*) express a collection of individuals or part of a whole. Follow the regular rules to choose the articles or determiners that precede the count noun following the word *of*.
Most women use their profits to repay the loans and invest **the rest of the** money in their businesses and families.	

B Read over your journal entry, and <u>underline</u> at least one sentence that you can revise to include a quantifier from the chart above. Write your revised sentence(s) below.

_____

_____

_____

C Edit the noun phrases with quantifiers to make the text below more specific. Some of the phrases may have two correct forms.

When Dr. Yunus first proposed his Grameen Bank Project, many of his ^ colleagues doubted that the poor would repay their loans. No banks in his region gave credit to anyone below the poverty line, especially women. Dr. Yunus spoke with several bankers because he hoped that a few might support his project. Instead, they all laughed at him. Then, he changed his strategy. All the loans borrowed that year came from some funds that Dr. Yunus had borrowed from one bank. After all loans were repaid, he had more success with his microfinance projects.

D Look at the current records of Mr. Haq, a local banker with Grameen Bank. Make sentences about Mr. Haq's loan groups, using the data from the chart and the words in parentheses. Follow the example.

Group 1273	Mrs. S	Mrs. F	Mrs. T	Mrs. W	Mrs. T
Amount requested	200	175	175	200	250
Amount received	200	150	175	175	
Amount repaid	200	150	155	160	

Group 1733	Mrs. T	Mrs. G	Mrs. W	Mr. H	Mr. M
Amount requested	150	175	200	175	175
Amount received	150	175			
Amount repaid	0	25			

Group 1349	Mrs. H	Mrs. S	Mrs. T	Mrs. U	Mrs. S
Amount requested	175	150	75	175	100
Amount received	175	150	75	175	100
Amount repaid	175	150	75	175	50

(Note: Bangladeshi currency, the taka, has been converted to approximate U.S. dollar amounts in the chart.)

1. (most/woman in Group 1349) *Most of the women in group 1349 have already repaid their loans.*

2. (hardly any/person in Group 1733) _____

3. (all/loan in Group 1349) _____

4. (almost all/borrower) _____

5. (quite a few/loan) _____

6. (more than half/borrower) _____

7. (none/payment from Group 1733) _____

8. (one/borrower in Group 1349) _____

E Read Mr. Haq's oral report to his supervisor. Mr. Haq is worried that his groups are not performing well, so he makes some misleading statements or mistakes to hide some of the problems in his groups. Find the mistakes by checking the information in the charts on page 76. On a separate piece of paper, write a short report with the correct information. Follow the example.

Supervisor:	Mr. Haq, I understand that some of your groups aren't performing as well as we had expected.
Mr. Haq:	No, sir, I wouldn't say that. I can report that all the groups are making progress on repayment.
Supervisor:	I'd like to hear some specific information.
Mr. Haq:	In the first group—Group 1273—the majority of the women requested $200 or more, and most of them have completed their repayments.
Supervisor:	Excellent. How's your newest group handling their loans?
Mr. Haq:	Group 1733? They had a rough start, but since the beginning of the month, I have received a couple of payments from each of the first two borrowers. Both of them requested smaller amounts, so I'm hoping that they will be more consistent now.
Supervisor:	That's a relief. What about the third group?
Mr. Haq:	All of the borrowers in this group requested less than $200, and we have received almost all of the money back. The fifth borrower should pay back the rest of the loan next week.
Supervisor:	How much is that?
Mr. Haq:	Five dollars.
Supervisor:	Well done, Haq.
Mr. Haq:	Thank you, sir.

Report on the Grameen Bank Project

Some of the groups are making good progress on repaying their loans, but not all of them.

F Read the case studies of borrowers from the Grameen Bank below. Then, comment on the way that each borrower probably spends her loan money and her profit. Also, speculate on the way that each person spends her time. Use quantifiers from this lesson in your comments. Follow the example.

Case Study 1: Mrs. Jamirun Haq in Jolarpar

Mrs. Haq is a member of the Village Phone system, which is run by GrameenPhone. With her loan, she got a cellular phone with a 50% discount on airtime. She charges villagers in her region the market rate for calls—about 20 cents per minute for local calls and more for long-distance calls. When villagers receive a call at her home, she makes an appointment with the caller for a return call. Then, she or her children go to the villagers' homes to tell them when to come for the return call. With her profit, Mrs. Haq has been saving money for her daughters' education.

Case Study 2: Mrs. Sufia Begum in Jobra

Mrs. Begum weaves bamboo stools with bamboo that she buys from a local merchant. She sells her stools at local markets. She has helped to raise her family above the poverty line.

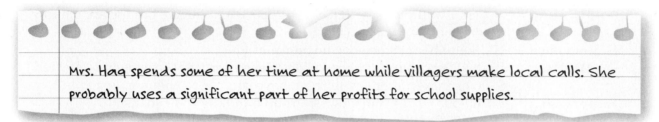

Mrs. Haq spends some of her time at home while villagers make local calls. She probably uses a significant part of her profits for school supplies.

■ COMMUNICATE

G **GROUP WORK** Talk with the members of your group about credit. Is credit readily available where you come from? Do you and your friends or coworkers have credit cards? Can you get a bank loan to buy a car or other major purchase? What are the attitudes of people where you come from about taking out a bank loan? Do you need collateral?

H **PAIR WORK** Talk with your partner about people who start small businesses in an area you're familiar with. Who are the owners or workers in these businesses? Are women encouraged to open their own businesses in that area? Do you have any idea how small business owners finance their businesses? Be prepared to tell your classmates about the information that you learned from your partner. Use quantifiers as you explain the information that you learned.

■ GRAMMAR IN CONTENT

A Reread the text at the beginning of this lesson, and <u>underline</u> the rest of the grammatical subjects that include quantifiers. Look at the main verbs in those sentences. Can you explain why some subjects take singular verbs and others take plural verbs?

Subject-Verb Agreement

Sample Sentences	Notes
First, **a team** of bankers evaluates loan applications. **The team** then meets with loan applicants to get more information. Later, **a committee** of advisors helps each borrower with her business plan.	**Collective nouns** (see the list at the bottom of the chart) usually take the singular verb form in American English.
In one village, **a number of** borrowers have repaid their loans, but **the number of** payments hasn't reached 100 yet. Before 1976 **the vast majority** of poor people was not eligible for bank credit. Since that time, Grameen Bank has shown that **a considerable majority of** poor Bangladeshis use their loans wisely. Until 1976 **none of** the poor villagers in Jorba was/were able to receive a loan. Since then, **none of the Grameen Bank branches** has/have asked for collateral from any of the poor. **Each of the borrowers** is/are making weekly payments. **Two hundred dollars** is the maximum for most loans.	Learn the differences: • *A number of* (similar in meaning to *some* or *several*) takes a plural verb. • *The number of* refers to a sum or total and takes a singular verb. • *The majority (of)* and *the minority (of)* usually take singular verbs, but a plural verb signals an emphasis on individuals. • *A majority (of)* refers to a specific group of individuals and takes a plural verb. • *None of* takes a singular verb in formal English. • Use a plural verb with *none of* + **plural noun** in informal English. • The same is true for *each of* and *every one of*. • Use a singular verb when a unit of time, distance, or money is expressed as a unit.

Collective Nouns

audience	club	couple	family	jury
cast	committee	crew	group	staff
class	council	crowd	institute	team

B (Circle) the correct verb. With a partner, discuss why you chose either the singular or plural form of the verb.

1. Everyone in the Vista Grande valley has to submit his or her loan application to a committee at the local microfinance institution (MFI). <u>The committee</u> (is/are) meeting
(1)
this Friday to discuss the applications on file and to revise the guidelines for next year. It is concerned about the loan balance that <u>current borrowers</u> (has/have) to pay
(2)
off. <u>Six hundred dollars</u> (has/have) been the average loan balance for a few years, but
(3)
<u>a number of the committee members</u> (has/have) mentioned that they would like to
(4)
see the loan balance decrease in the coming years.

2. Ms. Mendez is afraid that she will have to default on her loan of approximately $550. <u>None of her chickens</u> (has/have) laid as many eggs as she had anticipated. <u>The</u>
(5)
<u>number of eggs</u> (has/have) been so low that she had to consult with the advisory
(6)
team at the MFI. <u>The team</u> (wasn't/weren't) very sympathetic to her situation, but
(7)
agreed to take a look at her new hen house and make suggestions.

3. When a new MFI opened in the nearby town, many villagers in San Miguel made plans to apply for a loan to expand or create a small family business. In the first year, <u>the majority of borrowers</u> (was/were) able to see considerable improvements in family
(8)
income. Since then, the financial results haven't always been so visible, but gradually <u>each of the borrowers</u> (has/have) earned enough to change the lives of their families.
(9)

C Complete the sentences using one of the verb phrases in the box in the appropriate form.

~~meet with the villagers~~	caution the committee	become disappointed
divide into smaller teams	schedule a meeting	criticize various policies

1. Last year all of the researchers at an economics institute decided to work together on a microfinance project with one village in El Salvador. Since then, the institute
   _____ *has met with the villagers several times to plan the project.* _____

2. The villagers were extremely excited about the opportunity to work with the staff from the institute. Since then, none of the villagers _____

   _____

3. The villagers decided to form a committee to assist anyone who runs into difficulty with a loan. In the future, the committee _____

_____

4. Although the researchers at the institute support the villagers' decisions, a number of the economists _____

_____

5. In general, the members of the committee respect the advice of the researchers. However, a small minority of the committee members _____

_____

6. The institute researchers anticipated some criticism as they worked with the village. Next week the institute staff _____

_____

D **Look at the statistics on microfinance in Central America from 2004. Write three sentences about borrowers and loans based on this data.**

Microfinance in Central America						
Outreach Indicators	Central America	Costa Rica	El Salvador	Guatemala	Honduras	Nicaragua
# active borrowers	5,854	721	5,854	4,431	13,310	7,319
% female borrowers	65.7%	65.0%	61.0%	75.6%	81.3%	61.0%
Gross loan portfolio (US $)	3,008,127	651,862	4,903,319	989,743	3,780,661	3,935,179
Average loan balance/ Borrower	601	904	713	406	445	536

1. According to this information, 406 is the lowest average proportion of loan balance to borrower in Central America.

2. _____

_____

3. _____

_____

4. _____

_____

E Answer the questions below about Dr. Richard Browning's comments on microfinance in Central America. Dr. Browning of Microfinance Information eXchange (MIX) is a guest speaker in an economics class that has been discussing the Grameen Bank.

1. What is an MFI?

It's the acronym for microfinance institution.

2. How many MFIs are controlled by nongovernmental organizations?

3. How many of the MFIs have as many borrowers or services as the MFIs in Asia?

4. How many extremely poor borrowers are there in Central America?

5. What proportion of the borrowers in Central America are women?

6. In Honduras, how many of the MFIs work with village-level banks?

F Read each statement and (circle) the letter of the correct interpretation. The first one has been done as an example.

1. The committee has to wait until its meeting next week to announce the loans.
   a. The committee works as a unit.
   b. The people on the committee are working as individuals.

2. None of the farmers were able to make payments after the terrible floods.
   a. This is from a formal context.
   b. This is from an informal context.

3. The crowd is protesting against the increase in bank rates.
   a. The people in the crowd are acting as one unit.
   b. The people in the crowd are behaving as individuals.

4. Generally, the minority support political candidates for strong economic reform.
   a. This is from a formal context.
   b. This is from an informal context.

5. The team of graduate students were anxious to assist the poor villagers with their projects.
   a. The graduate students were going to work as a unit.
   b. Each student was going to work as an individual with the villagers.

6. The majority often demand their rights to the economic disadvantage of the minority.
   a. The majority in this context act like individuals.
   b. The majority in this context act as one large unit.

G There are five errors in the e-mail message below. The first one has been fixed. Find and correct the four errors that remain.

Jane-

I know that you would love the open-air markets here. Today at the market in the central square, most
~~of~~ *the* women were selling either food or crafts from their villages. A number of the craft items were very

elaborate, but the rest of them was quite simple. I bought a few pieces to decorate my room—take a look

at the attached photos.

The best part is that almost of the women keep the money that they earn. The majority of them are the

bosses of their little businesses. Remember when we learned about Grameen Bank in Econ? They have

something similar here in Malaysia. One of the women in my village has just one more payment of about $5.

That five dollars mean that she will be able to enjoy all of profits from her labor from now on.

You gotta do some volunteer work, too! It's the way to put your life in perspective.

Hugs-

Cora Mae

■ COMMUNICATE

H **GROUP WORK** Many people feel that Dr. Yunus deserved the Nobel Prize for his development of the Grameen Bank. Discuss his accomplishment with your group. How do you compare him with other recipients of the Nobel Prize? Many other individuals around the world have contributed to the welfare of the poor. How would you compare Dr. Yunus's contribution to theirs?

Dr. Muhammed Yunus, Winner of the 2006 Nobel Prize.

GRAMMAR AND VOCABULARY Write a composition on one of the topics below. Use as many words as possible from the Content Vocabulary on page 73. Use quantifiers where appropriate to express your ideas, and <u>underline</u> those words and phrases.

Topic 1: What's the best way for young people to learn the value of money? Use examples from your own experience and the experience of your friends or schoolmates.

Topic 2: Many nations have special programs to assist countries in the developing world. Some of these programs send money, and others offer advice from experts. Another strategy is to send volunteers to help with various projects in villages or regions outside large cities. In your opinion, what kind of aid is the most effective? Be as specific as possible and give examples.

PROJECT Interview at least one student on your campus about credit and credit cards. Find out the student's views regarding the following information and report on it at your next class meeting.

   a. Do most students have credit cards?
   b. How do most students get a credit card? Do their parents help them?
   c. If the student that you interview has a credit card, find out what the interest rate for that card is.
   d. Do most students pay off their balance each month?

 INTERNET Go online, and use the search phrase "student credit cards." Find a website that gives information about the risks that students face when they use credit cards. Choose two important points or suggestions, and report on that information in class.

Criminal Science: Juvenile Court

■ CONTENT VOCABULARY

Look up the words below that you do not know and enter them in your vocabulary journal. Write each word's part of speech, a definition, and an example sentence. Try to include them in your discussion and writing below.

to acknowledge	an incentive	an offense	a role model
a curfew	judicial	a prison sentence	to testify
empathy	a mentor	a procedure	testimony

■ THINK ABOUT IT

What are the roles of the people in a courtroom? What procedures are standard in a typical courtroom trial? What would you expect to see during a typical day in court? What is surprising about the people in the photo on the following page? Discuss your ideas with a classmate.

In your writing journal, write for five minutes about these questions. When you are finished, share your ideas with your classmates.

In your opinion, should courts of law treat teenagers who get in trouble with the law the same as adults? What should the police, judges, and lawyers consider when a young person commits a crime? What is the goal of the justice system when a young person commits a minor offense?

■ GRAMMAR IN CONTENT

CD1, TR17

A Read and listen to the passage below. The words in bold are phrases with gerunds or infinitives as subjects.

Getting a Second Chance

Since the 1970s, teen court has provided an alternative to juvenile court for teenagers who commit certain types of crimes. Every year 110,000 to 125,000 young people go before a jury or judge in teen court, or youth court as it is known in some states. By accepting this form of trial, first-time teenage offenders can avoid a criminal record and move quickly through the legal system. **Admitting guilt** is the first step in this process. Then, **appearing before a judge and/or jury** and **answering their questions** constitutes the next step. **Fulfilling the requirements of the sentence** is the third and final step.

One of the goals of youth court is to provide positive role models. Young people on the juries in teen court serve that function. Prior to working as jurors, teenage volunteers are given lessons in asking questions and in interpreting body language. Another part of their training is to learn about the law and courtroom procedures. There are strong incentives for participating as a juror aside from putting in volunteer hours. These young people gain valuable experience in public speaking and can develop leadership and mediation skills. In fact, it becomes a goal of many of the offenders **to serve as a juror.** In recent years, almost 30% of the jurors have been former offenders.

A teenager waits to hear his sentence at a hearing.

Another primary objective is to teach teens about the consequences of their actions. As mentioned above, **acknowledging mistakes** starts the process. Offenders may be in court for their conduct at school, such as excessive tardiness or disrespectful behavior to teachers, or for committing minor crimes like theft, disorderly conduct, or possession of marijuana or alcohol. Once the jury and judge have questioned offenders, it is the duty of the court **to decide on the sentence. Giving offenders a voice and then making them accountable for their conduct** is the philosophy behind the decisions, not **punishing them.** The sentences may be to perform community service, to attend counseling, to give a report, or even to pay back victims for their stolen or vandalized property. The idea is to connect the offenders with the community that suffered in some way from their behavior. By interacting positively with their families, teachers, and fellow citizens, the young people can create new opportunities for themselves.

a juvenile court: a court that hears criminal cases involving minors

a criminal record: a person's permanent record of criminal behavior

aside from: excluding, except for

mediation: a process of helping two sides solve a dispute or come to an agreement

to vandalize: to destroy or damage property intentionally

Sample Sentences	Notes
Lying is never a good idea, and **lying to your family** can be even worse.	Both **gerunds** and **infinitives** can function as the subject of a verb. They are often used interchangeably.
To err is human.	
Testifying in front of other teens isn't easy.	The subject of a verb can be a simple gerund or infinitive. The subject can also be a gerund or infinitive that is part of a longer phrase.
To act defiantly doesn't sound like a good strategy in youth court.	
Listening to testimony requires a lot of attention and empathy.	Always use a singular verb with a gerund or infinitive subject.
To give young people a second chance is one goal of teen court.	Generally, use a gerund to emphasize a real action that happens regularly, and use an infinitive to express an abstract possibility or a potential, unfulfilled action.
It takes courage **to admit mistakes**.	Place **an infinitive subject** after the verb phrase and the word *it* in the subject position. This word order is preferred, but the infinitive can precede the verb, especially if the infinitive is very short.
It wasn't smart **to act belligerently** during court.	
From the beginning, it hasn't been the job of youth court **to punish offenders**.	
Admitting mistakes takes courage.	Place **a gerund subject** in regular subject position in front of the verb. There are a few exceptions in informal English where you can use *it* in subject position and the gerund after the verb phrase:
It was no use **lying to the judge**.	• *It's no use . . .*
It wouldn't be any good **blaming someone else**.	• *It's no/not any good . . .*
	• *It's (not) easy/hard . . .*
It was difficult **testifying before the teen jury**.	
It's unacceptable **not to be** on time for a court date.	In a negative construction, follow these patterns:
	• *to* + *not* + simple verb
Not appearing at all is actually a crime.	• *not* + *-ing* verb

B **Read over your journal entry, and <u>underline</u> at least one sentence that you can revise to include a gerund or infinitive phrase used as a subject. Write your revised sentence(s) below.**

_____

_____

_____

C Write about the experience and emotions of an offender in youth court. Match one of the actions with an adjective, and write the sentence. Use either a gerund or an infinitive in each of your sentences. See the example.

Adjectives	Actions
difficult	answer/questions
embarrassing	admit/mistakes
frustrating	wait/sentence
intimidating	not have/criminal record
encouraging	sit/courtroom
frightening	perform/community service

1. _____ Admitting your mistakes is very difficult. _____

2. _____

3. _____

4. _____

5. _____

6. _____

D Look at the instructions that teen jurors receive when they learn about sentences for offenders in youth court. Write down the goals or objectives of juries when they assign each of these actions.

> **Guidelines for Sentencing**
>
> Remember, connect the sentence to the offenders' behavior so that they see the consequences of their actions. You can use one or more of these sentences:
> A. paying for the damages of vandalism with money earned by the offender
> B. participating in a safe-driving program
> C. tutoring a child in reading skills
> D. writing a letter of apology
> E. touring a jail
> F. meeting with a mentor weekly
> G. having a curfew from 10 P.M.–6 A.M.

1. _____ It's their goal to teach the offender the value of people's property. _____

2. _____

3. _____

4. _____

5. _____

6. _____

7. _____

E Read the statements, and then paraphrase the information using the phrases in parentheses. Use a variety of infinitives and gerunds.

1. Students have to work hard to get scholarships for college.

    (take hard work) _It takes hard work to get a scholarship for college._

2. Young people have to be patient and try hard if they want to be excellent in sports.

    (take patience and perseverance) _____

    _____

3. Young people have to work very hard if they want to have a part-time job and get good grades in school.

    (take a lot of effort) _____

    _____

4. Teenagers need to spend many hours cooperating with other group members if they want to finish a school project well.

    (involve time and teamwork) _____

    _____

5. Some families can't afford college tuition payments for their children.

    (cost too much for some families) _____

    _____

6. Some parents encourage their children to babysit or to get summer jobs so that they can learn to be more responsible.

    (teach teenagers responsibility) _____

    _____

7. It's hard for some young people to resist peer pressure.

    (require self-confidence) _____

    _____

8. It is often a hard decision when teens decide that they won't use drugs.

    (take determination) _____

    _____

F PAIR WORK Read the case studies from teen court below, and with your partner decide on an appropriate sentence for each offender. Use infinitives and gerunds as much as possible.

Putting Fred in jail doesn't serve any purpose. He should be given another chance.

But it's not a good idea **to let him off completely**. He should have some sort of punishment.

Case 1: Fred, who lives in an inner-city neighborhood, admitted that he cut the tires of his teacher's car in the school parking lot. His teacher made him stay after school because he hadn't handed in his homework on time.

Case 2: Natasha, who lives in a middle-class neighborhood, acknowledged that she had drank at a party and then went through a red light on her way home. She is a 17-year-old high school senior and attended the party at the home of one of her classmates. Natasha had run the red light when the police stopped her around 1:00 A.M. She failed the breathalyzer test and was arrested.

PART TWO	Gerunds and Infinitives as Subject Complements; Gerunds Following a Preposition

■ GRAMMAR IN CONTENT

A Reread the text at the beginning of this lesson, and (circle) the other gerunds and infinitives in the reading. Then, share your results with a partner.

Subject Complements	
Sample Sentences	**Notes**
A common problem for youth offenders is **not having positive role models.** The point of each sentence is **to make the offender accountable for his or her actions.**	Both **gerunds** and **infinitives** can function as subject complements. Use one of the following patterns: 1. Subject + **be** + Gerund 2. Subject + **be** + Infinitive The complement explains or elaborates on the subject of the sentence.
A common problem for youth offenders is **not having a stable home environment.** A common problem for youth offenders is **not to have any positive role models.**	Use this structure to emphasize the information in the gerund or infinitive. In English, the end of a sentence is typically the **focus of new information.**

Gerunds Following a Preposition

Sample Sentences	Notes
First, the judge spoke with Ken **about taking** responsibility for his actions. Then, in the interest **of teaching** Ken a lesson, the judge thought **of assigning** him some hours of community service. Instead, she sentenced the young man **to writing** letters of apology to every person in his neighborhood.	Use a **gerund** after any **preposition**. This rule even applies to the preposition *to*. Use this structure to make your sentences more dynamic. Many English structures allow speakers to include more than one action in a clause. Also, see Lessons 21, 22, 25.

B **Revise each sentence so that it has only one clause. Use one of the verbs from the original sentence as a gerund with a phrase in the box below.**

in preparation for	with regard to	as a consequence of
~~as a result of~~	in reference to	

1. Judge Klegg has volunteered at teen court for years, so he can interpret teenagers' body language very well.

   As a result of volunteering at teen court for years, Judge Klegg can interpret
   teenagers' body language very well.

2. Carl talked about his participation in gang activities, and he revealed that he had also encouraged his younger brother to join.

   _____

   _____

3. Carl was finally arrested because he and his brother stole a neighbor's car.

   _____

   _____

4. Before he heard the jury's recommendations, Judge Klegg reviewed the police report about Carl and his brother.

   _____

   _____

C Paraphrase one of the clauses with a gerund and a phrase from the box below.

be upset about	~~be afraid of~~	be guilty of
be familiar with	be used to	

1. Carl feared that he would reveal the names of other gang members.

   Carl was afraid of revealing the names of other gang members.

2. Carl tried to protect his brother during the trial.

   _____

3. Carl admitted that he had endangered his brother with his gang connections.

   _____

4. Carl didn't like the fact that he had to spend time with younger kids.

   _____

D How did Carl end up in teen court? What was the situation in his family? Use your imagination to answer the questions about his dysfunctional home life.

1. What did he argue with his father about?

   _____

2. What did his mother blame him for?

   _____

3. What did Carl always complain about?

   _____

4. What was his younger sister always talking about?

   _____

5. What did Carl's brother care about?

   _____

6. What did Carl feel like?

   _____

E Read what these community leaders have to say about their work with young people. Then, answer the questions that follow.

1. **Coach Tennyson:** Most kids nowadays want to be big sports stars, like Kobe Bryant or Tiger Woods, and earn millions of dollars. You know as well as I do that most of them will never be basketball or golf stars. What they have to learn is to work together and not to be selfish. When they grow up, those skills are going to help them get a job and keep it.

   According to Coach Tennyson, what's the point of team sports?

   The point is learning to work with other people and not being selfish.

2. **Ms. Davies:** Lots of people ask me why I waste my time with a bunch of teenage girls every week. For me, it's time that's well-spent. When the girls start out, all they care about is their hair, their clothes, or their cell phones. Many of them have never been outside the city. I love to see their faces when we go hiking on the weekend or when we cook over a campfire for the first time. They're just like kids again—instead of cool teenagers.

   What's the motivation of this Girl Scout leader?

   _____

3. **Mr. Henderson:** I believe that students learn history much better when they have a hands-on project. They have to negotiate among themselves and take responsibility for their part of the project. They can be creative—and see that history is much more than what's in their textbooks.

   What's Mr. Henderson's reason for assigning group projects?

   _____

4. **Judy Callahan:** Whenever I tutor one of my classmates, I realize that I probably learn more than the other person. You know, it's really hard to explain math if the other person feels like he can't get it. When the other person finally understands, I feel happy for him, but I also feel like I passed a big test, too.

   What's Judy's motivation for doing peer tutoring?

   _____

5. **Mr. Patterson:** When I was young, I was lucky to have a father who supported me and always gave me great advice. Even when I made mistakes, he stood behind me. When I graduated from college and went into business, there were other people who helped me along the way. Nowadays so many young men need that kind of positive support. I'm just following in my father's footsteps.

   What's Mr. Henderson's idea about being a mentor?

   _____

F If appropriate, edit the underlined sentence in each of the texts below so that the new information is at the end of the sentence. Explain your decision to edit or to leave the sentence in the same form.

1. Teenagers have to deal with an intimidating situation when they appear before the judge and jury in youth court. ~~It takes a lot of courage to face a judge and jury of your peers.~~ *Facing a judge and jury of your peers takes a lot of courage.* Teenagers with that kind of courage and determination will probably benefit from having a second chance.

   REASON: _____ *"Courage" is new information so it needs to be at the end.* _____

2. Many youths who appear in youth court made one bad decision. Making one wrong choice shouldn't be the reason for having a criminal record according to the philosophy of youth court. Instead, young people who admit their guilt and fulfill other requirements can avoid getting a record.

   REASON: _____

3. Teenage jurors shoulder a lot of responsibility as they decide on sentences for other teens. It takes a lot of training to make good decisions about another person's life. That training is an ongoing activity in teen court as judges help the jurors to understand their options in choosing the proper sentence.

   REASON: _____

4. Communities with teen courts have demonstrated an understanding that not all "troublemakers" are bad kids. Some teenagers get into trouble because of peer pressure. Saying "No" to your friends requires a lot of self-confidence at that age. Adults have seen that teenagers can gain that feeling of self-worth as they fulfill the requirements of their youth court sentences.

   REASON: _____

5. Some adults get involved in youth court because of their own experiences as teenagers. The reason that they become mentors is to help young people avoid such experiences. The mentors try to guide the teenagers so that they make different friends and better choices.

   REASON: _____

G Find and correct the four errors in the e-mail below.

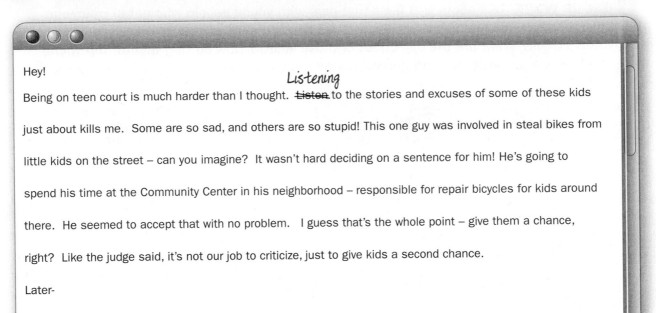

Hey!

Listening

Being on teen court is much harder than I thought. ~~Listen~~ to the stories and excuses of some of these kids just about kills me. Some are so sad, and others are so stupid! This one guy was involved in steal bikes from little kids on the street – can you imagine? It wasn't hard deciding on a sentence for him! He's going to spend his time at the Community Center in his neighborhood – responsible for repair bicycles for kids around there. He seemed to accept that with no problem. I guess that's the whole point – give them a chance, right? Like the judge said, it's not our job to criticize, just to give kids a second chance.

Later-

JR

■ **COMMUNICATE**

H **PAIR WORK** Brainstorm types of youth programs that teenagers can join outside of school. Choose one of the programs and prepare a list of the goals of that organization. Then, for each of the goals, develop a list of 2–3 actions or activities that teenagers or their mentors do in order to implement the goals. When you are finished, share your program description with your class.

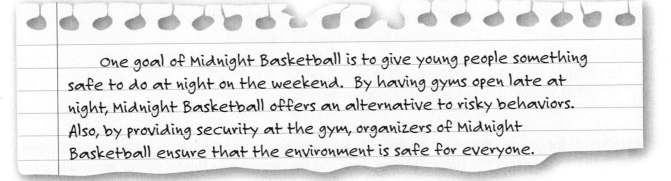

One goal of Midnight Basketball is to give young people something safe to do at night on the weekend. By having gyms open late at night, Midnight Basketball offers an alternative to risky behaviors. Also, by providing security at the gym, organizers of Midnight Basketball ensure that the environment is safe for everyone.

I GROUP WORK Talk about 2–3 films that deal with young people who get in trouble at school or with the law. What happens to the teenagers? Who are the adults that try to help them? What are the objectives of those adults? How do they mentor the young people? Use prepositions with gerunds as often as possible.

Radio was a movie about a great football coach. He gave his team a lesson **in respecting** one another.

I saw that movie, too. The coach prevented the players **from being** mean to Radio, who was mentally challenged. You could tell the coach cared **about giving** all the players an equal chance.

Connection Putting It Together

GRAMMAR AND VOCABULARY Write a composition on one of the topics below. Use as many words as possible from the Content Vocabulary on page 85. Use gerund and infinitive structures from this lesson to express your ideas, and <u>underline</u> those structures.

Topic 1: The parents of teenagers who break the law should receive a fine. If the crime is serious, the parents should also serve time in jail. Do you agree?

Topic 2: It's one of the goals of teen court to teach young people to be good citizens. Is the idea of civics, that is, lessons about good citizenship, still important in our modern world, or is it too old-fashioned?

PROJECT Interview at least one student on your campus about judicial affairs on campus. Find out the following information, and report on it at the next class meeting.

    a. Is there a judicial board or an honor board on campus?
    b. What is its purpose?
    c. What kinds of offenses does the board handle?
    d. What happens when students are guilty?

 INTERNET Go online, and use the search term "youth court" to find information on the federal youth court system in the United States. Find out the answers to the following questions and be prepared to present the information in class.

    1. Where are youth courts located? Select four states and find out how many youth courts operate there.
    2. What kinds of scholarship opportunities exist for young people who are involved in youth court?

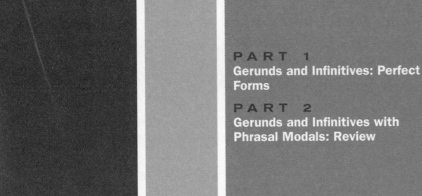

Environmental Chemistry: H$_2$O

■ CONTENT VOCABULARY

Look up the words below that you do not know and enter them in your vocabulary journal. Write each word's part of speech, a definition, and an example sentence. Try to include them in your discussion and writing below.

a compound	mercury	to ascertain	to discharge
distilled water	preliminary	to contaminate	to dispose of
lead	a residue	to dilute	toxic

■ THINK ABOUT IT

How do chemicals and pollutants enter our water supply? What are the short-term and long-term dangers associated with impure water? How can we purify our sources of water and keep them clean?

In your writing journal, write for five minutes about the questions below. When you are finished, share what you wrote with the class.

Are people in your community concerned about the environment? Do they tend to pay attention to reports on air or water pollution? Are they aware of the companies or businesses that may be guilty of having contaminated the air or water in your area?

■ GRAMMAR IN CONTENT

CD1,TR19

A Read and listen to the passage below. The words in bold are gerunds or infinitives in the perfect form.

Chemistry 091: Chemistry for Non-Majors

Dr. N. Sato
Semester Research Project

As we examine the role chemistry plays in our lives this semester, you will participate in a research project on the safety of the waterways near campus. In the past, several local industries were guilty of **having discharged** their wastewater directly into local streams. For example, Prestige Paper routinely got rid of the chlorine that they used in paper-processing in Maple Hill Creek until the early 1970s. Although conditions have improved since the Clean Water Act of 1972, some local farmers and small business owners still tend to use local streams and creeks as a way to dispose of wastewater, and unintentional run-off still occurs as well.

Your goal in this project is **to have measured** the quality of water in a particular stream or creek in three ways by the end of the semester. Local officials claim **to have monitored** these same waterways since the 1990s, but citizens have often complained about unpleasant odors and a slightly metallic taste in the tap water. In light of these complaints, you will perform a public service by ascertaining the current quality of our tap water and by following up on your results with recommendations for punishing those who seem to be responsible for **having contaminated** the water.

PROCEDURES
1. You will work in teams of 4. In this way, our class will manage to investigate all of the local waterways.
2. Each team will conduct a biochemical oxygen demand (BOD) test and a chemical oxygen demand (COD) test to check for organic material in the water. In both tests you will determine the amount of dissolved oxygen in the water samples.
3. The second tests will focus on inorganic substances, such as rocks, minerals, and metals, in the water. These tests involve filtering the water.
4. The last set of tests will measure the level of toxic chemicals, such as chlorine, ammonia, or petroleum products, in the water samples. For these tests you will monitor small organisms, such as algae or minnows, to ascertain the concentration of toxic compounds.

SCHEDULE:
The BOD and COD tests are conducted over a 5-day period. You should plan **to have completed** the first set of measurements by the end of this month. The other tests will be assigned as we cover the material pertinent to the research procedures.

run-off: an overflow of liquid or rainwater

an organism: a form of life

organic: materials made of carbon, such as plants and animals

algae: aquatic, photosynthetic organisms

a minnow: a small fresh-water fish

pertinent: relevant

Sample Sentences	Notes
Professor Irving's achievement was **having proven** the source of mercury in the water.	Use the perfect form of a gerund or infinitive to emphasize that the action happened before the action of the main verb.
TTR Industries denied **having done** anything illegal.	A perfect gerund takes this form: *having* + **past participle**.
You can't expect them **to have admitted** dumping mercury in the water.	A perfect infinitive takes this form: *to have* + **past participle**.
As a result of **not having disposed** of the mercury properly, the company will have to pay a large fine.	Put *not* before the gerund in a negative phrase: *not having* + **past participle**.
They pretended **not to have lied** about the mercury spill.	Put *not* before an infinitive in a negative phrase: *not to have* + **past participle**.
The Water Board expects **to have measured** the level of chlorine in all local streams by the end of next month.	An **infinitive in the perfect form** may be similar in meaning to an action expressed in future perfect, especially with the main verbs *expect, hope, plan*.
It's Senator Marksbury's ambition **to have revised** the law on clean water by this summer. Senator Marksbury **will have revised** the law on clean water by this summer.	The future perfect generally expresses greater certainty than does a perfect infinitive that the action will be completed by a future date or time.

B Read over your journal entry, and <u>underline</u> at least one sentence that you can revise to include a gerund or infinitive in the perfect form. Write your revised sentence(s) below.

_____

_____

_____

C Complete the sentences in the text below with the appropriate perfect gerund or infinitive. Use verbs from the box below.

neutralize	~~pour~~	add	make	measure
follow	demonstrate	use	lie	start

As a result of _____*having poured*_____ only distilled water into a beaker,
(1)

each student started last Tuesday's lab assignment with a completely neutral liquid

with a pH of 7.0. Then, they were supposed to mix an equal amount of an acid and a

base, but because of _____ a mistake in his measurement,
(2)

Ken had an acidic mixture. When his professor Dr. Fletcher checked the pH of the

liquid in his beaker, Ken denied _____ the liquids incorrectly.
(3)

As a consequence of _____ too much acid, Ken ended up with
(4)

a mixture that had a pH of 3.0 instead of 7.0. Dr. Fletcher used Ken's mistake in the

next step of her lesson since her goal was _____ the process of
(5)

neutralization by the end of class. She planned _____ with a
(6)

strong acidic mixture in her demonstration, so it was convenient to use the liquid in his

beaker. Dr. Fletcher measured and poured some of a base liquid into Ken's beaker, and as

a result of _____ the acid, she could prove to the students that
(7)

the pH of the liquid was back to 7.0. After class, Ken apologized to Dr. Fletcher for not

_____ her directions more carefully.
(8)

D Answer the questions on the next page using information from Professor Sato's project schedule. Use the verb in parentheses with a perfect gerund or infinitive.

Group/Leader	Waterway	Deadline	Chemical Analysis	Finding? mg/L
Team 1: Nick	Wolf Stream	Week 6	copper	1.3*
Team 2: Judy	Stone Creek	Week 7	sulfate	250
Team 3: Ryan	Maple Hill Creek	Week 8	lead	0.015*

*Action is required for chemicals at this level in drinking water.

1. According to Professor Sato's schedule, when should he receive results from the second round of testing? (anticipate)

   Professor Sato anticipates having received the results by week 8.

2. Ryan has been really busy this semester and wanted to do their experiment as soon as possible. What was his tentative schedule for Team 3's experiment? (hope)

3. Judy's team works very well together and did a good job on the previous experiment. When does Judy think that they will be able to complete this assignment? (expect)

4. Professor Sato is eager to start the next round of experiments. Which week looks good for starting that lesson? (plan)

5. The students have a final exam in this class in Week 15. When would they prefer to finish the final set of tests for this course? (want)

6. After each round of tests, the students report on their findings in class. When do the students think that they will present their test results? (anticipate)

E Look at the chart on page 100 again. Answer the questions about Professor Sato's class using the adjectives in parentheses and the perfect form of a gerund or infinitive.

1. Professor Sato was very surprised at the finding of Team 1, which has done very careless work in the past. How does he explain their results? (likely)

   They are likely to have made a mistake in their measurement.

2. How did Team 1 feel about discovering a high level of copper in the water? (worried about)

3. How did Team 3 feel about finding so much lead? (shocked at)

4. Team 3 realized that their finding could have a great impact on the health of the community. How did they feel about uncovering the dangerous level of lead? (proud)

5. Professor Sato had not anticipated Team 3's discovery of high levels of lead. How did he feel about assigning Team 3 to check lead in that particular river? (lucky)

F Revise the sentences below. Combine them by replacing the second sentence with a perfect infinitive or gerund.

1. *The Sentinel* has accused Lycome Corporation of water pollution. According to the article, the company has been discharging ammonia into Willow River for five years.

   The Sentinel has accused Lycome Corporation of having discharged ammonia into Willow River for five years.

2. According to their spokesperson, the company planned a solution to the ammonia problem. The solution was to dilute the ammonia to an acceptable level.

3. Another article congratulated Dale Franklin for improvements at his ranch. Franklin has eliminated the run-off of his cattle waste into Sydney Stream.

4. However, some of Franklin's neighbors claim the opposite. Supposedly they found evidence of wastewater from the ranch farther down the stream.

5. The paper suspected a local chicken farm of similar pollution. The farm may have dumped an illegal amount of their organic material in Queensland Creek.

6. A nearby pet food producer was charged with the same violations. The company got rid of large amounts of waste through their sewer lines.

7. Employees pretended otherwise, but it was obvious that they had known about the waste in the sewer lines.

8. The newspaper also blamed a large farm for deforestation. According to the report, the farm had cut all the trees in a local forest.

■ **COMMUNICATE**

G **GROUP WORK** Discuss problems of water pollution in your local region. Who or what has caused the pollution? What steps has the government taken, if any?

People usually blame the mining companies for having dumped toxic chemicals in the local rivers.

Yeah, and the mining companies deny having done anything illegal.

■ GRAMMAR IN CONTENT

A Reread the text at the beginning of this lesson, and <u>underline</u> the other gerunds and infinitives in the text.

Gerunds and Infinitives with Phrasal Modals

Sample Sentences	Notes
Our goal is **to be able to drink** water out of any stream in this area without ill effect.	Use *to be able to* + **verb** or *being able to* + **verb** to express ability.
I appreciate **being able to drink** water out of a river when I go hiking.	
Did the authorities acknowledge **not being able to find** the source of contamination?	Use the word *not* in front of the phrasal modal to express negation of the gerund or infinitive.
People get tired of **having to boil** their water and of **not being able to take** showers.	Use *to have to* + **verb** or *having to* + **verb** to express necessity.
We prefer **not to have to buy** bottled water, but in some places the water tastes bad.	

Gerund and Infinitive Review

Sample Sentences	Notes
The test for mercury **kept showing** a positive result.	Verbs such as *keep, fail, cause, continue, prefer, forget, remember, stop,* and *try* must be followed by a gerund or infinitive. See Appendix 1 for a complete list of these verbs.
The test **failed to show** any increase in copper.	
We should **continue monitoring/to monitor** the oxygen level daily.	For most verbs with both gerund and infinitive objects there is little difference in meaning.
Dr. Dix **forgot to get** a sample at Willow Creek, so he had to go back to get one. Maybe next time he'll **remember to go** there.	For the following verbs, however, the use of a gerund or infinitive object marks a difference in meaning: *forget, remember, stop, regret, try.*
Dr. Penn **remembered putting** the samples in the lab but completely **forgot turning** on the equipment. Luckily, Dr. Dix turned it off, and the machine **stopped filtering** the water. Dr. Penn **tried measuring** the solids on the filter and it worked.	With these verbs, remember that a gerund emphasizes a real action that occurred before the action of the preceding verb/the main verb and an infinitive expresses a possibility or a potential, unfulfilled action.

B (Circle) the letter of the correct interpretation of each sentence.

1. The water here appears to contain a lot of calcium and magnesium because we often get a white film on the faucet.

   a. The water must have calcium and magnesium in it.
   b. The water has calcium and magnesium in it.

2. Before class was over, Dr. Sato remembered to assign the second set of experiments.

   a. Dr. Sato realized that he had already assigned the experiments.
   b. Dr. Sato did not forget that he had to give the next assignment.

3. Dr. Sato's students managed to find a significant amount of lead in the river.

   a. It took a lot of effort, but the students succeeded in analyzing the lead content.
   b. The students organized themselves efficiently so that they could find the lead.

4. Students on Team 3 tried collecting their next samples from Maple Hill Creek according to Dr. Sato's instructions.

   a. The students wanted to collect the samples, but they weren't successful.
   b. The students hadn't collected samples this way before, but it worked.

5. Some people pretend to follow clean water laws.

   a. Some people say that they follow the laws, but they don't.
   b. Some people have the intention of following the laws.

6. While the students on Team 3 were testing the water for lead, they stopped to check their preliminary results.

   a. The students decided not to check their results any more.
   b. The students decided to discontinue their tests so that they could check the results.

7. After the mercury scare, Hendersonville has resumed testing its tap water regularly.

   a. The city has started testing the tap water again.
   b. The city has summarized the results of the water tests regularly.

8. Many citizens resent having to boil their tap water when the water supply is contaminated.

   a. Many citizens feel angry and irritated when they have to boil their tap water.
   b. Many citizens don't want to boil their tap water when it has been contaminated.

9. Dr. Sato regretted telling the teams about making recommendations to local officials now that they had actually found lead in the water.

   a. Dr. Sato was sorry that he had already told the students about making recommendations.
   b. Dr. Sato was sorry that he had to tell the students about the recommendations.

10. A local company neglected to neutralize the acids that it uses in one process before they discharged the wastewater from their factory.

   a. The company succeeded in neutralizing the acids.
   b. The company failed to neutralize the acids properly.

C Complete each sentence with the appropriate phrasal modal + gerund or infinitive, using the verb in parentheses.

1. To do their experiments, Dr. Sato's students need ___to be able to conduct___ various types of tests. (ABILITY/conduct)

2. At the beginning of the semester, some of his students may be anxious about

   _____ samples because they've never done it before.
   (NECESSITY/collect)

3. Dr. Sato is accustomed to _____ various experimental techniques before his students can begin their projects. (NECESSITY/demonstrate)

4. He expects all of them _____ liquids because it is so similar to using a coffee filter. (ABILITY/filter)

5. Many students can't imagine _____ the amount of dissolved solids in water until they see that it just involves filtering and boiling off the water, and then weighing the residue. (ABILITY/determine)

6. When the students evaluated their water samples for toxic compounds, the

   experiments involved _____ organisms in the samples.
   (NECESSITY/place)

7. Some of the students felt uncomfortable about _____ the lives of creatures in their research. (NECESSITY/endanger)

8. Dr. Sato wanted the students _____ the toxicity of the water so he assured them that the experiments were necessary. (ABILITY/measure)

9. A few students really resented not _____ the research without killing the minnows that they were using. (ABILITY/conduct)

CD1,TR20

D Listen to Dr. Sato's introduction to desalination and answer the questions below. Try to use a gerund or infinitive in your answers.

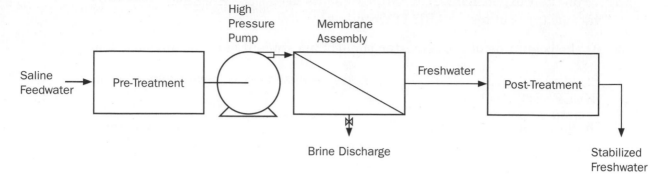

1. How do some arid regions manage to get drinking water?

_____

2. Why does Dr. Sato recommend using the Middle East as an example?

_____

3. What does desalination technology require?

_____

4. What do they need to have done before sea water can become drinkable?

_____

5. In reverse osmosis, what are the membranes in the system effective at doing?

_____

6. What is involved in producing drinking water from distilled water?

_____

7. What is a desalination plant capable of doing?

_____

E Find and correct the five errors in the e-mail message below.

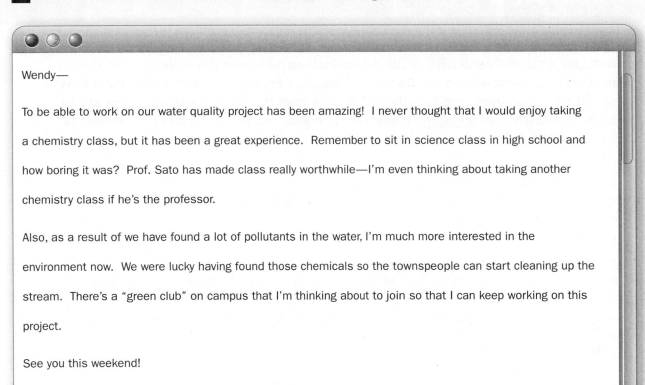

Wendy—

To be able to work on our water quality project has been amazing! I never thought that I would enjoy taking a chemistry class, but it has been a great experience. Remember to sit in science class in high school and how boring it was? Prof. Sato has made class really worthwhile—I'm even thinking about taking another chemistry class if he's the professor.

Also, as a result of we have found a lot of pollutants in the water, I'm much more interested in the environment now. We were lucky having found those chemicals so the townspeople can start cleaning up the stream. There's a "green club" on campus that I'm thinking about to join so that I can keep working on this project.

See you this weekend!

Greg

■ COMMUNICATE

F **PAIR WORK** Dr. Sato's students have found unacceptable levels of lead and copper in sources of local drinking water, and they are going to discuss their findings with town officials tomorrow. Prepare some questions that will help students during their meeting. Use the main verbs in the box below and appropriate gerunds or infinitives.

| manage | ~~arrange~~ | ~~demand~~ | resume | avoid |
| threaten | acknowledge | propose | expect | tolerate |

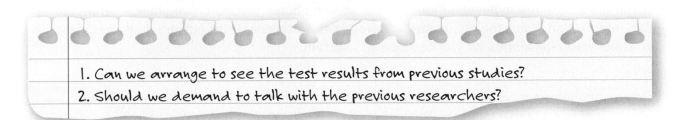

1. Can we arrange to see the test results from previous studies?
2. Should we demand to talk with the previous researchers?

G **SMALL GROUP WORK** Discuss the importance of water conservation. Put together a list of 4–5 pressing issues related to water. What is the best response to these issues? Discuss possible solutions, and then share your ideas with your classmates.

GRAMMAR AND VOCABULARY Write a composition on one of the topics below. Use as many words as possible from the Content Vocabulary on page 97, and (circle) them in your composition. Use gerund and infinitive structures from this lesson where appropriate to express your ideas, and underline those verb phrases, i.e., the verbs and the gerunds or infinitives that follow them.

Topic 1: Water has shaped the culture, history, and economy of countries around the world. What kind of impact has water had on your country? Are people in some areas concerned about being able to maintain a safe water supply? How secure is the water supply as a result of having diverted water for agricultural purposes? Explain and give concrete examples.

Topic 2: Many students complain about having to take chemistry classes because they consider chemistry to be irrelevant to their lives. In the media, stories about chemists and chemistry often highlight accidents or the harmful effects of chemicals even though scientists may deny having created the problem. How has chemistry actually contributed to making all of our lives better?

PROJECT Interview at least one student on your campus about the question of drinking bottled water. Find out the following information, and report what you found out to your classmates.

1. What kind of water does the student drink?
2. Is it safe to drink the water in public places in the U.S.?
3. Why do Americans tend to drink so much bottled water?
4. What kind of water does the student recommend drinking?

 INTERNET Go online to the website of your local water authority and check the water quality in your area. Ask your instructor for the name of the organization in your area, for example, the "Sewerage and Water Board of New Orleans." If possible, check the water quality in nearby cities or counties for comparison. Bring your findings to class and discuss them. Should you drink bottled water in your area?

If you are interested in desalination, use the search phrase "desalination plant diagram" to find information about the equipment involved in this process. Print out the diagram if possible to show your classmates as you describe the system.

Review the information on the costs of desalination plants that use distillation technology and plants that use reverse osmosis. Present the information to your classmates.

A Circle the letter of the word that correctly completes each sentence, and then write the word in the blank space.

1. Reporters have been investigating the contamination of a nearby river by local

   companies, and they _____ release their results soon.

   a. must   b. should   c. would

2. According to the reporters' preliminary results, Oxtle Corporation _____
   have disposed of toxic compounds in the river because the chemical analysis shows
   a low level of pollutants related to their business.

   a. can't   b. may not   c. must not

3. The reporters _____ have tried to find eyewitnesses to the
   contamination, but they relied on the chemical analysis of the river water instead.

   a. could   b. might   c. can

4. Once the analysis becomes available, the reporters may reveal that _____
   companies along the river were guilty of polluting the water to some degree.

   a. all the   b. all of the   c. either a. or b.

5. None of the companies _____ responded to the reporters' allegations.

   a. has   b. have   c. either a. or b.

6. The spokesperson for Oxtle Corporation has objected _____ chemical
   formulas that Oxtle has developed to outside researchers.

   a. to providing   b. to provide   c. for providing

7. According to town officials, it is no use _____ because the court will
   require companies to reveal the compounds that they produce.

   a. to object   b. objecting   c. either a. or b.

8. After the trial began, Oxtle Corporation regretted _____ with the
   reporters' investigation.

   a. not to have cooperated b. not to cooperate   c. not having cooperated

9. An eyewitness _____ testify against Oxtle when the company lawyer
   interrupted and asked to speak to the judge.

   a. was to   b. was about to   c. was able to

10. The president of Oxtle was unhappy about _____ pay a $500,000 fine,
    but he preferred it to going to jail.

    a. having to   b. to have to   c. have to

B Use the correct form of the verb in parentheses. Add negation when necessary for the meaning of the sentence.

1. Our university committee on ethical research always _____ (ascertain) how experiments will protect the health of test subjects.

2. The number of experiments with animal test subjects _____ (decrease) since 1990.

3. Before then, there _____ (must be) some problems with unethical procedures since the committee has shown much more concern about test subjects in recent years.

4. In some labs they still _____ (could use) procedures that the committee has not approved, but researchers know that they should follow the guidelines.

5. They _____ (be supposed to follow) any procedures that may endanger the physical or psychological health of human subjects.

6. For the last decade, researchers _____ (have to submit) research proposals to the committee for review.

7. It takes the committee several months _____ (review) each research proposal.

8. With regard to _____ (approve) a proposal, the committee members prefer careful consideration over speed.

9. The committee also wants to avoid any bad publicity for the university as a consequence of _____ (consider) a research proposal carefully.

10. The long approval process irritates some researchers who resent _____ (be able to begin) their work for many months.

LEARNER LOG Check (✔) Yes or I Need More Practice.

Lesson	I Can Use . . .	Yes	I Need More Practice
6	Academic Phrasal Modals and Other Modal Verbs		
7	Modal Verbs in the Past Logical Scale and Other Perfect Modals		
8	Quantifiers and Subject-Verb Agreement		
9	Gerunds and Infinitives as Subjects and Subject Complements; Gerunds Following a Preposition		
10	Gerunds and Infinitives in Perfect Forms and with Phrasal Modals		

PART 1
Review of Adverbials

PART 2
Adverbs in Sentence-Initial
Position

Lesson (11)

Human Resources: The Multigenerational Workplace

■ CONTENT VOCABULARY

Look up the words and phrases below that you do not know and enter them in your vocabulary journal. Write each item's part of speech, a definition, and an example sentence. Try to include them in your discussion and writing below.

the bottom line	hands-on	savvy	a work ethic
to buy into	haphazardly	to socialize	a workforce
friction	multitasking	to take up the slack	a workload

■ THINK ABOUT IT

Look at the photo on the following page. What do you notice about the types of employees working at this particular restaurant? Would you find the same kind of staff at a similar restaurant in your neighborhood or community? Why, or why not? Discuss your ideas with a classmate.

In your writing journal, write for five minutes about the questions below. When you are finished, share what you wrote with the class.

In your experience as an employee, have you worked with people of different ages? What was your relationship with co-workers or supervisors of various ages? What kinds of problems or conflicts did your co-workers have because of age differences? If you've ever been an employee, write about a work conflict you may have seen or heard about.

■ GRAMMAR IN CONTENT

CD1,TR21

A Read and listen to the passage below. The words in bold in the text are adverbials.

Working with Grandpa

Across the U.S., Americans are encountering co-workers and colleagues who are quite different in age and outlook. In fast food restaurants, home repair centers, and many other retail stores, teenagers and people the age of their grandparents are working **side by side**. Managers in such businesses have realized that their bottom line depends on a workforce that spans generations. For corporate and public sector administrators, leading **effectively** means finding ways for their employees, who may have **fundamentally** different values and expectations, to work **cooperatively**. This attitude toward leadership differs **significantly** from those held **when the workforce was predominantly made up of white men of the pre-World War II generation**. Experts in the field of human resource management have identified characteristics that help managers understand the motivations and issues important for each generation of employees in the workplace.

For the most recent generation in the workforce, known as Generation Y, technology plays a **quite** important role in their worldview. Members of Generation Y, who were born between 1982 and 2002, incorporate computers and other technology in their private and work lives **seamlessly**. The parents of these "Millennials" or "Echo Boomers" involved themselves **actively** in the lives of their children, who now interact **positively** with older co-workers and tend to prefer project-oriented work assignments.

In contrast to the Millennials, members of Generation X perform job-related tasks **more independently**. Preferring results over a cooperative work-style, Generation X-ers view authority figures **more skeptically** than their younger colleagues. **Clearly**, this attitude can **potentially** lead to conflict in the workplace as these adults, born between 1965 and 1981, set very clear boundaries between their work and private lives.

Members of the largest and currently the most powerful generation differ **considerably** from the younger generations. Baby Boomers, born during the years of great cultural and social change from 1946–1964, tend to view the world **optimistically**. Characterized **quite accurately** as workaholics, they desire acknowledgment of their own personal accomplishments and respect the accomplishments and power of others. For this generation, work always comes first.

Although the number of workers from the Traditionalist (or Silent) Generation, who were born from 1927 to 1945, is decreasing, these people **still** influence the workplace. Some of them continue in their jobs **long past the traditional retirement age**. Also, many retired workers have been re-joining the workforce to earn money as part-time employees or to contribute as volunteers. Employers value their loyalty and positive work ethic.

Faced with global competitive pressures, managers need to ensure that their employees perform **efficiently** so that tasks and projects are completed **on time** and products or services are delivered **properly**. Excellent managers have to build a team based on the strengths that all of these workers bring to the workplace and to build respect among the team members for smooth working relationships.

an outlook: perspective, point of view

to span: to go across, to range

predominantly: mostly

acknowledgment: recognition

Sample Sentences	Notes
The VPs **unanimously** selected Jim Green and Pam Connors to work on the Harris project. Green moved **overseas when he got a promotion.** Connors has been e-mailing Green **constantly because of the project deadline.**	Most adverbials answer one of these questions: · How? · Where/In which direction? · When/How often? · Why? · To what extent?
The deadline is **especially** important for their client. Ms. Carlson may send Connors **to Asia eventually** since she and Green have performed **so well.**	Adverbs that answer "To what extent?" modify or intensify adjectives, for example, *very careful, extremely powerful.* Adverbs that answer "To what extent?" can also modify other adverbs, as in *quite slowly.*
The tech team meets **every week /at 12:00/ on Wednesdays.** The newer members of the team sit in the chairs **toward the back of the room.** Some old-timers voluntarily sit **in the back of the room** to talk with the newer staff. **In the back,** staff can come and go **as they please.** **During the meeting,** everyone shares ideas **freely.**	Adverbials can take the form of simple words (*very, completely*), phrases (*every day, in a minute, at home*), and clauses (*when we arrived in Beijing*). Put adverbials at the end of the sentence in this order: *How? Where? When? Why?* The order of adverbials that tell *How?* and *Where?* can be switched. The same is true for *When?* and *How often?* and *Where?* and *In which direction?* Less frequent positions for adverbials: Where? ⎤ When? ⎬ in sentence-initial position Why? ⎦ How? ⎤⊢ in the same position as frequency adverbs
We can **usually** find an empty table in the lunchroom. I am **always** the first person to arrive.	Some frequency adverbs (*always, usually, sometimes, rarely,* etc.) appear after the first auxiliary verb. If there is no auxiliary verb, adverbs appear after *be* but before other verbs.

B Read over your journal entry, and <u>underline</u> at least one sentence that you can revise to include an adverbial. Write your revised sentence(s) below.

_____

_____

C **Circle** the letter of the correct completion(s) to the sentences below.

1. As soon as he read the e-mail from his boss, Martin Cates walked

   a. purposefully toward the 3rd floor meeting room.
   b. toward the 3rd floor meeting room purposefully.
   c. both of the above.

2. A staff meeting had already begun when Cates entered

   a. the meeting room about 5 minutes late.
   b. about 5 minutes late the meeting room.
   c. both of the above.

3. Gina Tatum was explaining their new marketing strategy

   a. at the head of the table at that moment.
   b. at that moment at the head of the table.
   c. both of the above.

4. Gina and Martin had been working on the strategy

   a. to impress their boss in their spare time.
   b. in their spare time to impress their boss.
   c. both of the above.

5. Martin could tell that Gina had introduced their marketing concept

   a. before his entrance capably.
   b. capably before his entrance.
   c. both of the above.

6. Gina was going through their slide presentation

   a. with handouts instead of a projector due to a problem with the equipment.
   b. due to a problem with the equipment with handouts instead of a projector.
   c. both of the above.

7. Gina and Martin had printed the handouts

   a. the previous afternoon quickly in the company copy center.
   b. quickly in the company copy center the previous afternoon.
   c. both of the above.

8. Now he was very glad they had taken that precaution because the staff was responding

   a. so positively during her presentation.
   b. during her presentation so positively.
   c. both of the above.

D Use one of the adverbs in the box below to modify an adjective or adverb in each sentence. Many of these adverbs are interchangeable, and there are more adverbs than necessary to complete the exercise.

| extremely | completely | highly | fairly | appreciably | a little |
| ~~quite~~ | amazingly | perfectly | somewhat | rather | a bit |

(1) Of all her employees, Mrs. Lawrence is _{quite} ∧impressed with the newest staff member, Karen Bunting. (2) Hired right out of college as an accountant, Ms. Bunting has learned the company's system quickly. (3) Normally it takes a new accountant several months to handle the workload comfortably. (4) During Ms. Bunting's job interview, she seemed competent, but not as well-prepared as she appears to be. (5) Mrs. Lawrence feels confident that within a short time Ms. Bunting will be one of her star employees.

(6) In contrast to Karen Bunting, Mrs. Lawrence is concerned about Richard Acton, a long-time employee in the sales department. (7) Several co-workers have mentioned that he seems depressed lately. (8) Recently two younger sales representatives have joined that department and added to the competitive atmosphere there. (9) Up until now, Acton has always met his sales goals satisfactorily and contributed positively to the company's bottom line. (10) If his sales numbers get lower, Mrs. Lawrence may have to speak with him about his performance.

E Edit the sentences with "X" to show where the adverbial in parentheses can be added to the text.

1. Younger co-workers may criticize older employees when they ˣfollow company rules.ˣ **(rigidly)**
2. Workers in the Silent Generation have tended to remain at the same workplace. **(until retirement)**
3. It is unrealistic to think that everyone born in a certain generation will have the same work ethic. **(inherently)**
4. Colleagues from different generations can work together effectively if they respect each other's strengths and weaknesses. **(eventually)**
5. A good manager will praise a Baby Boomer in public while she will give a Gen X-er positive feedback in private. **(explicitly)**
6. All employees will perform their jobs in a new way if their supervisor insists on it. **(temporarily)**
7. If employees are motivated to continue with new procedures, their services or products may improve. **(qualitatively)**
8. New procedures will not make services better unless the employees buy into the need for change. **(automatically)**

F Edit the paragraph to improve its coherence. Place adverbials in sentence-initial position when the information is already known from the text.

Evan Gibbons started his new job at Patterson, Inc. and ran into some trouble in the first week. *That week h*His boss assigned him to an ongoing project ~~that week~~. Most of his new colleagues were more experienced, and they had also been working together for years. His colleagues had become friends during that time, and their families often socialized together. Although his co-workers treated him politely, he felt isolated and wondered how to improve his situation. He finally made an appointment to talk to his supervisor because of his negative feelings.

G **PAIR WORK** Brainstorm adverbials that can be used to describe good job performance for the tasks and behaviors listed below. Then, define "excellent" performance by adding an intensifier to the description.

- Interact *very politely* with the public

- Respond to inquiries or requests for information

- Fulfill one's job duties

- Follow the supervisor's directions

- Respond to feedback

- Assist colleagues/co-workers

- Handle payments

- Process paperwork

H **PAIR WORK** Ms. Guzman has written a draft of a letter of recommendation for Susie Dawson. Add appropriate adverbials to make the letter even more positive. Use at least six appropriate adverbs.

To Whom It May Concern:

Ms. Susie Dawson requested that we send a letter of recommendation to you. Ms. Dawson worked as a cashier for us last summer from June 1 to August 15. When she began her job, she had no experience. Our accountant gave her a one-week training course and reported that Ms. Dawson learned our procedures. After her training, she worked in our gift shop. She performed her job, cashiering and interacting with our customers. Many customers commented to us about her work. We were sorry that she had to leave.

We recommend Ms. Dawson for the position in your company. If you have any questions about Ms. Dawson's job performance, please contact us.

Sincerely,
Elena Guzman

■ GRAMMAR IN CONTENT

A Reread the text at the beginning of this lesson, and (circle) the example of an adverb in sentence-initial position. What is the function of this adverb?

Adverbs in Sentence-Initial Position

Sample Sentences	Notes
It will take awhile for Ms. Aguilar to understand how our company works. **Typically,** new managers need time to understand a company's culture.	Use particular adverbs in sentence-initial position to comment on or to express an attitude about the information that follows. Use a comma to separate these adverbials from the main clause.
The interns have complained about Mr. Johnson's e-mails. **Evidently,** he is having trouble communicating with some younger workers.	**Probability:** *certainly, surely*
There have been some clashes between our senior staff and the new recruits. **Regrettably,** the age difference has led to some misunderstandings.	**Frequency:** *frequently, occasionally* **Typicality:** *generally, typically*
Technically, all new employees have 10 vacation days annually, but not everyone takes them.	**Clarity/Obviousness:** *obviously, clearly, evidently* **Viewpoint:** *luckily, (un)fortunately, hopefully, regrettably*
Fortunately, their supervisors are monitoring them closely, so we can tell if anyone is getting burned out.	*Fortunately* shows that things are more positive than expected.
Unfortunately, many talented computer techs don't stay long at one job.	*Unfortunately* is used to show regret.
	The following adverbials don't require the use of a comma.
Perhaps they need to be encouraged to take their vacation days.	*Perhaps* is more formal than *maybe,* and is often used to persuade the listener.
Maybe the employees don't want to appear lazy.	*Maybe* is often used with negatives.
Of course we know that none of them is lazy because their work has been excellent so far this year.	*Of course* is more common in speech than in writing. Its use assumes the listener has the same background information as the speaker/writer.

Other Adverbs Used in Sentence-Initial Position

frankly	naturally	possibly	actually	ultimately
superficially	technically	theoretically	strangely	(not) surprisingly

B With a partner, comment on the job performance of Franco Drake, 25, and Sylvia Cates, 49, who are working together on an advertising project for an important client. Decide which of you will play the role of the supportive supervisor or the critical supervisor, and then take turns giving your feedback.

1. Franco and Sylvia are seriously behind schedule.

   Supportive: _Technically, they are behind schedule, but they have improved the original concept substantially._

   Critical: _Unfortunately, they have disagreed about every aspect of this project._

2. Franco and Sylvia often argue loudly, but then they get back to work.

   Supportive: _____

   Critical: _____

3. Franco has much more artistic imagination even though Sylvia has a degree in design.

   Supportive: _____

   Critical: _____

4. Sylvia's children have been sick with the flu this week, so Franco has had to take up the slack.

   Supportive: _____

   Critical: _____

5. Franco expects a bonus when the project is complete.

   Supportive: _____

   Critical: _____

6. Sylvia originally felt uncomfortable about working with such an inexperienced colleague.

   Supportive: _____

   Critical: _____

7. They have generated impressive graphics, but the message still needs to be revised considerably.

   Supportive: _____

   Critical: _____

8. The clients prefer to speak with Sylvia when they contact the advertising agency.

   Supportive: _____

   Critical: _____

C Listen to the statements of various employees at Freeman Services, and comment on their attitudes or work ethic, using information in the chart below. If their dates of birth are not given, try to determine which generation they belong to based on the information given.

	Work-life vs family-life?	Approach to authority?	Optimistic?	Personal achievement?	Technological know-how?
Silent Gen. (1927–45)	separate	strong respect	so-so	obedience is more important	no
Boomers (1946–64)	workaholic	little respect	yes	yes	so-so
Gen X (1965–81)	balanced	casual	no	important outside workplace	yes
Gen Y/ Millennials (1982– present)	work-oriented	respect	yes	yes	yes

1. Don, born 1950: *Obviously, Don doesn't have very strong computer skills, as with many other Boomers.*

2. Olivia, born 1982: _____

3. LeShanda: _____

4. Richard, born 1939: _____

5. Juanita: _____

6. Will, born 1962: _____

7. Aisha: _____

8. Jerry, born 1985: _____

Find and correct the four errors in the informal e-mail message below.

Kerry—

Hi, honey! Thanks for your email – I enjoy hearing about your life on campus. I can understand your stories a lot better now since I started working part-time in a fast-food restaurant. Did I tell you that most of my co-workers are only 19 or 20?!? Fortunately we're getting along real well. They are actually very funny – at least most of them. A couple of them are amazing LAZY!!!

The work is pretty easy. I spend most of my time as a cashier, but I flip sometimes burgers if they need help in the kitchen. In the early morning at the cash register I work and then at lunch time the boss may ask me to help out in the kitchen. So far, so good!

Love,
Mom

■ COMMUNICATE

E **SMALL GROUP WORK** Talk about your expectations of a workplace where you can perform your job comfortably and confidently. How should your employer treat you? Include the following ideas in your conversation.

a. providing a mentor or coach
b. giving feedback
c. assigning projects
d. providing technology
e. offering flexible working hours
f. working on a team
g. providing training for professional development

Be prepared to share your ideas with another small group in your class.

GRAMMAR AND VOCABULARY Write a composition on one of the topics below. Use as many words as possible from the Content Vocabulary on page 111, and (circle) them in your composition. Use sentences with adverbials to express some of your ideas, and underline those sentences.

Topic 1: New employees need orientation to the organization and job training for their specific duties. Of course supervisors can help new employees become valuable employees. The next time that you start a new job, how can your supervisor train you effectively? Would you like to read a manual, listen to explanations, do hands-on activities by yourself, or have a mentor? Explain and give concrete examples.

Topic 2: During a job interview, prospective employers often ask candidates about their strengths and weaknesses for a particular job. In preparation for such an interview, write an analysis of yourself for a job in a workplace that includes people of different generations. Select a specific job that would interest you for this composition.

PROJECT Interview at least one student on your campus who has a job. Ask him or her questions about intergenerational relations at the workplace.

Here are some ideas:

1. Where has the student worked?
2. Who else was on the staff at that workplace? Was everyone about the same age?
3. Were there ever any misunderstandings or conflicts among the staff?
4. Did the ages or values of the co-workers result in any friction?

Give a short oral report on the results of your interview to your class.

 INTERNET Go online, and use the search phrase "managing millennials." Find a website with information or tips about managing Millennials successfully. If you are a Millennial, choose 2–3 tips that would be good advice for your future boss. Share this information with your class, and tell why you chose the tips.

If you are not a Millennial, choose 2–3 tips that would be difficult for you to follow if you were the supervisor of a Millennial. Share this information with your class and tell why following the tips would be difficult for you.

Counseling: Rites of Passage

■ CONTENT VOCABULARY

Look up the words and phrases below that you do not know and enter them in your vocabulary journal. Write each item's part of speech, a definition, and an example sentence. Try to include them in your discussion and writing below.

endurance	an initiation	a ritual	to signify
a gang	a myth	to distance oneself from	a transition
guidance	an ordeal	to mature	a vision

■ THINK ABOUT IT

When you see younger people today, what is your impression? Do you identify with them? Why or why not? Discuss your ideas with a classmate.

In your writing journal, write for five minutes about the questions below. When you are finished, share your information with the class.

There are many ceremonies and "rites of passage" associated with the transition from adolescence to adulthood. Some of them are formal, while others are not. What are some of these rites of passage in different cultures you know?

■ GRAMMAR IN CONTENT

CD1, TR23

A Read and listen to the passage below. The words in bold in the text are sequential connectors.

The Journeys of Life

What's up with the green hair? Parents and teachers wonder what ever happened to that sweet child Katie, who now has a pierced navel and a tattooed ankle and a chip on her shoulder. How about Eugene, who seems to wear the colors of the local gang?

As families fret about their teenagers, counselors and anthropologists have an explanation for the weird appearance and outrageous behavior of many teenagers. It's not just "a phase" that these adolescents are going through. They are in the middle of a journey from childhood to adulthood, a journey that experts call a "rite of passage." In the modern version of this rite of passage, young people separate themselves from childhood and find their own ways toward the meaning of being an adult. Similarly, young people throughout history have made this journey, but there was an important difference. For youths from traditional cultures, the elders strictly guided their change of identity and taught them the meaning and obligations of adulthood. Their time of transition often involved special initiation rites, which involved separation from everything that they knew, tests of endurance, and sacrifice. Once the difficult passage was over, the whole community celebrated as the new adults took their places in society.

Initiation into adulthood isn't clearly defined in some cultures anymore, but some counselors advise parents and troubled teens to view the experiences of these years in terms of the traditional pathway. We can re-invent myths, those traditional stories about ancient heroes, in a way that young people can understand and incorporate in their lives. David Oldfield, a mental health professional, advocates the use of these stories so that youths have positive role models and can learn what life is really all about as they realize the steps that all people take as they mature. **First,** a youth answers a "call of adventure," which means leaving the safety of home. In most stories, the hero has no choice and must leave to handle a problem. **Second,** the young person "finds a path" while learning to be independent and developing a view of life. Another name for this step is a vision quest. **Third,** "entering the labyrinth" means that the hero has to endure some kind of testing or ordeal. Young persons overcoming such an ordeal prove themselves worthy of being an adult. **Fourth,** the hero encounters "the woods between the worlds," in which he or she must express a new vision of life to others in the community. Young adults express that vision in words, in music, or in art. **Finally,** the community celebrates the end of the journey with a ceremony. This ceremony often includes special clothing, food, decorations, gifts, and perhaps even a new name.

Teenagers are not the only members of society who experience a rite of passage. Marriage and the birth of a child mark milestones in people's lives. Modern society offers other opportunities for celebrating transitions, such as high school graduation, a new job, or retirement from the workforce. In each case, there are special rituals that we can follow to signify someone's transition from one identity to a new one. Modern sophisticates may scoff at or ridicule such ceremonies, but these celebrations link us strongly to our communities and to past generations at the same time that they recognize our progress through life.

to have a chip on your shoulder: to resent, to have a negative attitude

to fret: to worry

a milestone: a distance marker; a sign of an important event

a sophisticate: a person with experience and knowledge of the world

a labyrinth: a confusing, complex path

Sample Sentences	Notes
Rick's family made all the preparations for his marriage to Cindy. **First of all**, they found a nice restaurant for the rehearsal dinner. **Second of all**, they sent out invitations to all of the wedding party.	Use the sequential connectors below to express the order of events or ideas. · *first, second, third, last/finally* · *first, next, then, last/finally* · *firstly, secondly, lastly/finally* · *in the first place, in the second place, last/finally* · *first of all, second of all, last of all* · *after that*
Rick's father planned to make a toast at the rehearsal dinner. **After that**, he wanted to give Rick and Cindy a special gift.	
There were different reasons for boys to leave home for their initiation rites. **In the first place**, they needed to make a break from their mothers and the comfort of home. **In the second place**, they had to learn about manhood from the men of the community.	Connectors may express · a real-time relationship of events · the author's order of ideas or events The author's order may be from least to most important or from most to least important.
Cindy's parents needed several months for her wedding preparations. **First**, they had to rent a place for the reception many weeks ahead of time and send out invitations to all the guests. **Next**, they needed to order Cindy's dress. Cindy wanted a custom-made dress so they knew it would take several weeks; **then**, she had to find all of the accessories for the dress.	Connectors that express a sequence are the type of adverbials that connect two independent clauses. Follow the rules of punctuation below for connectors in this category: a. clause$_1$; connector, clause$_2$ b. clause$_1$. Connector, clause$_2$ Choose option b if you want to emphasize the connector or if the clauses are quite long.
Cindy's parents were very patient during the hectic preparations. Cindy wanted a custom-made dress **first**, and they agreed to it. She **then** saw a dress that she really liked in a magazine. **Finally**, she found one at the local mall.	English speakers sometimes use a connector from this category after the subject or at the end of the clause. Don't use a comma in these cases. **NOTE:** *At first* means "at the start of a process or situation" and *at last* means "finally after much effort, time, or worry." These phrases are not connectors.

B **Read over your journal entry, and <u>underline</u> at least one sentence that you can revise to include a sequential connector. Write your revised sentence(s) below.**

_____

_____

_____

C Add two more sequential connectors to the text below, where appropriate. Add the appropriate punctuation.

Many people think that some aspects of military service are similar to traditional initiation rites of young men. Nowadays both young men and women enter military service in some countries. During "boot camp" they undergo training that can be compared to those older rites. *first of all, t*These young people go to a training base away from their homes. A master sergeant there takes a group of youths under his or her wing. Under this supervision, the young soldiers learn what it means to be a soldier. Boot camp always involves a number of physical tests as they gain new skills. The young soldiers must demonstrate skills in handling equipment and must know how to survive under dangerous conditions.

D Imagine that you took the notes below during a class lecture. Reorganize the information into a clearer order, and write up the notes with the appropriate connectors. Be prepared to explain the order of your notes.

Transitions in the workplace
a) Summer interns return to the university
b) New employees successfully complete their probation period
c) Apprentices earn their master's letters
d) Employees retire
e) Employees receive a promotion
f) Employees begin new job

Some transitions in the workplace are more important than others. First, . . .

E Edit the text so that there are sequential connectors between the appropriate clauses.

When young people graduate from high school, their community celebrates this step toward adulthood. For many youths, graduation signifies the transition from being a child to becoming a contributing member of society. The school is at the center of the ceremony. *first of all, the staff* ~~The staff first~~ plans the location and date of the graduation ceremony. They prepare the diplomas. The diplomas are usually printed in elegant lettering and proclaim each student's graduation in formal language. The students receive their caps and gowns, which they will wear for the ceremony, shortly before graduation day. Parents often finish the big day with a party for their graduate at home with family and friends.

■ **COMMUNICATE**

F **PAIR WORK** With a partner, talk about wedding preparations in your culture, from the engagement to the wedding day. Tell about the order of events for each wedding tradition.

I'm from a small town with very traditional values. The man **first** asks his girlfriend to marry him and **then** he talks to her father. **After that** they can tell other people about it.

Oh, really? The place I'm from is even more conservative. A man has to get permission from his girlfriend's father **first**. He formally asks her to marry him **after that**.

■ GRAMMAR IN CONTENT

A Reread "The Journeys of Life" at the beginning of this lesson, and <u>underline</u> the clause that is introduced with one of the connectors in italics below.

Connectors of Equivalence

Sample Sentences	Notes
In some traditional African cultures, boys receive new names as men; **similarly,** Native American youths received their adult names during their vision quest.	Use the connectors of equivalence below to highlight similar ideas or to clarify information by providing a restatement or an example.
Boys had spiritual lessons from the elders; **by the same token,** girls learned about the meaning of life from older women in the community.	For similar ideas or information, use *similarly, likewise, in the same way, by the same token.* For elaborating ideas or information, use *for example, for instance.*
Young adults showed the death of their childhood in a new appearance; **for example,** they often received new clothes.	Connectors in this category, like sequential connectors, are adverbials. Follow the rules of punctuation below: a. clause$_1$; connector, clause$_2$ b. clause$_1$. Connector, clause$_2$
Young men in traditional cultures often had a haircut as they separated from their families. **In the same way,** gang members usually have a distinctive haircut or hairstyle.	Sometimes connectors introduce identical ideas in a phrase, not a clause. See Lesson 29, Part 2.

B Using your own personal knowledge, complete the following sentences about rites of passage from around the world. If you are unfamiliar with a particular rite or culture, write what you think may be true. You can discuss your answers with your classmates.

1. For centuries adults had different hairstyles from those of children. For example,

   European women and girls had long hair but only girls wore their hair down.

2. After some rites of passage, adults change their names; for example,

   _____

3. In some cultures, when a spouse dies, the surviving spouse may wear black for the funeral and for a time afterward. In the same way,

   _____

4. On her wedding day, a bride often wears a dress of a significant color. For instance,

   _____

5. On his wedding day, a bridegroom might wear a very formal suit; likewise,

_____

6. Guests at a wedding reception often give the newlyweds advice. For example,

_____

7. Some religions observe special rites for young people. For example,

_____

8. Likewise, boys used to prove themselves by hunting or fighting; in the same way,

_____

C Add the correct punctuation to each sentence. If necessary, add capital letters.

1. Youths in traditional societies underwent initiation with a group of peers ͵ similarly ͵ many modern young people mature with their teammates in various sports.

2. In traditional societies, village elders provided instruction for teenagers by the same token coaches nowadays teach young athletes skills and proper behavior.

3. Parents also trusted the mentors to guide their children for instance modern parents rarely contradict a coach's instructions to their children.

4. Village elders had to teach that life has both light and dark sides likewise coaches help athletes to accept winning and losing.

5. Youths benefit from having peers in the transition to adulthood for instance young athletes can share their frustration and joy with teammates.

6. Adults look back often on the lessons of their initiation into adulthood for example they remember the praise of their mentors and try to follow their advice.

D Listen to a short lecture on an updated version of rites of passage and answer the questions below.

CD1,TR24

1. Who or what is most likely to provide "rite of passage" experiences for young Americans?

_____

_____

_____

2. What example did the lecturer give for each type of "rite of passage" experience?

_____

_____

_____

E **GROUP WORK** Brainstorm a list of 3–5 movies that follow the story of a rite of passage. The character may follow the journey from childhood to adulthood or make the transition to some other phase of life. Then, describe the steps or phases that the character experiences during the film.

Connection | Putting It Together

GRAMMAR AND VOCABULARY Write a composition on one of the topics below. Use as many words as possible from the Content Vocabulary on page 123, and (circle) them in your composition. Use sentences with sequential connectors and connectors of equivalence to express some of your ideas, and underline those sentences.

Topic 1: Tell the story of an important mythical (or fictional) hero from your culture with David Oldfield's five steps, which were explained in "The Journeys of Life" on page 124. Use at least one example for each step on your journey.

Topic 2: How do young people in your culture prove themselves? What are the typical tests, sacrifices, and ordeals that a young person must endure before older people respect them as adults? Give specific examples.

PROJECT Interview at least one student on your campus about initiation rites for students who join clubs such as fraternities or sororities. Find out the following information, and prepare a brief oral report on your interviewee's comments.

1. What does "hazing" mean?
2. Has your interviewee heard of any hazing on campus?
3. What kinds of rituals do students on campus go through to join special clubs? to be part of the "in-crowd"? to be cool?

 INTERNET Go online and use the search phrase "name meanings." Find a website where you can find an analysis of the meanings of different names. Select 3 or 4 names and give a short oral report on those meanings in class. Also, in your report tell your classmates about the customs in your culture regarding a change of names. If people change their names, does the change usually coincide with a transition in their lives?

Engineering: Emergency Preparation and Management

■ CONTENT VOCABULARY

Look up the words below that you do not know and enter them in your vocabulary journal. Write each word's part of speech, a definition, and an example sentence. Try to include them in your discussion and writing below.

an aftermath	to comprise	to mitigate	to stock
a building code	a fault line	to precipitate	to upgrade
a buoy	imminent	to scrutinize	vulnerable

■ THINK ABOUT IT

The photo on the next page shows the impact of Hurricane Katrina on the infrastructure of the New Orleans area. What other kinds of public structures are often affected by natural disasters? Can you remember any specific examples from other natural catastrophes around the world? Discuss your ideas with a classmate.

In your writing journal, write for 5–10 minutes about the questions below. When you are finished, share what you wrote with the class.

Describe briefly what happened in a recent natural disaster. How did emergency workers respond? What were the needs of the people in the disaster, and what did various responders do to meet those needs?

■ GRAMMAR IN CONTENT

CD1,TR25

A Read and listen to the passage below. The words in bold in the text are connectors of causality.

Emergency Management: Planning and Responding

Current wisdom inclines toward the view that disasters are *not* exceptional events. They tend to be repetitive and to concentrate in particular places. With regard to natural catastrophes, seismic and volcanic belts, hurricane-generating areas, unstable slopes, and tornado zones are well known. Moreover, the frequency of events and **therefore** their statistical recurrence intervals are often fairly well established—at least for the smaller and more frequent occurrences—even if the short-term ability to forecast natural hazards is variable. Many technological hazards also follow more or less predictable patterns, although these may become apparent only when research reveals them. Finally, intelligence gathering, strategic studies, and policy analyses can help us to understand the pattern of emergencies resulting from conflict and insurgence. **Thus**, there is little excuse for being caught unprepared.

The main scope of emergency planning is to reduce the risk to life and limb posed by actual and potential disasters. Secondary motives involve reducing damage, ensuring public safety during the aftermath of a disaster, and caring for survivors and the disadvantaged. Inefficiencies in planning translate very easily into loss of life, injuries, or damage that could have been avoided. **Thus**, emergency planning is at least a moral, and perhaps also a legal, responsibility for all those who are involved with the safety of the public or employees. When a known significant risk exists, failure to plan can be taken as culpable negligence. Moreover, planning cannot successfully be improvised during emergencies: this represents one of the worst forms of inefficiency and most likely sources of error and confusion. Fortunately, however, 50 years of intensive research and accumulated experience have furnished an ample basis for planning.

Given that disasters tend to be repetitive events, they form a cycle that can be divided into phases of mitigation, preparedness, response, and delivery, including reconstruction. The first two stages occur before catastrophe strikes and the last two afterwards. The actions taken, and **therefore** the planning procedures that predetermine them, differ for each of the periods, as different needs are tackled. Mitigation comprises all actions designed to reduce the impact of future disasters. These usually divide into structural measures (the engineering solutions to problems of safety) and non-structural means, which include land-use planning, insurance, legislation, and evacuation planning. The term *preparedness* refers to actions taken to reduce the impact of disasters when they are forecast or imminent. They include security measures, such as the evacuation of vulnerable populations and sandbagging of river levees as floodwaters begin to rise (**thus** the *planning* of evacuation is a mitigation measure, whereas its *execution* is a form of preparedness). Response refers to emergency actions taken during both the impact of a disaster and the short-term aftermath. The principal emphasis is on saving and safeguarding human lives. Victims are rescued and the immediate needs of survivors are attended to. Recovery is the process of repairing damage, restoring services, and reconstructing facilities after disaster has struck. After major catastrophes it may take as long as 25 years, although much less time is needed in lighter impacts or disasters that strike smaller areas.

Principles of Emergency Planning and Management by David Alexander, Oxford University Press, 2002, pp 4-5.
By permission of Oxford University Press, Inc.

an insurgence: a rebellion or revolt

culpable negligence: legal responsibility for a failure to prevent injury or damage

Connectors of Causality

Sample Sentences	Notes
Strong winds can lift houses off their foundations. **As a result**, the entire structure can be damaged beyond repair.	Connectors of causality introduce the result or consequence of an idea or action.
Hurricane Katrina destroyed many oil rigs in the Gulf of Mexico; **therefore**, oil production in the U.S. was significantly affected in the days after the disaster.	*Therefore* signals a result or consequence that readers/listeners could infer or predict themselves from the situation.
In 2005, hurricane winds rose above 90 mph; **consequently**, several boats from the harbor were lifted out of the water and landed on the beach highway.	*Consequently* and *as a result* signal a situation that was actually caused by previous actions or conditions, but may not be predictable.
Ocean waves that are generated by earthquakes can be detected by a network of buoys in the Indian Ocean; **thus/hence**, coastal residents may be alerted to flee to higher ground before a tsunami strikes.	*Thus* and *hence* are used primarily in formal contexts.
Preparing efficient routes away from the coast facilitates mass evacuations; **therefore**, traffic engineers should devise systems to increase the flow of vehicles. OR Preparing efficient routes away from the coast facilitates mass evacuations. **Therefore**, traffic engineers should devise systems to increase the flow of vehicles. OR Traffic engineers should, **therefore**, devise systems to increase the flow of vehicles.	Follow the rules of punctuation below for this category of adverbial connectors: a. $clause_1$; connector, $clause_2$ b. $clause_1$. Connector, $clause_2$ Connectors in this category can also be used in the middle of a result clause. In that case, two commas often separate the connector from the clause. The connector usually appears after the subject or the first auxiliary verb.

B Read over your journal entry, and <u>underline</u> at least one sentence that you can revise to include a causal connector. Write your revised sentence(s) below.

_____

_____

_____

The shaded area of this map is known as "Tornado Alley."

C Replace "so," which is an informal oral causal connector, with the appropriate word or phrase to connect the two clauses, and revise the punctuation. Use each connector from the chart on page 133 at least once.

1. Natural disasters affect some areas of the world more frequently than others, ~~so~~ ; therefore, ^ scientists closely monitor weather conditions in those areas.

2. U.S. meteorologists know "Tornado Alley" may have more than 500 tornadoes per year, so they track weather conditions that may cause these "twisters."

3. Other dangerous weather phenomena such as hurricanes and typhoons are also seasonal, so meteorologists scrutinize particular weather data during those months.

4. Rain or snowfall may precipitate avalanches or mudslides, so meteorologists and engineers have to cooperate to assess the threat of such phenomena.

5. Extensive monitoring equipment measures the seismic activity along fault lines, so scientists can analyze the chances of an earthquake or a volcanic eruption.

6. Earthquake movement can extend to the ocean floor, so people thousands of miles away can be in as much danger as those who live near the fault line.

D In each text below, connect two clauses with one of the causal connectors in this lesson. Follow the example.

1. One way to prepare for water-related disasters is to raise the land. For centuries people have built levees along ~~rivers. Water that~~ *rivers; as a result, water that* rises during heavy rains or very high tides remains in the river channel and does not damage property.

2. The levee system along the Sacramento River in California originally protected farmland from flooding. The population of Sacramento, the capital of California, has grown to more than 400,000 people, and approximately 2 million live in the Greater Sacramento area. Engineers are repairing parts of the levees that offer minimal protection to the surrounding homes.

3. Planners and residents in Sacramento are very concerned about the levee situation in the aftermath of Hurricane Katrina. The levees in New Orleans failed catastrophically due to inadequate maintenance. They were also below the height that experts recommended for severe local hurricane conditions. Engineers in Sacramento are re-examining local needs and want to upgrade their system.

4. The Dutch also have an elaborate system of dikes, or levees. Much of the land of the Netherlands is below sea level. It flooded regularly until they began an ambitious project of raising the land above sea level. They also invested billions in the construction of protective walls that they close during storms and extremely high tides. The Dutch have almost eliminated the threat of floods.

E Complete each of the sentences below with another clause. The first one has been done as an example.

1. Emergency officials need to communicate information about imminent dangers to their population. Therefore, <u>they should work closely with the local media./they should</u> <u>broadcast announcements on all radio stations.</u>

2. In some emergencies the population needs to collect food and other supplies before dangerous storms hit; thus, _____

   _____

3. At other times, people have to leave the area as fast as possible; consequently,

   _____

   _____

4. In some areas, there may be many foreign tourists who don't speak the local language. Therefore, _____

   _____

5. _____
   As a consequence, the police may have to drive around the area and announce the news.

6. _____
   Hence, an alarm siren may be the most suitable strategy for communicating a warning.

7. _____;
   consequently, all TV and radio programming should be interrupted to give important information.

■ **COMMUNICATE**

F **PAIR WORK** Emergency experts recommend a personal plan for everyone who has to evacuate a disaster area. Imagine evacuating for a few days and staying in a shelter. What will you take with you? Make a list of at least 7–8 items that you will need to take along. Share your list of items with the class.

The shelter will probably have some simple meals; therefore, we need to take some fruit, sandwiches, and other snack food.

■ GRAMMAR IN CONTENT

A Read the text on page 132 again, and (circle) any examples of concessive connectors such as *although, whereas,* and *while.* Compare your answers with a partner.

Concessive Connectors

Sample Sentences	Notes
Sometimes people have to evacuate for their own safety **although** they really don't want to go.	Concessive connectors express an unexpected contrast between two clauses. Both clauses are true, but the concessive clause highlights the importance of the main clause and de-emphasizes the information in the dependent clause, which begins with the concessive connector.
Even though evacuating can be inconvenient and costly, it is better than an injury or even death.	*Though* is more informal and **even though** is more emphatic than **although.**
Evacuees often complain about shelters though they are also thankful.	
While/Whereas emergency shelters may be uncomfortable, they protect people from threatening weather conditions.	*While* is not used as frequently as the other connectors for this meaning. **Whereas** is formal and is used less frequently than the other connectors.
To secure a structure for natural disaster, structural engineers have developed many special construction techniques. In hurricane zones, engineers recommend that home builders use special hurricane straps for roofs. **Although** the straps may add to the price of the roof, this precaution may keep the roof from blowing off.	These adverbial connectors introduce a dependent clause, which modifies the main, or independent, clause. Never use a dependent clause without an independent clause in the same sentence.
The angle of a roof can protect a structure from high velocity winds. **Even though** a roof with a lower angle might seem to be safer, houses with steeper roofs have a better chance of escaping catastrophic wind damage.	Follow the rules below for adverbial connectors: 1. Main clause + **although** + dependent clause. 2. **Although** + dependent clause +□+ main clause. Choose 1. when the information in the dependent clause is closely linked to the main clause. Choose 2. when the subordinate clause is more closely linked to previous information.
Although the wind was extremely strong, ~~but~~ my roof sustained very little damage.	Do not use *but* along with another connector to express a concessive relationship.
Don't think that a steep roof will protect you in every storm, **though.**	Use *though* in final position informally. Use a comma in front of *though* at the end of the sentence.

B Select the clause that is more appropriate for completing each sentence below. (Circle) the letter that shows your choice. Follow the example.

1. People tend not to evacuate their homes even though
   a. local officials may strongly recommend that they leave the area.
   b. they make their own preparations and stock emergency supplies.

2. In past hurricane seasons, some evacuations from American cities involved terrible traffic on the highways although
   a. people don't want to evacuate any more.
   b. officials had advised voluntary evacuation in time for people to leave.

3. While _____, citizens still need to obey the order for mandatory evacuation.
   a. an evacuation can be stressful and inconvenient
   b. they are preparing themselves for a natural disaster

4. Although _____, traffic engineers have devised new systems of "contraflow" on highways to ease traffic congestion.
   a. traffic will move at a steady, but slower pace
   b. traffic will always be heavy during peak evacuation times

5. During "contraflow" all cars on the highway move in only one direction away from the danger even though
   a. highways are designed for two-way travel.
   b. officials want as many cars as possible to leave the area quickly.

6. While _____, traffic engineers plan ways to direct drivers to the correct lanes.
   a. this strategy might sound dangerous
   b. local officials are announcing the evacuation

7. Though _____, local transportation officials realize that some drivers won't know about the plan and will need their help.
   a. a contraflow plan is always widely publicized in the local media
   b. a contraflow plan is the safest way to move more people more quickly

C **Read the sentence, then look at the clause below it. Should the clause go in (a) or (b)? Decide on the appropriate location for the clause, and write X on the blank. Add commas where necessary. Then write the reason for putting the clause in that position.**

1. After a natural disaster, residents of the affected area may need temporary housing.

   __X,__ the housing needs to protect people from the weather conditions _____.
   (a)   (b)

   Clause: although it is temporary

   Reason: _The word "temporary" is linked closely to the previous sentence._

2. In some cases emergency workers face great difficulty in supplying shelter for people

   who live in remote areas. _____ emergency agencies need to act fast _____.
                              (a)   (b)

   Clause: while delivering basic shelters to outlying areas is very difficult

   Reason: _____

3. After the tsunami in 2004, people around the world donated supplies to help the

   victims. _____ the supplies took weeks to reach some of the survivors _____.
            (a)   (b)

   Clause: although governments used high-tech equipment to deliver them

   Reason: _____

4. The situation of the earthquake survivors in the mountains of Pakistan in 2006

   touched people around the world. _____ emergency workers were able to deliver
                                     (a)

   only simple tents for many of the survivors _____.
                                                (b)

   Clause: even though the winter weather conditions were very bitter

   Reason: _____

5. In the aftermath of some disasters, it is clear that rebuilding will take a very long

   time. _____ temporary housing rarely offers the comforts of a real home _____.
         (a)   (b)

   Clause: although it provides shelter for some people for months or years

   Reason: _____

6. Many residents of Kobe, Japan, lived in containers during the reconstruction of

   their city after their big earthquake. _____ the people resigned themselves to such
                                           (a)

   difficult living conditions and stayed in their hometown _____.
                                                             (b)

   Clause: although the rebuilding process took years

   Reason: _____

D Take notes on the short lecture on Jamaica and the threat of natural disaster there. Then, summarize the information according to the categories below. Use concessive clauses in your summary sentences.

CD1,TR26

1. Terrain: *Even though Jamaica has coastal areas with beaches, it also has the tallest mountains in the Caribbean.*

2. Economy: _____

_____

3. Rural/Urban Populations: _____

_____

4. Potential Natural Disasters: _____

_____

5. Safety of Housing: _____

_____

E Complete the sentences below to create a question about the best ways to respond to natural disasters.

1. Although the victims of natural disasters need immediate help, *what can the average citizen do to help them* ?

2. While many organizations ask people to donate money for disaster victims,

_____ ?

3. Even though the Red Cross or the Red Crescent are supposed to help disaster victims,

_____ ?

4. Although millions of dollars may be collected for disaster relief, _____

_____ ?

5. Should we send only money even though _____

_____ ?

6. Is it a good idea to travel to the affected area as a volunteer although

_____ ?

7. Does my small donation really help even though _____

_____ ?

8. While the media often forgets about victims soon after a disaster, _____

_____ ?

F Edit the text below to include some of the connectors in the box below. Place the appropriate connectors in the text, connecting clauses near the slash marks.

while ~~although~~ consequently therefore

Once a disaster has occurred, engineers assess the damage and study ways to improve safety in future catastrophic events. / ~~They~~ *Although they* have to think in terms of costs and benefits. ~~Engineers~~ *, engineers* have to give risks to human life the highest priority. They can often design new structural ways to control natural hazards for public safety.

/ They are trained to find ways to strengthen buildings or to control the forces of nature. The strategy of improving construction has proven very successful in earthquake and hurricane zones. Construction can also harm the environment. / Environmental change can lead to unforeseen dangers, such as a levee system actually causing increased flooding.

■ **COMMUNICATE**

G **SMALL GROUP WORK** Tell a chain story about the experience of a group of university-age volunteers who went to Southeast Asia to help with recovery efforts after the 2004 tsunami hit. For every sentence of your story, begin with *although* + the main clause of the previous sentence.

Although they didn't know anybody in Thailand, Victor, Jim, and Will decided to go there to help after the tsunami.

Although they decided to go there, they had no idea exactly where to go.

Although they didn't know exactly where to go, they . . .

GRAMMAR AND VOCABULARY Write a composition on one of the topics below. Use as many words as possible from the Content Vocabulary on page 131. Use sentences with connectors of causality and concessive connectors to express some of your ideas, and <u>underline</u> those sentences.

Topic 1: After a natural disaster, victims need a lot of assistance; as a result, there are many opportunities for young people to play a part in the recovery. What is the best way for young adults from your country to help victims of a natural disaster? How is this different from the kind of help that you might expect from older adults in your country? Give concrete examples if you can.

Topic 2: Although many people live in areas where natural disasters may strike, most people face greater dangers in their everyday lives. The number of people who die in natural catastrophes is much lower than the number of people who die of other causes. Compare or contrast the safety of citizens in your hometown with the safety of the place where you are living right now. Give concrete examples.

PROJECT Interview at least one student on your campus about threats of natural disasters in your area. Find out the following information and give an oral report to your classmates.

1. What kind of natural disaster is the most likely in this area?
2. What should you do in case such a disaster occurs?
3. What does the student plan to do in case of such a disaster?

 INTERNET With your classmates, make a list of some colleges or universities that are located in "Tornado Alley," earthquake zones, and areas threatened by hurricanes or typhoons. Include your own school if it is affected by any of these potential threats. Select two or three of the schools, and check their websites for emergency instructions. In class, compare the information from various schools that might experience the same type of disaster. Then, decide which university seems to have the best disaster preparedness plan.

Education: Service Learning

■ CONTENT VOCABULARY

Look up the words below that you do not know and enter them in your vocabulary journal. Write each word's part of speech, a definition, and an example sentence. Try to include them in your discussion and writing below.

appreciation	a food bank	literacy	to reinforce
to empower	to implement	a partnership	to revitalize
to enhance	insight	to reflect	self-motivating

■ THINK ABOUT IT

Should your grade in a high school or university class depend on your work as a volunteer in your community? Discuss your ideas with a classmate.

In your writing journal, write for five minutes about the questions below. When you are finished, share what you wrote with the class.

Has one of your teachers or professors ever assigned a "hands-on" project in your community? Have you ever volunteered in your community as part of a school project? How do people from your culture view volunteer work? If you have done this kind of work, what have you learned from it?

■ GRAMMAR IN CONTENT

A Read and listen to the passage below. The words in bold are phrases in which the author omitted repetitious words.

Education in the "Real World"

For students who complain that their economics courses have little to do with their lives, service learning can be a welcome relief — **something new and different** for most economics students. But by the end of the semester, students who choose the service option also are often surprised **when they look back and see** how effectively their service-learning experience increased their awareness of what economics is and how it can be used. Through their experience and through a self-reflective process by which they analyze that experience, students gain a new appreciation for how **economic theory and analysis** can help us not only understand problems but also begin to *solve* them. One of the reasons for this increased awareness is that while students often initially approach their service with skepticism, at some point during their service most allow their whole being to get involved—the physical and intellectual, the emotional, and often the spiritual. This total immersion experience seems to increase student learning significantly (relative to a nonservice option) while providing students with **meaningful and rewarding experiences.** Although I see **an increased awareness of what economics is and how it can be used** as service learning's most important contribution to economics classes, many other benefits are also involved. Service provides a real-world issue on which students can focus. Students gain an appreciation for how real people in the world are trying to solve concrete development problems. Agencies often invite students who provide the best service to work as paid employees. Thus, service provides students with valuable contact opportunities that may help in their future careers. A related benefit is that service often helps students learn job skills and helps prepare them for careers after college. Another benefit for students is that their service helps them retain **important concepts they learn in class.** Service also enhances personalized education for the students and teaches positive attributes, such as leadership, citizenship, and personal responsibility (students may not care about a D or an F as much as about the impression they make in the real world and the fact that they learn about local economic problems). Service learning invites students to become involved members of their communities, and students frequently **say they will continue to volunteer after the course ends.** Furthermore, service learning empowers students as learners, teachers, achievers, and leaders. Service learning also contributes to a university's collaboration and partnerships, broadening the concept of service in which faculty must be engaged, and giving faculty a service option that integrates service with teaching and reinforces both. Service learning also contributes to people in need through nonprofit agencies, nongovernmental and governmental agencies, and even some private-sector companies.

skepticism: a feeling of doubt or disbelief

relative to: compared to

to engage in: to be involved in, to be active in

Sample Sentences	**Notes**
"Hope you're OK." "Got an umbrella?" "Catch you later." "I know ~~that~~ you'll enjoy our literacy project." The woman ~~who~~ you were talking to has been my supervisor on the project ~~for~~ 2 months. Have you ever met Ms. Dixon, ~~who is~~ the director of the literacy project? "Budget at ~~the~~ Senior Center ~~was~~ Reduced" "Senior Center ~~is~~ Anticipating ~~an~~ Increase in ~~the~~ Number of Student Volunteers" Jim is so excited about his project at the Senior Center, and I am ~~excited~~, too. Whoever wants to ~~ride in the van~~ can ride in the van to the training site.	Avoid repeating words in order to improve your English style. One way to avoid redundancy is to delete or omit words or phrases that are repetitious. Use ellipsis (or deletion) when the missing words can be understood from your speech or writing. **Ellipsis can be situational:** In conversations, we know the missing words at the beginning of common expressions and sentences. **Ellipsis can be structural:** We know the missing words from our knowledge of grammar. Headlines are good examples of this kind of ellipsis. **Ellipsis can be textual:** We know the missing words from other words in the text or conversation.
Do you know if the 4:00 van for the Senior Center is the last ~~van~~ this afternoon? One university van leaves at 4:00 and another ~~van~~ is scheduled for 4:30. I enjoy the feedback from Dr. Winters, but I don't get much out of Dr. Sun's ~~feedback~~. Dr. Winters didn't come to the last session, but he should have ~~come~~. He forgot to give us our assignments, and he's not going to ~~give us our assignments~~ until next week. Rachel got her new assignment by e-mail, but I didn't ~~get my assignment by e-mail~~.	When a noun is deleted, the modifiers of that noun remain in the sentence. Avoid repetition by substituting *one* for a noun: *Do you know if the 4:00 van for the Senior Center is the last **one** this afternoon?* *One university van leaves at 4:00 and another **one** is scheduled for 4:30.* When a verb or verb phrase is deleted, the subject and the auxiliary verb(s) remain.

B **Read over your journal entry, and <u>underline</u> at least one sentence that you can revise by omitting repetitious words. Write your revised sentence(s) below.**

_____

_____

C Read the informal conversations below, and <u>underline</u> phrases where ellipsis has occurred. Then, write the missing words above the phrase.

1. **Karen:** OK, everybody, <u>ready to go</u>? *(are you)* The van's out in front.

   Greg: Pat isn't here yet. Can we wait a few more minutes?

   Karen: No problem. It only takes about 10 minutes to get to the Literacy Center.

2. **Karen:** OK, you guys, we'll pick you up in about 2 hours.

   Betty: Right here on the corner?

   Karen: It's probably better if we wait for you behind the Center. Got all of your equipment for today's activities?

   Greg: I think we're set. See you later.

3. **Mr. Newton:** Glad to see that you all made it today. Any trouble finding a place to park?

   Karen: Karen just dropped us off, so we didn't have any hassle.

   Mr. Newton: OK, then, let's get down to business.

4. **Greg:** Hey, Pete, bring that book that we were working on last time?

   Pete: Sure, I did all the homework that you gave me, too. See?

   Greg: Looking good. I can see that you're getting more serious about reading.

D Interpret the headlines below in complete sentences. Follow the example.

1. Local Teens Donate Time at Senior Center

   Local teens have been donating their time at the Senior Center.

2. Volunteer Offers Yoga Wednesdays at Sports Complex

   _____

3. Free Swimming Classes Open to All

   _____

4. Student Club IDs New Projects Based on Report Findings

   _____

5. Air Quality Increase Due to Jackson Plant Closing

   _____

E Create headlines from the first sentence of these newspaper articles. There is more than one possible headline for each sentence.

1. The Houston City Council voted to cut the Arts Council budget by 15%.

   Arts Council Budget Cut by 15% ; City Council Cuts Arts Budget 15%

2. The Baltimore AIDS Taskforce is promoting more information sessions in local high schools and technical schools.

3. The Back Bay district has continued its revitalization efforts through university volunteers who help plan and implement changes in the neighborhood.

4. Local volunteers held a book drive and other fundraising activities to raise over $300,000 for the Kerry Library.

5. For their course on public administration, Parklane University students have identified over 50 streetlights that are missing bulbs in the Highland Park area.

6. The proceeds from last night's benefit dinner at Clancy's will finance a new playground in Oaklawn Park.

7. According to students at Dawson State, the parking needs at Memorial Hospital are growing annually by 3–5% as the hospital gains importance in this region.

F **PAIR WORK** Brainstorm a list of 3–5 ways that a service-learning project could change your relationships with classmates. What benefits could you gain from such cooperative work? Then, write sentences comparing the normal type of student-student relationship with the relationships that you have brainstormed.

Normally you don't care if the other students behave responsibly, but in this type of project you have to.

■ GRAMMAR IN CONTENT

A Reread the text at the beginning of the lesson, and <u>underline</u> phrases or clauses that are grammatically similar within a sentence. (The first example of parallelism, or grammatical similarity, is in the second sentence.) Compare your answers with one of your classmates.

Parallelism	
Sample Sentences	**Notes**
We haven't heard **where the Center is** or **what we need to do.** **If you want to get some practical training** and **if you like to work with kids**, you should volunteer for the after-care project. Some students don't like **to write papers** or **do academic research.**	Use parallel structures to emphasize the connection of ideas. When structures are parallel, they are connected by a coordinate conjunction and are grammatically the same. Use ellipsis to avoid redundancy in sentences with parallelism.
You can hand in your project report **right now** or **anytime tomorrow.** Leave it **here** or **in my box.**	In the case of adverbials, the structure may not be structurally parallel, but the expressions of time, place, or manner should be parallel in meaning.

B Use the phrases or clauses in parentheses to complete each sentence. Edit for appropriate grammar structures, add words when necessary, and check for parallelism.

1. (select a project / establish a vision)

   To make a service-learning project effective, professors should interest their students
   _____*in selecting a project and establishing a vision.*_____

2. (solve interpersonal problems / interact appropriately with people in the community)

   _____

   can be very important lessons that students take away from their service-learning

   experience.

3. (have great success / meet all the goals)

   Professors shouldn't expect every project-team _____

   _____

4. (write journals or reflective essays / make formal presentations)

At the end of the semester, students may have a choice of _____

_____ about their projects.

5. (apply business analysis to real-life situations / understand social issues in the community)

An effective service-learning project for business students demands _____

_____

6. (put a human face on a social issue / make students feel responsibility for project results)

The goal of professors that assign students service-learning projects is _____

_____

CD1,TR28

C Read the questions below. Then, listen to a telephone conversation between Barbara Reilly, an economics professor, and Jim Brewer, the manager of the Millvale Food Bank and Community Kitchen, as they make final arrangements for Professor Reilly's service-learning project. Take notes on their conversation, and use the information to answer the questions below.

1. How will the students get to the project site?

   The students will go there in Professor Reilly's car or in the university van.

2. What are Professor Reilly's goals for the project?

   _____

3. What are Mr. Brewer's concerns about the students?

   _____

4. What will most of the students be involved in during the first weeks of the project?

   _____

5. How will the students assist the staff and clients in the second part of the project?

   _____

■ **COMMUNICATE**

D **GROUP WORK** Brainstorm a list of projects that a group of students could do in order to accomplish a goal in health care, education, journalism, or engineering. When you are finished, share your ideas with your classmates.

GRAMMAR AND VOCABULARY Write a composition on one of the topics below. Use as many words as possible from the Content Vocabulary on page 143, and (circle) them in your composition. Use sentences with ellipsis and parallelism to express some of your ideas, and underline those sentences.

Topic 1: Many Americans criticize U.S. colleges and universities for preparing young people for their careers but not for citizenship. These critics feel that institutions of higher education should prepare such young adults to be sensitive to less fortunate citizens and to enhance their communities. Do people in your community share this view of the purpose of higher education? Give examples.

Topic 2: According to Herbert Spencer, an English philosopher who lived from 1820 to 1903, "The great aim of education is not knowledge, but action." Do you agree or disagree? Give examples.

PROJECT Interview at least one student on your campus about service learning. Find out the following information, and give a brief oral report on it to your classmates.

1. Is there a special office on your campus that provides information about service-learning opportunities?
2. Has the student ever participated in a service-learning project?
3. If so, what was the project and what did the student learn from the experience?
4. If the student hasn't had this kind of experience before, what does he/she think about having a service-learning option in an academic course?

 INTERNET Go online and use the search phrase "National Service-Learning Clearinghouse." Find out what "Service-learning Projects" are under way in your state and/or city, and select one or two topics that you find interesting. Read about the projects and choose one to describe to your class. Report briefly on the program at your next class meeting.

Public Policy and Administration: NIMBY

■ CONTENT VOCABULARY

Look up the words and phrases below that you do not know and enter them in your vocabulary journal. Write each item's part of speech, a definition, and an example sentence. Try to include them in your discussion and writing below.

to advocate	a controversy	ill-advised	property values
a building permit	a developer	an initiative	to sign a petition
circumstances	a group home	a phenomenon	zoning laws

■ THINK ABOUT IT

How would you feel about living near a nuclear power plant? A rehabilitation center for drug addicts? Why? How can urban and regional planners decide on the best locations for such facilities? What criteria are the most appropriate? Discuss your ideas with a classmate.

In your writing journal, write for five minutes about the questions below. When you finish your writing, share your ideas with your classmates.

Near your family's home, are there any buildings, businesses, or other facilities that are very unpopular in your neighborhood? Why do your family members or your neighbors feel unhappy about the situation? What can you do about it?

■ GRAMMAR IN CONTENT

A Read and listen to the passage below. The words in bold are negative elements.

CD1,TR29

"NIMBYism" Blocks Construction of Elementary School

WILLIAMSBURG, VA. Residents along Brickyard Road have successfully brought plans for the construction of Henry Elementary School to a halt. Their opposition to the school, a classic case of "not in my backyard" (NIMBY), has resulted in a second court case that will delay any resolution of the situation for several more months. Not only families on the road where the school is to be built but also people on nearby residential streets where the school buses will have to go are claiming that the proposed school will affect their property values and their quality of life. Meanwhile, both teachers and parents of local elementary school students strongly defend the need for another school in town.

"**Not once** did I think that the people on Brickyard Road had such an anti-education attitude," commented one of the members of the local school board. "I knew that they were concerned about the traffic, but this is really unreasonable. In fact, **seldom** have I heard such a selfish point of view when we're talking about improving our children's educational opportunities."

Valarie Newcomb, Williamsburg's city manager, was also perplexed by the reaction. "Either they haven't listened to our plans for traffic control, or they just don't understand that we have to find a solution that is fair for all members of our community. **At no time** did they come forward with their complaints before they filed the court case."

The NIMBY phenomenon is nothing new. When the atomic power facility in Surry County was built two decades ago, hundreds of citizens protested. Neither their protests nor local politicians' proposals for alternate locations had any effect on the state energy commission. State energy officials had to balance the needs of the whole region against the interests of one sparsely populated county. Such controversies arise all across the nation, and **rarely** do local politicians have it easy in pushing for development while satisfying the concerns of their constituents.

to claim: to assert, to state an opinion

perplexed: confused, at a loss

to file a court case: to register a case with the court

a constituent: a citizen, a voter

Sample Sentences	Notes
Never had the mayor heard such nonsense when it came to new school construction.	Put negative words or phrases at the beginning of the sentence (or clause) for emphasis. With this word order, invert the subject and verb, and use the auxiliary *do* if necessary.
Under no circumstances should an official ignore the strength of NIMBY attitudes.	
At no time did the opponents of the school talk to the press.	
I don't like their attitude about the school, and **neither do** a lot of residents.	
Seldom are city council meetings without controversy.	Follow the same rule for words and phrases with a negative meaning or very restrictive meaning, such as *few, little, rarely, least of all*, and *seldom*.
Little do some city planners realize how upset citizens can become about a park.	Such sentences are often very formal or literary in style.
Least of all would one expect a new park to upset local residents.	Formal constructions such as these often have a main verb in passive voice.
Few words could be spoken without upsetting the audience members further.	

B Read over your journal entry, and <u>underline</u> at least one sentence that you can revise to include one of the negative elements in the chart above in initial position. Write your revised sentence(s) below.

_____

_____

_____

C Rewrite the underlined text in each conversation, emphasizing the negative elements. In some cases you will have to revise the sentence considerably.

1. **Frank:** I can't believe that they are talking about building a new racetrack close to the kids' playground.

   Marcie: <u>I can't either.</u> It doesn't make any sense. Is the mayor out of his mind?

   Neither can I.
   _____

2. **Mayor Clark:** I'm thinking about putting our plan for a new racetrack on the agenda for the town meeting tonight.

   Mr. Dunner: Mr. Mayor, <u>I have seldom heard you make such an ill-advised statement.</u> You know very well that more than half the town hates that idea.

   _____

3. **Council-member Wagner:** Mayor Clark, I wholeheartedly agree with Mr. Dunner. <u>You cannot mention one word about the racetrack.</u> Don't even say "horse!"

   _____

4. **Mayor Clark:** John, what do you think? Is the time right?

   Council-member Owens: <u>There is no way that you can mention it without causing a big uproar.</u> The press will be all over you.

   _____

5. **Mayor Clark:** Men, I think that you are over-reacting. Ms. Yoder, what's your take on the racetrack?

   Council-member Yoder: With all due respect, Mayor, <u>you shouldn't bring up the track under any circumstances.</u> Our polls show that it is a political disaster waiting to happen.

   _____

6. **Mayor Clark:** Ms. Yoder, I'm really surprised at you. <u>I would expect such advice least of all from you.</u> Don't you own several racehorses?

   Council-member Yoder: Be that as it may, I stand by my words.

   _____

7. **Mayor Clark:** I'll bow to your expert advice. <u>I have little hope that the racetrack will be approved without all of your support.</u>

   _____

D **Choose one negative element in each of the letters to the editor below, and rewrite that sentence to emphasize it. Give your reason for emphasizing a particular negative element.**

---

1. I firmly believe that our community needs at least five more group homes for our fellow-citizens with developmental disabilities. (Such homes pose no danger to families and property values in the neighborhood.) Research studies have shown this to be true in cities across the U.S. Our citizens need to inform themselves about the facts and not listen to false information about dangers. Families of these citizens don't want their loved ones to live far away, and I don't either. It's not fair!

Negative Statement: _No danger is posed to families in the neighborhood._

Reason: _The main argument is the lack of danger, so it should be emphasized._

---

2. Just as our citizens' committee had warned, the new motel on Jamestown Road has increased traffic in our neighborhood. I used to let my children walk to school and cross at the intersection of Jamestown and First Streets. I can no longer do that in good conscience. I can never be sure that they will cross the street without some out-of-town visitor running them over. I have never before felt so betrayed by my elected officials.

Negative Statement: _____

Reason: _____

---

3. I call on the City Council to oppose the mayor's ill-advised plan to relocate the city jail to Morningside, a section of town five miles from the closest police station. I have never heard of a politician with so little concern for the welfare of taxpayers. We elected Mayor Burns for his innovative ideas on economic development, but he didn't give us reason at any time during the campaign to believe that our lives would be in danger as a result of his ideas.

Negative Statement: _____

Reason: _____

---

4. We should all be very alarmed that the Bluebird Café has applied for a liquor license. Many of us concerned neighbors don't want to see college students making noise late at night with their drunken friends. This neighborhood has never had many college students, but now they will be around at all hours of the day and night. The City Council should in no way consider this application seriously. In fact, there's no way in a million years that we will put up with it. I strongly urge everyone to send a letter to the City Council.

Negative Statement: _____

Reason: _____

E Read the following situations and make an emphatic response that expresses NIMBY. Use one of the phrases in the box below at the beginning of your sentence.

no way	never in a million years	not for all the money in the world
rarely	in no uncertain terms	not for a million dollars
~~not for one minute~~	never once	at no time

1. The City Council has introduced a plan to build a health-care clinic in the next block.

   Not for one minute will I support this plan because the traffic and parking will be terrible around my house.

2. You read in the newspaper that a local developer wants to convert an apartment building nearby to housing for poor people.

3. A person asks you to sign a petition that supports the construction of a new soccer field across the street from your house.

4. You attend a City Council meeting and listen to the mayor's proposal for a waste treatment plant in your town.

5. One of your neighbors asks you to join a local planning committee. The committee advocates building a wind energy park with 25 turbines at the edge of town near your house.

6. On the local TV news, they have been reporting all week about the need for a new landfill in the region. It seems that your county is at the top of the list because the population is so low.

7. In the governor's campaign for reelection, she has said that the solution to traffic congestion on the highway near your town is to build more on- and off-ramps. One of the proposed exits will cut through your neighborhood.

F PAIR WORK Discuss your reaction to the construction of a high school, a group home for adults with developmental disabilities, a casino, a nightclub, a 10-story hotel, and a solar power plant in your neighborhood.

> Not for a moment would I consider a nightclub being built in my neighborhood.

> Neither would I. It wouldn't be a good influence on my kids.

PART TWO	Correlative Conjunctions

■ GRAMMAR IN CONTENT

A Reread the text on page 152, and <u>underline</u> all of the sentences with one of the following pairs of connecting words: *either . . . or, neither . . . nor, both . . . and, not only . . . but also.*

Correlative Conjunctions

Sample Sentences	Notes
Either Fred **or** George will speak first at the meeting.	Connect elements in your sentences with the correlative conjunctions below.
Both Fred **and** George will support the plan.	• *Either . . . or* Only one of two items is true. • *Both . . . and* Both items are valid.
Neither Fred **nor** George can predict the results.	• *Neither . . . nor* Both items are false. • *Not (only) . . . but (also)* The first statement is unexpected or surprising and so is the second one.
Not only did Fred speak effectively, **but** he **also** won the election.	
Either George will volunteer for the recycling center, **or** he will find another project to work on.	Follow the rules of subject-verb inversion when a negative correlative element begins a clause. Use parallel structures after correlative elements in formal English.
Not only does George volunteer a lot, **but** he **also** donates to community projects.	Use *either . . . or* and *not (only) . . . but also* to connect clauses. Use a comma after the first clause.
Neither they **nor** Fred is surprised that the recycling center won approval.	When *neither . . . nor* or *either . . . or* connect two subjects, follow the proximity rule of subject-verb agreement: "the verb agrees with the closer subject." If, however, both subjects are pronouns, English speakers prefer a plural verb.
Neither they **nor** he have heard any criticism of the center.	
Both his co-workers **and** his wife think that Fred is going to do a great job.	Subjects connected with *both . . . and* and *not only . . . but also* always have plural subject-verb agreement.

B Combine the sentences below using one of the pairs of correlative conjunctions. There may be more than one way to combine the sentences.

1. When citizens protest against the construction of a group home in their neighborhood, they are concerned about falling property values. These citizens are also worried about more traffic in their neighborhood.

   <u>Citizens that protest against the construction of a group home in their neighborhood</u>
   <u>are concerned about both falling property values and more traffic in their neighborhood.</u>

2. Homeowners generally agree that a community needs to provide housing for people with disabilities. Politicians tend to agree that a city should provide housing for citizens who cannot care for themselves.

   _____

   _____

3. Selecting a particular street for a group home doesn't seem fair to the neighbors there. Changing the zoning laws on a particular street doesn't seem right to the local residents.

   _____

   _____

4. When increased traffic seems a real possibility, officials should look for a location outside a quiet residential neighborhood. When personal safety may be an issue, planners need to consider an alternative site.

   _____

   _____

5. According to public policy analyses, group homes have no statistical effect on the property values in a neighborhood. The analyses also show that such homes do not have any negative impact on the character of the neighborhood.

   _____

   _____

6. Effective city planners choose projects that will bring about the greatest benefits to the community. Good administrators also select projects that produce the least harm to society.

   _____

   _____

7. Being part of a group enriches the lives of people with disabilities. Living in a group setting gives them opportunities for social interaction and shared responsibilities.

   _____

   _____

C Select the best verb from the box to fill each blank, and be sure to use the proper form of the verb for the context.

be	~~advocate~~	oppose	voice
urge	support	consult	interview

About three months ago, T-Mart announced its interest in opening a new store in the vicinity of Beaumont. In recent weeks, neither Mayor Nichol nor City Council members _____*have advocated*_____ (1) having a T-Mart in the city limits. They support local businesses instead. However, all this week, both the T-Mart representative and their corporate lawyers _____ (2) with local citizens' groups who would like to see a T-Mart store in the community. A sizeable proportion of the local population _____ (3) the initiative to build a T-Mart. The local media _____ (4) people from each side. Not only the mayor but also the City Council _____ (5) citizens to consider the impact of T-Mart on local small businesses very carefully. Also, they have cautioned the T-Mart supporters that either the empty field by Lafayette School or the acres of marshland by Lake Kennesaw _____ (6) the only available site for the giant retailer. The mayor has already heard that neither the environmentalists nor the School Board _____ (7) the use of city land for the construction of a T-Mart.

D On a separate piece of paper, write a summary of the opinion poll results below for your boss, Mayor Gregson. Use correlative conjunctions in your memo.

Survey Question: In the upcoming referendum on proposed city development, will you vote for the following projects in your neighborhood?

	Absolutely	Maybe	No Way
a. a police substation	25%	15%	60%
b. a drug rehabilitation center	10%	15%	75%
c. a recycling center for garden waste	25%	40%	35%
d. a children's day-care center	40%	40%	20%
e. a group home for juvenile offenders	5%	15%	80%

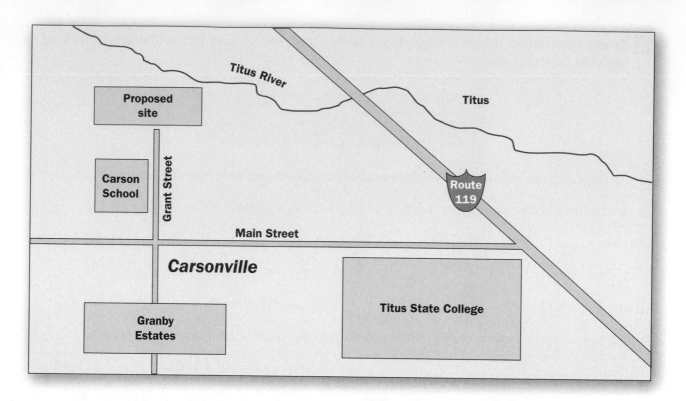

E Listen to some community leaders in Carsonville give their recommendations for the location of the new recycling center. After listening to each speaker, (circle) the letter of the correct interpretation.

CD1, TR30

1. a. The Green Club neither supports the construction of the center nor the mayor's recommendation for its location.
   b. The Green Club both supports the construction of the center and recommends a different site for its location.

2. a. The Sierra Club recommends both accepting household chemicals and locating the center in a different location.
   b. The Sierra Club recommends either changing the location of the center or changing the items that the center will accept.

3. a. The Carsonville School Board agrees with either the Green Club or the Sierra Club.
   b. The School Board is worried not only about the chemicals but also about the noise.

4. a. Titus State College supports neither the location on Grant Street nor the alternative site by Route 119.
   b. TSC both understands the concerns of the other speakers and suggests finding a different alternative location.

5. a. Jim Samuel has not only investigated sites in Carsonville but has also discussed a site near Titus.
   b. Jim Samuel recommends the site either at one end of Grant Street by the school or at the other end beyond Granby Estates.

6. a. Mr. O'Malley either wants the recycling center near the school or near the TSC campus.
   b. Mr. O'Malley both objects to the recycling center near his neighborhood and threatens to resist this idea strongly.

There are four errors in the e-mail message below. Find and correct the errors.

Dear Steve,

You should have been at the meeting on the recycling center last night. It got pretty tense. There was supposed to be a time limit for each speaker. Not only the mayor let them talk as long as they wanted, she also asked a lot of questions. I thought that we would be there till midnight!

I guess that most of the speakers actually presented their opinions both clearly and they talked politely. One of the last guys was the worst. Seldom I have heard such an arrogant person. It was incredible. He kept neither to the point nor tried to be respectful to the other groups in the meeting. We were all happy when it was over.

Now we have to make the final recommendations to the City Council. There should be some more fireworks at that meeting!

What's the latest on your end?

Lenny

■ COMMUNICATE

G **SMALL GROUP WORK** Prepare a short presentation to local homeowners who are very concerned about a new 100-occupant dormitory that your school wants to build in the neighborhood. The neighbors are worried about noise, traffic and parking, trash, and the general appearance of the property as well as drugs and alcohol.

Not only will the dorm residents keep the property clean, we will also be responsible for garbage cans on garbage pick-up days.

GRAMMAR AND VOCABULARY Write a composition on one of the topics below. Use as many words as possible from the Content Vocabulary on page 151, and (circle) them in your composition. Use sentences with fronted negative elements and correlative conjunctions to express some of your ideas, and underline those sentences.

Topic 1: Changes in a neighborhood or city district concern those who live there. For example, safety issues worry not only homeowners but also renters. Residents also complain about changes that could lead to more noise, pollution, or traffic. Explain one example of the NIMBY phenomenon in your town or city in detail.

Topic 2: Not only on the local level will one find the NIMBY phenomenon. It also exists on the state and national level in the U.S. Other countries also practice NIMBY. Discuss the NIMBY phenomenon in your region or country. Give concrete examples.

PROJECT Interview at least one student on your campus to find out that person's attitudes about NIMBY. Find out the following information, and give a brief oral report at the next class meeting.

1. How would you describe your neighborhood?
2. How would you or your family feel if your town/city decided to build one of the following in your neighborhood? Why?

   a. a high school
   b. a group home for adults with developmental disabilities
   c. a nightclub
   d. a 10-story hotel
   e. a solar power plant

3. How can a community both respect families and their homes and provide important services (like schools, rehabilitation centers, housing for the poor, etc.) for everyone in the community?

 INTERNET Go online, and use the search phrase "NIMBY headlines" to find a website with current articles about NIMBY issues. Then, select and read two different articles. Write a brief summary of one of the articles, using at least one pair of correlative conjunctions. In class, tell your class about the NIMBY issue in the other article that you read.

A Select the appropriate connector or adverbial from the box to complete the idea in each pair of sentences. Add punctuation where necessary.

thus	first of all	ultimately	while
evidently	even though	both	similarly

1. Many college students work part-time during their studies. _____

   they probably have some experience interacting with older co-workers.

2. Many experienced employees enjoy working with young people.

   _____ they listen politely to the ideas and suggestions of their

   younger co-workers, the employees may not accept their ideas easily.

3. New, inexperienced employees could feel frustrated for several reasons.

   _____ they might have the feeling that their co-workers don't take

   their ideas seriously. They might also feel like their supervisors are scrutinizing them.

4. A new employee may share her ideas with her supervisor. _____ the

   supervisor will decide whether to implement the new idea.

5. Residents in some towns protest changes in zoning laws to protect the value of their

   property. _____ homeowners in other places are against school

   construction close to their neighborhood.

6. In some cities, residents protest against any change. _____ jails and

   schools are particularly controversial.

7. Protesting against school construction may seem incredible. _____

   families benefit from having new schools, most people don't want to live near one.

8. Recently the local school board voted against building a new school in our district.

   _____ no one could agree on the location of the new construction.

B (Circle) the letter of the best completion for each sentence below.

1. _____ miss the opportunity to join a service-learning project.

   a. Under no circumstances should you
   b. Under no circumstances you should

2. During her project at the Food Bank, Tamika has not only shared her accounting experience _____

   a. but also her organizational skills.
   b. but also used her organizational skills.

3. Tamika and two classmates work _____ to fulfill a service-learning requirement for a course that they are taking.

   a. every week there
   b. there every week

4. _____ and her classmates are glad that they chose the service-learning option.

   a. Both Tamika is enthusiastic
   b. Both Tamika

5. Neither her classmates nor Tamika _____ signing up for this course option.

   a. regrets
   b. regret

6. _____ fulfill the course requirement with this project, _____ have made useful contacts in the community.

   a. Not only do they . . . but they also
   b. Not only they . . . but also they

7. Tamika hasn't decided which courses she'll take next year or _____

   a. what to major in.
   b. what she'll major in.

8. However, she is _____ that she will participate in another service project.

   a. quitely sure
   b. quite sure

LEARNER LOG Check (✔) *Yes* or *I Need More Practice.*

Lesson	I Can Use . . .	Yes	I Need More Practice
11	Adverbials and Adverbs in Sentence-Initial Position		
12	Sequential Connectors and Connectors of Equivalence		
13	Connectors of Causality and Concessive Connectors		
14	Ellipsis and Parallelism		
15	Fronted Negative Elements and Correlative Conjunctions		

PART 1
Review of the Passive Voice

PART 2
Passive Options with Verbs
Taking Two Objects

Lesson 16

Cultural
Anthropology:
The Gullah

■ CONTENT VOCABULARY

Look up the words below that you do not know and enter them in your vocabulary journal.
Write each word's part of speech, a definition, and an example sentence. Try to include them
in your discussion and writing below.

to carve	a grain	means	a practice
to commence	to investigate	norms	to transmit
to compile	to isolate	oral history	unscrupulous

■ THINK ABOUT IT

What do you know about the American South? Who settled there? What was the basis of their
economy? What was the importance of these states during the 1700s and 1800s? Discuss
your ideas with a classmate.

In your writing journal, write for 5–10 minutes about the questions below. When you are
finished, share what you wrote with the class.

The topic of this lesson is the culture and language of a particular group of Americans who
have a "rice culture." Do you belong to a rice culture? If not, what dietary culture do you
belong to? What does it mean to belong to a culture that is defined by a type of food?

■ GRAMMAR IN CONTENT

A Read and listen to the passage below. The words in bold are verbs in the passive voice.

The Gullah: Cultural Isolation and Preservation

Gullah communities in the Sea Islands and neighboring mainland regions in Georgia and South Carolina provide a unique opportunity to study some of the distinctive elements of African cultural influences on African American culture in the United States. . . . One significant characteristic of these communities, for example, is that most residents are descendants of enslaved Africans who worked on these islands as early as the seventeenth century. Beginning in that period, Africans **were captured and transported** as slaves from various regions in Africa, extending from Angola to the Upper Guinea Coast region of West Africa. Between 1670 and 1800, however, Africans from rice-cultivating regions in West Africa, such as Liberia, Sierra Leone, Senegal, Gambia, and Guinea, **were sought** because of their knowledge of cultivation of rice, which was then a lucrative crop in Georgia and South Carolina. Rice planters were particularly interested in enslaving Africans from the "Rice Coast" of West Africa because the planters themselves lacked knowledge about rice cultivation under tropical conditions. . . .

Dependence on rice as a staple food is the most significant way the Gullah express cultural identity through food practices. Rice is the main food that links Gullah dietary traditions with the food traditions of West African food cultures; women play a primary role in fostering the continuance of these practices. In such cultures a person **is not considered** to have eaten a full meal unless rice **is included.**

Although most Gullah families no longer cultivate rice regularly, people are still conscious of its significance. Rice **was described** as the central part of the main family meal by at least 90% of the women I interviewed. . . .

One way of promoting [traditional values] through food practices is in the observance of strict rituals of rice preparation. In Gullah and West African rice cultures, for example, it is typical to commence the preparation of rice by picking out any dirt or dark looking grains from the rice before washing it. Then the rice **is washed** vigorously between the hands a number of times before it **is considered** clean enough for cooking. As a girl growing up in Sierra Leone, I **was taught** to cook rice in this way. I still follow this practice faithfully, even though most of the rice available for sale today in the U.S. **is labeled** as prewashed. . . .

Gullah culture **is influenced** strongly by rules and norms of West African food preparation. Many women who cook perpetuate these practices daily. One of these practices involves the selection, the amounts, and the combination of seasonings for food. These elements differentiate Gullah cooking practices from those of other cultures, according to many women I interviewed. Although the Gullah identify certain foods as their own, such as Hoppin' John (rice cooked with peas and smoked meat), red rice, rice served with a plate of shrimp and okra stew, and collard greens and cornbread, the interaction between European American, Native American, and African American food systems in the South has carried these popular Southern dishes across ethnic lines. One way in which Gullah women try to control cultural boundaries in their way of cooking these foods, as distinct from other Southern practices, is to assert that although similar foods **are eaten** by others in the South, their style of preparation and the type of seasonings they use are different.

lucrative: profitable

to foster: to promote and protect

okra: a green vegetable used in soups and stews

collard greens: kale, a green leafy vegetable

Sample Sentences	Notes
Because European planters had no experience with growing rice, slaves **were put** in charge of its cultivation. Rice **was introduced** to South Carolina agriculture in the late 1600s. The name "Gullah" **might have been derived** from Angola, which was home to many slaves in South Carolina. To avoid punishment, a house slave might say, "The rice platter **was broken**" or "The dinner **was overcooked**." Slaves also developed means of irrigating the rice fields. Elaborate systems **were dug** and **monitored** for water levels that were appropriate for cultivating rice.	Use **passive structures** to focus attention on the person or thing that experiences or receives an action, not the agent or doer of the action. Focus on the object when • the agent is obvious or very general • the agent is unknown • the agent is known, but you want to avoid naming that person or thing • the object is more important to the text than the agent. In scientific and technical texts this is common. The context of a sentence often determines whether the agent or object is the focus of attention.
In the 1780s after the Revolutionary War, slaves were transported to South Carolina **by Danish ships.** The first rice crops were ruined **by the poor farming techniques** of the white planters. The slave trade was directed **by Henry Laurens,** who was President of the Continental Congress in the 1770s.	Include the agent in the sentence if • the agent is new information • the agent is not a person (because this is unexpected) • the agent is well-known or famous
In England **they** imported tons of rice from South Carolina. The adaptable Asian white-grained species, *Oryza sativa,* **was introduced** into West African agriculture and replaced *O. glaberrima,* which had been cultivated in Senegambia since 1500 BCE.	English speakers prefer active rather than passive sentences in many instances. • In conversation, use "they" for obvious, general, or unknown agents to avoid passives. • In scientific writing, however, use passive voice to emphasize the topic of interest/focus of research.

B **Read over your journal entry, and <u>underline</u> at least one sentence that you can revise to include a verb in the passive voice. Write your revised sentence(s) below.**

_____

_____

_____

C Explain the steps in cultivating and harvesting rice on a South Carolina farm using the illustrations. Use the past passive.

1. ___First, the irrigation canals and ridges were created.___

2. _____

3. _____

4. _____

5. _____

6. _____

PART TWO Passive Options with Verbs Taking Two Objects

■ GRAMMAR IN CONTENT

A Look at the passive verb forms in bold print in the text at the beginning of the lesson. Which one of those verbs can have both a direct object and an indirect object?

Passive Options with Verbs Taking Two Objects

Sample Sentences	Notes
Nowadays, **children** are read the traditional African stories of their ancestors. **The elderly** have always been shown respect in Gullah culture. Respect has always been shown **to the elderly** in Gullah culture. Special rice dishes are cooked **for children** on their birthdays.	Choose the **direct** or **indirect object** as the subject of a passive verb according to the focus of your sentence. See list of verbs on next page. Use *to* with the indirect object when the direct object is the passive subject. Passive forms of verbs with *for* + indirect object usually take only the direct object as the subject.
Did the slaves **get kidnapped** from their homes in West Africa? Sometimes African families **got separated** on their arrival in America. Gullah children didn't **get educated** with white children, so they only learned the language that their parents spoke. In the early 1900s, the Gullah **got criticized** for their language.	Use *get* instead of *be* for a more informal passive construction. Typically this option · specifies no agent · has a human grammatical subject · has an action verb This construction often implies that something negative happened to the grammatical subject (who may or may not have responsibility for the negative consequence). In contrast to some other languages, in English only passive sentences with this "get" structure can imply a negative consequence except with this structure.
During the hurricane one boat **was sunk** by an oar that crashed through its hull. Nearby a small rowboat **was sunk** in just a few feet of water. Several small fishing boats **sank** during the storm. Several others **capsized** but did not actually **sink**.	Use ergative verbs in passive structures or in the middle voice. (See Lesson 4.) · Choose the passive form of an ergative verb to stress that an agent of the action exists even if you do not specify the agent. · Use the active form of ergative verbs in the middle voice if the agent is not relevant or if there are many possible agents.

D <u>Underline</u> agents that should be omitted, and then write the reason for omitting or keeping the agent. Consider the information in previous sentences as you decide whether to omit an agent.

1. The isolation of the Gullah is mentioned <u>by researchers</u> in many academic research projects.

   Reason: _____ *The context makes "researchers" obvious.* _____

2. Their separation from slave owners was greater than in other regions because the planters' houses were built far away from the rice fields.

   Reason: _____

3. Many planters were infected with malaria or yellow fever by the slaves, so slave owners kept their distance.

   Reason: _____

4. The diseases were transmitted by the slaves but did not affect them due to the Africans' inherited resistance to those illnesses.

   Reason: _____

5. Also, the planters and their families were affected by the humid, semitropical climate of the coastal region; consequently, they spent many months of the year farther inland.

   Reason: _____

6. While the families stayed away, the plantations were managed by a few European supervisors and some trusted slaves.

   Reason: _____

7. Finally, slaves from other American colonies or from the Caribbean weren't bought by the planters because only Africans from the Guinea Coast knew how to cultivate rice.

   Reason: _____

8. The language and customs of the slaves on coastal rice plantations were constantly renewed by Africans of the same background so that they were able to keep their cultural identity.

   Reason: _____

E Edit the following passages to adjust the focus of the information. Read the entire passage before you change any verb forms to passive. Give the reason(s) for your edits.

1. Numerous linguists have conducted research on the language of the Gullah since the 1930s. Before that, however, ~~outsiders considered the language~~ *the language was considered* a simplified, even barbaric means of communication. Plantation owners in particular thought the Gullah way of talking wasn't a "real" language.

   Reasons: *The first sentence introduces new information on the language of the Gullah. The language, not the outsiders, is the topic of the next sentence, with new information at the end of the sentence. The final sentence also continues the focus on the language.*

2. Perceptions of the language of the Gullah began to change thanks to the research of Lorenzo Turner, who was an African American linguist. He lived among the Gullah for many years, recorded their speech, and compared it to African languages. The languages of the Guinea Coast showed a number of similarities in grammar, vocabulary, and pronunciation. A company published his book on those linguistic similarities in 1949.

   Reasons: _____
   _____
   _____

3. In contrast to the work of some other linguists, Turner discovered thousands of words that Gullah speakers share with speakers of African languages. Some of those words were in stories, songs, and prayers that Turner learned in the Gullah community. Also, he found hundreds and hundreds of other words, but these words were personal names that are used only within the family. Having two kinds of names is not uncommon in traditional African societies.

   Reasons: _____
   _____
   _____

4. As Turner gained the trust of the Gullah, he found out about their naming practices. For example, "Joe" appears to be an English nickname, but it could also be the shortened form of "Cudjo" for a male child born on Monday. Along the Guinea Coast parents often named children for the day that they were born.

   Reasons: _____
   _____

5. Modern linguists agree that Gullah is a Creole language. Such languages develop in situations where people of different cultures need to communicate. Gullah made communication possible among speakers of various African languages and with the white planters and their families.

   Reasons: _____
   _____
   _____

■ **COMMUNICATE**

F **SMALL GROUP WORK** Discuss the isolation of groups in a society. Talk about any examples of an ethnic or social group that was isolated from a mainstream culture. How was the group isolated? What happened to the language or culture of that group? Can you compare that group to the Gullah in any way?

G **PAIR WORK** Discuss naming practices in your community and culture. Who is involved in selecting the name(s)? Are names chosen for particular meanings? For family reasons? Try to find some interesting similarities or differences between your cultures. Use passive constructions whenever appropriate.

In some parts of Mexico, names **are passed down** from one generation to the next. I **was named after** my grandfather, for example.

In Japan, we **aren't necessarily named after** our grandparents, but names are often chosen by them.

Verbs Commonly Taking an Indirect Object as the Passive Subject

bring	hand	owe	send
deny	lend	promise	show
give	offer	read	teach

B **Change the focus, or topic, of the sentences below by using a passive construction.**

1. Gullah women show their children the way to prepare rice in the traditional style.

   New focus: the way to prepare rice

   The way to prepare rice in the traditional style is shown to Gullah children.

2. Men taught some young boys wood-carving so that they could continue the tradition.

   New focus: some young boys

3. Slave traders brought South Carolina plantation owners slaves from the Guinea Coast because they needed them for cultivating rice.

   New focus: South Carolina plantation owners

4. The plantation owners offered top dollar for slaves from Sierra Leone.

   New focus: top dollar

5. Sometimes agents bought families of slaves so they could stay together.

   New focus: families of slaves

6. Owners sometimes lent other planters in South Carolina their slaves.

   New focus: slaves

7. Planters in South Carolina didn't deny the slaves the chance to earn a little money.

   New focus: the slaves

8. Planters promised each slave a small piece of land for growing vegetables.

   New focus: a small piece of land

9. Gullah speakers have taught many linguists the Gullah language in recent years.

   New focus: many linguists

C Paraphrase the statements below with a passive sentence with *get* to make the statement less formal. Use one of the verbs in the box below as the main verb.

exploit	cheat	lose	catch
swindle	deceive	attack	mistreat

1. The Gullah, like all other enslaved Africans, felt that Europeans had taken advantage of them.

   Similar to other African slaves, the Gullah got exploited by Europeans.

2. Many planters punished slaves, including the Gullah, very severely for a variety of reasons.

   _____

3. Although planters found many slaves who tried to escape, hundreds of Gullah escaped to Florida.

   _____

4. In Florida they lived with the Indians there and fought with them when Europeans invaded their villages.

   _____

5. After people began to appreciate Gullah culture, outsiders bought their baskets and other homemade items and handicrafts at extremely low prices.

   _____

6. Sometimes unscrupulous researchers used stories and other family information in their publications that the Gullah had shared only in private conversations.

   _____

7. Outsiders are still coming into Gullah communities and buying beach property at extremely low prices.

   _____

D Listen to the comments of Sharon Carpenter, a visitor to the Sea Islands of South Carolina, and explain what happened to her and her friend.

CD2,TR2

1. _____ *The bus left without her.* _____

2. _____

3. _____

4. _____

5. _____

6. _____

7. _____

E There are four errors in the e-mail message below. Find and correct the errors.

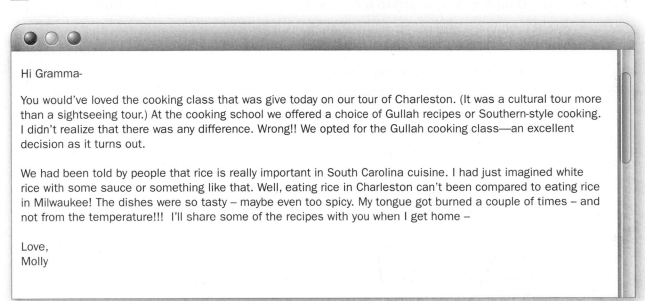

Hi Gramma-

You would've loved the cooking class that was give today on our tour of Charleston. (It was a cultural tour more than a sightseeing tour.) At the cooking school we offered a choice of Gullah recipes or Southern-style cooking. I didn't realize that there was any difference. Wrong!! We opted for the Gullah cooking class—an excellent decision as it turns out.

We had been told by people that rice is really important in South Carolina cuisine. I had just imagined white rice with some sauce or something like that. Well, eating rice in Charleston can't been compared to eating rice in Milwaukee! The dishes were so tasty – maybe even too spicy. My tongue got burned a couple of times – and not from the temperature!!! I'll share some of the recipes with you when I get home –

Love,
Molly

■ COMMUNICATE

F **PAIR WORK** Children often learn traditional crafts, traditional ways of preparing food, and other traditional activities. Discuss what you were taught, shown, given, read, and/or offered while you were growing up. Who taught you these traditional things? How were you taught? Use passives whenever appropriate.

In my country, children **are taught** to show respect from an early age.

What's one way they do that?

For example, if you give them something, they don't just grab it. Both hands **are cupped together** to receive it.

GRAMMAR AND VOCABULARY Write a composition on one of the topics below. Use as many words as possible from the Content Vocabulary on page 165, and (circle) them in your composition. Use sentences with verbs in the passive voice to express some of your ideas, and underline those sentences.

Topic 1: In many ethnic or cultural groups, maintaining traditional norms and practices is very difficult in our busy modern world. Some research shows that traditions are kept alive and transmitted to the younger generation by women. Why and how is this role taken on by the female members of such groups? Use concrete examples.

Topic 2: Select an ethnic or cultural group that you are familiar with and explain some of their traditions and customs. For example, what food customs were practiced by these people and have they been transmitted to younger members of the group? What kinds of occupations did members of the group have and how were their job tasks performed? Use concrete examples.

PROJECT Interview at least five students on your campus about their names. Find out the following information, and give a brief oral report on your findings at your next class meeting.

1. the students' complete names (including the spelling)
2. who named them
3. why they were named this way
4. the reason for the spelling of the name (if there is a choice of spellings)
5. family traditions for naming

 INTERNET Go online and use the search phrase "Gullah video" or "Gullah storytelling." Listen to a story in Gullah, and make notes on the basic plot of the story. Write a brief summary of the plot that you will hand in at your next class meeting. Also, be prepared to talk about the characters in the story in class.

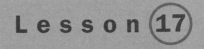

PART 1
Gerunds and Infinitives in the Passive Voice

PART 2
Passive Voice in Other Complex Sentences

Lesson ⑰

Industrial Design: Modern Wheelchairs

■ CONTENT VOCABULARY

Look up the words and phrases below that you do not know and enter them in your vocabulary journal. Write each item's part of speech, a definition, and an example sentence. Try to include them in your discussion and writing below.

access	a component	to donate	mobility
assembly	to deny	high performance	to mold
assistive technology	a disability	to maneuver	a strap

■ THINK ABOUT IT

Take a look at the two wheelchairs shown on page 180. What adjectives could you use to describe their general appearance? Have you ever seen a wheelchair similar to the one on the right? Where did you see it and what was the person in the wheelchair doing? Discuss your ideas with a classmate.

In your writing journal, write for five minutes about the questions below. When you are finished, share your information with the class.

In your opinion, what needs to be done in your hometown so that people with disabilities have easier access to public places? Is your school or place of work accessible to people with disabilities? What else needs to be done?

■ GRAMMAR IN CONTENT

CD2,TR3

A Read and listen to the passage below. The words in bold are phrases with the passive form of the gerund or the infinitive.

High-Tech Wheelchairs

There's a revolution going on in the field of wheelchair design. People whose lives used to be severely restricted by their lack of mobility have benefited greatly from advances in materials science and in the aerospace industry. Engineers and researchers have been inspired to incorporate new lightweight materials into more user-friendly wheelchair designs. Some new wheelchairs are intended to enhance wheelchair athletes' performance, others are meant to be easier for people with severe disabilities to use, and still others are expected to be distributed to people with disabilities in developing countries.

Exotic materials **permit wheelchairs to be constructed for various functions.** The standard wheelchair, made of a common steel alloy, provides temporary mobility for people in such places as hospitals. For this traditional type of wheelchair, weight, long-term comfort, and ease of maneuvering do not concern designers. However, weight, comfort, and maneuverability acquire much greater importance when engineers design a wheelchair for an individual's long-term use. **In addition to being constructed** of high performance aluminum or titanium, lightweight or ultralight wheelchairs may also have certain components that are molded from advanced composites, such as carbon fiber, fiberglass, and Kevlar®. Wheelchair users can be assured of greater freedom of movement and will avoid repetitive stress injuries to their arms and shoulders with such wheelchairs.

Some designers specialize in chairs for wheelchair athletes, who can now participate in sports from road racing to rugby to fencing. For example, **being involved in wheelchair sports** has a special meaning at the University of Illinois in Urbana-Champaign. Since the 1940s, students in wheelchairs have participated in competitive wheelchair sports, starting with basketball. On another part of campus, students in industrial design classes have put their minds to solving mobility problems faced by the student athletes. One design team, for example, tackled the braking system for basketball players. The brakes on their chairs **needed to be applied** while they held the ball. The student engineers developed a braking system in the seatback.

Making wheelchairs available to 100–150 million needy people around the world is the mission of other designers and their nonprofit organizations. Some of these organizations have been prompted to design wheelchairs of cheap, readily available materials. The Free Wheelchair Mission, for instance, has distributed more than 175,000 of its wheelchairs in more than 60 countries since 2005. **In order to be redistributed later,** used wheelchairs are cleaned and refurbished by other organizations. They feel that wheelchairs **need to be custom fit** to the new owner and reject the "one-size-fits-all" mentality. Finally, some nonprofit organizations design new wheelchairs for the lifestyle and environment of the user and find local workers who can build and maintain the chairs. Regardless of the views of wheelchair suppliers, bringing assistive technology, like the wheelchair, to people who don't have it certainly means some kind of improvement in their lives.

fiberglass: a material made of fine glass fibers

Kevlar®: a strong material used for bulletproof vests and radial tires

to put one's mind to: to concentrate on

to tackle: to deal with, to work hard on

to prompt: to move into action

Sample Sentences	Notes
Wheelchair athletes risk **being injured** just like any athlete. Nowadays, marathon racers expect **to be included** in any marathon. The coach wouldn't allow the team **to be photographed** without their trophy.	Make passive gerunds and infinitives by applying the basic rules for each form to the auxiliary *be:* Gerund: *being* + past participle Infinitive: *to be* + past participle
Being respected for your efforts makes hard work worthwhile. My goal for this year is **to be chosen** for the assistive technology research team. Weren't you sad about **being rejected** by that team?	Use **passive gerunds** and **infinitives** for the same functions that you use the active form of these phrases.
Trish denied **having been contacted** by our competitor's research team. Ted preferred **to have been included** in the project even though he had other work to do. Ted didn't admit **having been offered** a higher salary by our competitors.	Use the perfect form of the passive constructions to emphasize a time that contrasts with the time of the main verb: Gerund: *having been* + past participle Infinitive: *to have been* + past participle These forms are infrequently used.

B Read over your journal entry, and <u>underline</u> at least one sentence that you can revise to include a gerund or an infinitive in the passive voice. Write your revised sentence(s) below.

_____

_____

_____

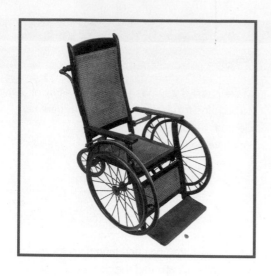
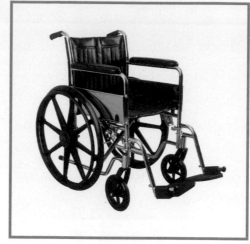

C <u>Underline</u> the correct form of the gerund or infinitive in each sentence.

1. Lightweight wheelchairs need (to construct / <u>to be constructed</u>) of titanium, high performance aluminum, or advanced composites.

2. (Propelling / Being propelled) the wheelchair by the hand rims is hard on bumpy terrain.

3. The standard wheelchair is not designed (to lift / to be lifted), so its weight is not that important.

4. Other kinds of wheelchairs, however, often require (lifting / being lifted) because they are transported in vans and car trunks.

5. Designers try to design wheelchairs so that users can avoid (treating / being treated) for repetitive stress injuries.

6. The goal of many wheelchair designs is for the user (to see / to be seen) before the chair; in other words, for the wheelchair to blend into the background.

7. In the interest of (riding / being ridden) more comfortably, users of ultralight wheelchairs often have specially molded seats to fit their bodies.

8. Some designs enable wheelchairs (to adjust / to be adjusted) manually to the widths of doors and other narrower spaces.

9. Designers also have to protect young wheelchair users from (injuring / being injured) if the wheelchair is not the right size for them.

D Select a phrase in the box to complete each sentence.

~~choose for a wheelchair rugby team~~	release from the hospital	confine to a wheelchair
select for the Paralympics in the next Olympiad	~~take seriously as an athlete~~	sideline with an injury
train in wheelchair techniques	offer a rugby scholarship	equip with a safety strap
fit for an ultralight wheelchair	worry about rough play	injure on the court

1. Jamaal is interested in _____ *being chosen for a wheelchair rugby team.*

2. Since his motorcycle accident, he has wanted _____ *to be taken seriously as an athlete.*

3. Before the accident, he had hoped _____

4. For a while Jamaal was very depressed about _____

5. To help Jamaal return to sports, his physical therapist encouraged him

    _____

6. Now his goal is _____

7. As he has become accustomed to his wheelchair, Jamal is putting his energy into

    _____

8. It's hard to avoid _____
    because rugby is a rough sport, even in a wheelchair.

9. However, he doesn't want to risk _____
    during the Paralympic trials, so he tries not to push too hard.

10. For that reason he admitted _____
    when he spoke with his physical therapist.

11. After that, the therapist authorized Jamaal's wheelchair _____

    _____

E Paraphrase each of the sentences below with a sentence that includes at least one passive gerund phrase. Use the verb in parentheses as your only main verb.

1. When a wheelchair user participates in sports, he often says that he was motivated by the competition. (admit)

   A wheelchair user who participates in sports often admits being motivated by the competition.

2. When wheelchair users get an ultralight chair, they have to be measured for the seat. (involve)

   _____

3. When wheelchair athletes participate in some sports, they have to be strapped into their chairs. (require)

   _____

4. When the athlete returned to the locker room, he said that he was not exhausted by the game. (deny)

   _____

5. One athlete was angry because a player had hit him from behind. (recall)

   _____

6. When the player hit his opponent from behind, the referee could have ejected him from the game. (risk)

   _____

7. When a wheelchair is made out of titanium, it is lighter and stronger. (mean)

   _____

F Read the text below and <u>underline</u> all of the gerund and infinitive phrases. Then, change the gerund or infinitive to the perfect form if appropriate.

        Nathan Dearborn was proud of <u>being chosen</u> *having been chosen* for the wheelchair design team in his industrial design class. He recalled seeing prototypes of several types of lightweight chairs, and Nathan was hoping to be involved in another groundbreaking innovation. When Professor Hadley interviewed him about his project preferences, Nathan couldn't deny being fascinated by racing wheelchairs at an early age. Seeing the Boston Marathon every spring had introduced him to marathon racers, and he had pursued that interest in learning more about the mechanical side of the sport. Now Professor Hadley was encouraging him to contribute his ideas to the new semester project.

G **PAIR WORK** Talk about different types of assistive technology that benefit people with disabilities. Use gerunds and infinitives in the passive voice whenever possible.

> How do people with a particular disability **need to be helped?**

> I think they need **to be given** more mobility and access. Too many places are hard to access by wheelchair.

PART TWO	Passive Voice in Other Complex Sentences

■ GRAMMAR IN CONTENT

A Reread the passage at the beginning of this lesson, and <u>underline</u> all other passive constructions. Then, find any examples of a passive verb that is followed by an infinitive or a *that* clause.

Passive Voice in Complex Sentences

Sample Sentences	Notes
The designers **have been authorized** to use the highest grade titanium for their projects. Barbara's design **is expected** to win a design award. She **was warned** that she might lose to Joe. Joe and Barbara **were informed** that she had won the top prize. **Was Joe told** that the award included a $1,000 prize?	Most **passive constructions** with complex complements follow one of two patterns: 1. Direct object + passive verb + infinitive 2. Indirect object + passive verb + *that* clause. In both cases, the object functions as the subject of the passive verb.
Barbara **was named** the winner of the competition. Although Barbara won, Joe **was made the** head of the research team. Barbara **wasn't elected** the team leader due to her poor leadership skills. Has a specific wheelchair design ever **been declared** the best design of that competition?	When using the passive in sentences with a direct object and an object complement, follow this pattern: Direct object + passive verb + object complement See Lessons 21, 23, and 25 for other complex passive structures. Verbs with direct objects and object complements in the passive include: *appoint, call, certify, choose, declare, elect, make, name,* and *vote.*

B Change the topic of the second sentence by using a passive construction.

1. Don Schoendorfer contacted his Chilean distribution agent Steve Colón about the new shipment of Free Wheelchair Mission wheelchairs. ~~Schoendorfer authorized Colón to pick up the container shipment at the warehouse.~~

   Colón was authorized to pick up the container shipment at the warehouse.

2. Schoendorfer didn't know about a problem in the shipment in Chile. Colón notified Schoendorfer that some of the wheelchair assembly kits were missing the instructions.

3. Under normal circumstances the wheelchairs are shipped with illustrated instructions and assembly tools for local workers. Schoendorfer expects the workers to assemble the wheelchairs for people.

4. The Free Wheelchair Mission depends on donations from churches and other groups. Schoendorfer notified the donors that the cost of each wheelchair was $44.40 including shipping.

5. Although many donors support the distribution of their wheelchairs, the Free Wheelchair Mission has many critics. The availability of Schoendorfer's wheelchairs has not convinced other organizations that such wheelchairs are actually good for people with disabilities.

6. Critics agree with Schoendorfer's goal of making wheelchairs available, but they aren't sure that the chair really meets the medical needs of everyone who has one. Schoendorfer's goal constrains it to be "one-size-fits-all."

7. When he travels around the world to monitor the program, people with disabilities always thank him for the dramatic change in their lives. As a result, the response of wheelchair recipients has encouraged Schoendorfer to continue with his mission.

CD2,TR4

C Listen to each conversation, and then (circle) the letter of the correct interpretation.

1. a. Sam persuaded Kirk to photograph the team.
   b. Kirk persuaded Sam to be photographed.

2. a. The coach allowed Kirk to interview Jeff.
   b. Jeff was allowed to be interviewed.

3. a. Kirk encouraged Sam to help Jeff with his equipment.
   b. Kirk was encouraged to help Jeff.

4. a. The coach prompted Sam to introduce Jeff to the others.
   b. Sam was prompted to be introduced to Jeff.

5. a. Sam expected Kirk to pass him the first ball of the game.
   b. Sam was expected to pass Kirk the first ball of the game.

6. a. Sam doesn't permit Kirk to check his wheelchair.
   b. Sam isn't permitted to check Kirk's wheelchair.

7. a. Only the coach is authorized to load the wheelchairs in the van.
   b. The coach has authorized only one person to load the wheelchairs in the van.

8. a. This season the coach made Kirk captain of the team.
   b. Next season Sam will be made captain.

■ COMMUNICATE

D **GROUP WORK** What devices have been invented or refined to increase our mobility? Discuss the design, purpose, and benefits of these inventions. Use gerunds and infinitives with passive constructions whenever possible.

Elevators **were invented** to help people get to the top of a high building.

What about escalators? They **are used** for going up just one or two levels.

Nowadays there are even moving sidewalks, especially at airports. They **might have been invented** for people who can't walk, but lots of people use them because they're tired or want to move more quickly.

GRAMMAR AND VOCABULARY Write a composition on one of the topics below. Use as many words as possible from the Content Vocabulary on page 177, and (circle) them in your composition. Use sentences with gerunds and infinitives in passive voice and other complex passive structures to express some of your ideas, and underline those sentences.

Topic 1: There are many people with disabilities who are not chosen to compete in the Olympic Games although they are excellent athletes. The Paralympics and Special Olympics provide an opportunity for those members of society to be selected for national teams. How do athletes with disabilities benefit from being included in world-class competition?

Topic 2: In previous generations, people with disabilities had little access to public facilities. In fact, they were not encouraged to participate in school or sports activities, and they were expected to stay home. Explain how the opportunities for people with disabilities have changed in your lifetime where you live.

PROJECT Interview at least one student on your campus about services available for students with disabilities. Find out the following information, and report on your findings at the next class meeting.

1. Are all of the buildings required to be built for wheelchair access?
2. In what other ways do students with disabilities have access to school facilities?

 INTERNET Go online to one of the university websites below and check out their wheelchair sports teams. Follow the links, and report to your class about (1) the sports that male wheelchair athletes can participate in and (2) the sports for female wheelchair athletes. Tell your classmates about other information you got from that part of the university's athletics website.

   a. University of Illinois at Urbana-Champaign: www.uiuc.edu
   b. University of Alabama: www.ua.edu
   c. University of Texas-Arlington: www.uta.edu
   d. University of Wisconsin-Whitewater: www.uww.edu
   e. Edinboro University of Pennsylvania: www.edinboro.edu
   f. University of Arizona: www.arizona.edu

If you prefer to investigate the world of wheelchair basketball, go to www.nwba.org, which is the website for the National Wheelchair Basketball Association. Then, give a brief oral report on the other opportunities for wheelchair basketball players.

PART 1
Restrictive vs. Nonrestrictive
Relative Clauses

PART 2
Reduced and Special
Nonrestrictive Relative Clauses

L e s s o n 18

History of Philosophy of Science

■ CONTENT VOCABULARY

Look up the words below that you do not know and enter them in your vocabulary journal. Write each word's part of speech, a definition, and an example sentence. Try to include them in your discussion and writing below.

an artery	to determine	a hypothesis	a phenomenon
a blood vein	empiricism	to incorporate	to pursue
a breakthrough	a figure	logic	a substance

■ THINK ABOUT IT

During the 1500s and 1600s, many important inventions enabled scientists to discover and understand natural phenomena. Brainstorm 2–3 inventions from these centuries with a classmate.

In your writing journal, write for 5–10 minutes about the questions below. When you are finished, share your ideas with the class.

During the 1500s and 1600s, scientists changed the way that people understood the universe and our world. Some of these pioneers were Galileo, Isaac Newton, and Linnaeus. Do you know what any of these scientists were famous for? What were some important scientific ideas from this period?

■ **GRAMMAR IN CONTENT**

CD2,TR5

A Read and listen to the passage below. The words in bold are nonrestrictive relative clauses.

> ### The Scientific Revolution: New Ways to Analyze the World
>
> During the sixteenth and seventeenth centuries, the Scientific Revolution, **which brought about a new understanding of the universe and the world of living things,** took place in Western Europe. When Europe emerged from the Middle Ages, other centers of learning in the world were far ahead. Muslim scientists and thinkers, **who had come in contact with the philosophy and science of the ancient Greeks during the expansion of Islam,** further developed many of their ideas on mathematics, astronomy, physics, alchemy, geography, astrology, and medicine. Then, during the 1300s scholars in Europe began translating the Arabic and Greek scientific writings into Latin, used exclusively for written works at European universities, to disseminate their discoveries. At approximately the same time, various Chinese inventions, such as printing, paper, explosives, and the compass, became available in Europe as a result of growing commercial contacts between Europe and Asia. The Chinese, **whose technical expertise was famous along the Silk Road,** provided the Europeans with tools and technology for their emergence from the Dark Ages.
>
> Science, **which was called "natural philosophy" in those centuries,** expanded dramatically as men observed, measured, and experimented in new ways. For example, astronomers had begun to question the concept that Earth was the center of the universe and that the universe was finite and unchanging. The Danish astronomer Tycho Brahe, **who observed a comet beyond the moon in 1577,** demonstrated that the universe did indeed change. His precise observations of celestial, or heavenly, objects also enabled him to predict positions of the moon. Using Brahe's detailed information, Johannes Kepler determined not only that planets had elliptical orbits but also that their orbital speed depended on their distance from the sun. Other characteristics of the planets and their moons became observable with the invention of the telescope, **which Galileo used in his discoveries in the early seventeenth century.**
>
> The study of natural philosophy became more sophisticated as researchers developed devices to measure phenomena more accurately. For instance, advances in astronomy relied heavily on improvements in the study of optics. As the quality of telescopes rose, astronomers could both see objects more clearly and measure angles in space. Another groundbreaking invention in this period was the air pump, **which resulted from the discovery that air has both weight and pressure.** With the invention of this instrument, researchers pursued the concept of a vacuum.
>
> Finally, thanks to experimentation, scientists were able to demonstrate important properties of natural phenomena. Sir Isaac Newton, **who directed sunlight through a prism in his famous optical experiment,** was able to show that light is made up of various colors. Previously, people had believed that light was transformed into different colors. Magnetism, emerging as a completely new scientific field, resulted from William Gilbert's experiments. Thanks to his laboratory work on magnets and compass needles, new explanations of Earth's rotation and ocean tides became available.
>
> The observations, measurements, and experiments performed by European natural philosophers paved the way for later scientists, such as Charles Coulomb, Antoine-Laurent Lavoisier, and Carl Linnaeus. Fields of study that had been born during the Scientific Revolution contributed to the birth of new sciences like chemistry or botany. With the dawning of the Age of Enlightenment, also known as the Age of Reason, in the eighteenth century, science gained an increasingly stronger impact on society, which has continued to the present day.

alchemy: a mystical philosophy that sought to understand how materials may be chemically combined

to disseminate: to spread, especially ideas and information

elliptical: in an oval shape

Sample Sentences	Notes
The man **who/that was the most famous astronomer at the beginning of the 1600s** was Tycho Brahe.	Restrictive relative clauses identify and define a noun, making it more specific.
Kepler, **who worked as Brahe's assistant,** published a book in 1609. That book described Kepler's first important analysis, **which involved the orbit of Mars.** Kepler's work disputed the circular orbit of celestial bodies, **which was the commonly held view up to this time.**	Nonrestrictive clauses describe and add information about the noun. They give nonessential information about a noun that is unique or already clear from the context or situation. These nonrestrictive clauses modify proper nouns or definite proper nouns.
Brahe, **whose data Kepler used in his analyses,** did not share Kepler's views on Earth's role in the universe. Galileo, **with whom Kepler was in contact,** had devised his first telescope with a concave eyepiece. Also working in the field of optics, Kepler suggested using a convex lens in the eyepiece, **which improved telescopes considerably.**	Use commas to separate any nonrestrictive clause from the main clause. In conversation, English speakers pause slightly at the beginning and end of these clauses. Use only *who, whom, whose,* and *which* as relative pronouns in restrictive clauses.

B **Read over your journal entry, and <u>underline</u> at least one sentence that you can revise to include a nonrestrictive relative clause. Write your revised sentence(s) below.**

_____

_____

_____

_____

C <u>Underline</u> all of the relative clauses in the sentences below, and add commas where appropriate.

1. Philosophers in ancient Greece gained their knowledge through logic, <u>which they used to understand the basic characteristics of objects.</u>

2. Natural philosophers considered the rules of correct thinking which Aristotle and his followers had applied to be inadequate for the complexity of natural phenomena that they were discovering.

3. During the Scientific Revolution researchers began to use inductive reasoning which bases hypotheses and theories on observation and experimental results.

4. Francis Bacon who advocated empiricism felt that knowledge would grow the fastest if facts could be collected from observation and experiments.

5. According to Bacon, experiments that show aspects of nature which we cannot observe will lead to new knowledge to benefit humankind.

6. Advocates of "mechanical philosophy" who believed that nature works like a machine focused their experiments on the motion of objects.

7. Having mastered the translated texts which ancient Greek and Islamic mathematicians had written Europeans were able to solve problems in navigation engineering and even clock-making as they further developed mathematical analyses.

8. Europeans began to learn about the new scientific methods and knowledge in such books as John Wilkins's *A Discourse Concerning a New World & Another Planet* which was published in English in 1640.

D (Circle) the letter of the correct interpretation of the sentences below.

1. European scientists who performed experiments on air pressure used the newly invented air pump.

   a. All European scientists used the air pump.
   (b.) Not all of the European scientists used the air pump.

2. Robert Boyle's early experiments, which focused on air pressure, led him to understand the relationship between air pressure and the volume of air.

   a. All of Boyle's early experiments focused on air pressure.
   b. Not all of his early experiments focused on air pressure.

3. Later scientists were influenced by Kepler's Law which explained the motions of all planets.

   a. Kepler developed only one law.
   b. Kepler developed more than one law.

4. In addition to his expertise in performing experiments, Robert Hooke is known for Hooke's Law, which explains the power of springs.

   a. Hooke developed only one law.
   b. Hooke developed more than one law.

5. Many important observations were made possible by the microscope, which was greatly improved as techniques of lens grinding were refined.

   a. All microscopes improved in quality.
   b. Only one particular microscope improved in quality.

6. The microscope which Robert Hooke used in his experiments had a mirror for added light.

   a. Hooke's microscope had a mirror.
   b. All microscopes had mirrors.

7. The Scientific Revolution came about due to the efforts of the natural philosophers, who incorporated observation, measurement, and experimentation in their work.

   a. All natural philosophers used these methods.
   b. Not all natural philosophers used these methods.

E Write a summary sentence from the class notes below about each of the men involved in the discovery of the circulation of blood in the human body. Use nonrestrictive relative clauses in your sentences.

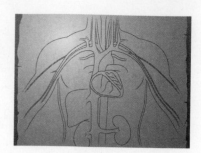

Realdo Colombo (1510-1559): "pulmonary circulation"
  pulmonary vein: blood (not air!!!) from heart (right side) → lungs
  lungs → heart (left side) = blood is much brighter & redder

Girolami Fabrici (1533-1619): "valves in the veins"
  = blood only flows toward heart

William Harvey (1578-1657): "blood circulation"
  blood = maintains body organs, NOT for heat distribution
  heart contraction = only action: from heart → lungs → heart →
    arteries → veins → heart

Marcello Malpighi (1628-1694): saw capillaries that connect arteries and veins
  = one of most important microscope discoveries of century (= in 1661)

1. Realdo Colombo, who did research on pulmonary circulation, discovered the purpose of the pulmonary vein.

2. _____

_____

3. _____

_____

4. _____

_____

D <u>Underline</u> agents that should be omitted, and then write the reason for omitting or keeping the agent. Consider the information in previous sentences as you decide whether to omit an agent.

1. The isolation of the Gullah is mentioned <u>by researchers</u> in many academic research projects.

   Reason: _____ *The context makes "researchers" obvious.* _____

2. Their separation from slave owners was greater than in other regions because the planters' houses were built far away from the rice fields.

   Reason: _____

3. Many planters were infected with malaria or yellow fever by the slaves, so slave owners kept their distance.

   Reason: _____

4. The diseases were transmitted by the slaves but did not affect them due to the Africans' inherited resistance to those illnesses.

   Reason: _____

5. Also, the planters and their families were affected by the humid, semitropical climate of the coastal region; consequently, they spent many months of the year farther inland.

   Reason: _____

6. While the families stayed away, the plantations were managed by a few European supervisors and some trusted slaves.

   Reason: _____

7. Finally, slaves from other American colonies or from the Caribbean weren't bought by the planters because only Africans from the Guinea Coast knew how to cultivate rice.

   Reason: _____

8. The language and customs of the slaves on coastal rice plantations were constantly renewed by Africans of the same background so that they were able to keep their cultural identity.

   Reason: _____

E Edit the following passages to adjust the focus of the information. Read the entire passage before you change any verb forms to passive. Give the reason(s) for your edits.

1. Numerous linguists have conducted research on the language of the Gullah since the 1930s. Before that, however, ~~outsiders considered the language~~ _the language was considered_ a simplified, even barbaric means of communication. Plantation owners in particular thought the Gullah way of talking wasn't a "real" language.

   Reasons: _The first sentence introduces new information on the language of the Gullah. The language, not the outsiders, is the topic of the next sentence, with new information at the end of the sentence. The final sentence also continues the focus on the language._

2. Perceptions of the language of the Gullah began to change thanks to the research of Lorenzo Turner, who was an African American linguist. He lived among the Gullah for many years, recorded their speech, and compared it to African languages. The languages of the Guinea Coast showed a number of similarities in grammar, vocabulary, and pronunciation. A company published his book on those linguistic similarities in 1949.

   Reasons: _____

   _____

   _____

3. In contrast to the work of some other linguists, Turner discovered thousands of words that Gullah speakers share with speakers of African languages. Some of those words were in stories, songs, and prayers that Turner learned in the Gullah community. Also, he found hundreds and hundreds of other words, but these words were personal names that are used only within the family. Having two kinds of names is not uncommon in traditional African societies.

   Reasons: _____

   _____

   _____

4. As Turner gained the trust of the Gullah, he found out about their naming practices. For example, "Joe" appears to be an English nickname, but it could also be the shortened form of "Cudjo" for a male child born on Monday. Along the Guinea Coast parents often named children for the day that they were born.

Reasons: _____

_____

_____

5. Modern linguists agree that Gullah is a Creole language. Such languages develop in situations where people of different cultures need to communicate. Gullah made communication possible among speakers of various African languages and with the white planters and their families.

Reasons: _____

_____

_____

■ C O M M U N I C A T E

F **SMALL GROUP WORK** Discuss the isolation of groups in a society. Talk about any examples of an ethnic or social group that was isolated from a mainstream culture. How was the group isolated? What happened to the language or culture of that group? Can you compare that group to the Gullah in any way?

G **PAIR WORK** Discuss naming practices in your community and culture. Who is involved in selecting the name(s)? Are names chosen for particular meanings? For family reasons? Try to find some interesting similarities or differences between your cultures. Use passive constructions whenever appropriate.

In some parts of Mexico, names **are passed down** from one generation to the next. **I was named after** my grandfather, for example.

In Japan, we **aren't necessarily named after** our grandparents, but **names are often chosen by them.**

■ GRAMMAR IN CONTENT

A Look at the passive verb forms in bold print in the text at the beginning of the lesson. Which one of those verbs can have both a direct object and an indirect object?

Passive Options with Verbs Taking Two Objects	
Sample Sentences	**Notes**
Nowadays, **children** are read the traditional African stories of their ancestors. **The elderly** have always been shown respect in Gullah culture. Respect has always been shown **to the elderly** in Gullah culture. Special rice dishes are cooked **for children** on their birthdays.	Choose the **direct** or **indirect object** as the subject of a passive verb according to the focus of your sentence. See list of verbs on next page. Use *to* with the indirect object when the direct object is the passive subject. Passive forms of verbs with *for* + indirect object usually take only the direct object as the subject.
Did the slaves **get kidnapped** from their homes in West Africa? Sometimes African families **got separated** on their arrival in America. Gullah children didn't **get educated** with white children, so they only learned the language that their parents spoke. In the early 1900s, the Gullah **got criticized** for their language.	Use *get* instead of *be* for a more informal passive construction. Typically this option • specifies no agent • has a human grammatical subject • has an action verb This construction often implies that something negative happened to the grammatical subject (who may or may not have responsibility for the negative consequence). In contrast to some other languages, in English only passive sentences with this "get" structure can imply a negative consequence except with this structure.
During the hurricane one boat **was sunk** by an oar that crashed through its hull. Nearby a small rowboat **was sunk** in just a few feet of water. Several small fishing boats **sank** during the storm. Several others **capsized** but did not actually **sink**.	Use ergative verbs in passive structures or in the middle voice. (See Lesson 4.) • Choose the passive form of an ergative verb to stress that an agent of the action exists even if you do not specify the agent. • Use the active form of ergative verbs in the middle voice if the agent is not relevant or if there are many possible agents.

F Combine sentences (a) and (b) to create one sentence with a nonrestrictive relative clause.

1. a. European scientists experimented with material substances.
   b. They continued the work of medieval Islamic alchemists.

   European scientists, who experimented with material substances, continued the work of medieval Islamic alchemists.

2. a. Gerber was a famous eighth-century Persian alchemist.
   b. Gerber believed that matter had both visible and hidden qualities.

   _____

   _____

3. a. A magical "elixir" was known as "the Philosopher's Stone."
   b. This "elixir" was supposed to cure illnesses as well.

   _____

   _____

4. a. Paracelsus lived from 1493 to 1541.
   b. He pursued his work on chemical elements in the human body to cure illnesses.

   _____

   _____

5. a. Alchemists believed that they could find the way to "grow" metals.
   b. They developed many alloys, or mixtures of metals, during their experiments.

   _____

   _____

6. a. Isaac Newton's interest in alchemy lasted for 25 years.
   b. His work on attraction and repulsion was influenced by his work on the "active principles" of alchemy.

   _____

   _____

7. a. Alchemy was sometimes condemned by the Catholic Church.
   b. It was encouraged by many European rulers.

   _____

   _____

G **GROUP WORK** Share information about important scientists and other thinkers from your culture who have contributed to the growth of knowledge about our world. Use nonrestrictive relative clauses whenever possible.

> Al-Khwarizmi, **whose Latinized name is Alghorismus,** worked on square roots and complex fractions.

PART TWO	Reduced and Special Nonrestrictive Relative Clauses

■ GRAMMAR IN CONTENT

A Reread the text at the beginning of the lesson, and <u>underline</u> examples of phrases or clauses that have been separated from the main clause by commas. Do not underline adverbials, examples, or connectors.

Nonrestrictive Relative Clauses

Sample Sentences	Notes
Advocates of mechanical philosophy, **who believed** that the world worked like a machine, investigated motion. Advocates of mechanical philosophy, **believing** that the world worked like a machine, investigated motion. Advances in science depended to a great extent on the microscope, **which was used** to unlock many secrets of nature. Advances in science depended to a great extent on the microscope, **used** to unlock many secrets of nature.	Like restrictive relative clauses, nonrestrictive relative clauses can also be reduced. Make the following changes: · Omit the relative pronouns *who* or *which* when they function as subjects in the relative clause. · Omit any auxiliary verbs. · Use **the present participle** for active verbs and **the past participle** for passive verbs. Use commas to separate any nonrestrictive phrase from the main clause. Use the context of the sentence to understand the time of the verb in the phrase.
Natural philosophers advocated observing and experimenting, **which** was a major change in the way that people understood natural phenomena. The mathematical concept of zero was frightening to ancient people, **which** surprises many people today.	Use a nonrestrictive clause to comment on the information in the entire preceding main clause. This kind of clause · always comes at the end of the sentence · is always separated from the main clause by a comma · always begins with *which*

B **Reduce the relative clauses if possible and add commas where necessary.**

1. Christiaan Huygens, who worked *working* on mechanics, invented the pendulum clock and then improved it in 1673.

2. In the early 1600s, telescopes which provided magnification up to 15 diameters at that time made the discovery of distant celestial bodies possible.

3. During the late 1600s, the lenses of microscopes which were ground to a much finer quality than ever before enabled scientists to examine cells in plants and animals.

4. Robert Hooke is credited with the invention of the universal joint with which a machine can combine rotary motion and movement in different directions.

5. The air pump that von Guericke experimented with in the seventeenth century couldn't produce a total vacuum.

6. Galileo's first thermometer which dates to the late 1500s was a glass bulb with water inside.

7. The instrument which was invented by Islamic scientists to distill liquids is called a retort.

8. Scientists who studied electricity could store energy in Leyden jars which consisted of a glass jar with metallic foil inside and outside and a wire which passed through the opening in contact with the inside foil.

9. Blaise Pascal's experiments on air pressure which involved instruments with tubes of mercury led to the invention of the barometer.

C Edit each text, reducing one of the nonrestrictive relative clauses in each text to a phrase. Follow the example. <u>Underline</u> any other relative clauses that you could reduce.

1. Learning from Greek texts, Arab mathematicians made significant progress in algebra, ~~which is~~ derived from the Arabic word *al-jaber*. The Arab world provided Europe not only with their understanding of algebra but also with Arabic numerals, which are used in mathematics today. However, these numbers, which took the place of Roman and Greek numerals, were not used in the first algebraic equations. Instead, Arab mathematicians wrote words, which may seem surprising since they already had the numeric symbols.

2. For ancient people, zero was a number that did not function like other numbers, which put it into a troublesome category. It represented emptiness, which signified chaos and darkness to the ancients. The Greeks learned about zero from the Babylonians, whose texts show that zero had the function of a placeholder. It wasn't until the 1600s that zero was commonly used.

3. Warfare in the sixteenth and seventeenth centuries, which depended greatly on cannonballs and other projectiles, benefited from a better understanding of both natural and violent motion. Niccolo Tartaglia, who experimented with the angles of cannons and the weights of cannonballs, performed experiments on types of motion. Consequently, he was able to predict the most effective position for such armaments, which led to more death and destruction.

D Listen for Professor Jensen's comments about information she presents during a science class. Use the verb indicated, as in the example, to paraphrase her comments.

1. suspect: _She suspects that students will think it is strange to learn about the people behind the ideas._

2. consider: _____

   _____

3. realize: _____

   _____

4. mention: _____

   _____

5. expect: _____

   _____

E There are four errors in the e-mail message below. Find and correct all four errors. (The commas for one clause count as one error.)

Jill-

Have you ever taken a course in the History of Philosophy? Or the History of Science? The Philosophy Department, that is supposed to be one of the best in the country, offers an intro class, that I'm thinking about taking. Do you know anything about Professor Jensen? I heard that she's tough. My advisor who has always pushed me toward these kinds of courses thinks that I can handle it. I really don't mind a lot of reading and I'd rather write papers than take exams, what means that I guess I'd enjoy the class. Maybe it's a good idea to talk to Jensen before I register. Any thoughts?

N.

■ **C O M M U N I C A T E**

F **GROUP WORK** Discuss the importance of learning about the people behind the history of science and philosophy. Should students have to learn about the people behind great scientific breakthroughs? Give some examples to support your opinion.

When I take a math or science course, I don't see the point of learning about the people involved in those fields.

But don't you think that it's interesting or important to know that Al-Khwarizmi, who is known as the "Father of Algebra," was Persian—or that Liu Hui, who lived in China round 300 BCE, found the approximate value of pi?

GRAMMAR AND VOCABULARY Write a composition on one of the topics below. Use as many words as possible from the Content Vocabulary on page 187, and (circle) them in your composition. Use sentences with nonrestrictive and restrictive relative clauses to express some of your ideas, and <u>underline</u> those sentences.

Topic 1: Throughout the centuries scientists have made discoveries that contradict people's perceptions of the world and religious teachings. This happened during the Scientific Revolution, and it is happening today. What is the responsibility of the scientists when their work goes against society's ethical, religious, or moral values? Use concrete examples in your writing.

Topic 2: Do people respect scientists and their work? What is the perception of scientists in popular culture, for example, in movies and on TV? How do the media treat scientists in your culture? Use concrete examples in your writing.

PROJECT Interview at least one student on your campus about his or her knowledge about prominent individuals from the history of science. Find out the following information, and report on it at your next class meeting.

1. Ask your interviewee about four to five of the scientists mentioned in this lesson. Report on how much information your interviewee knew about each one.
2. Ask how important it is to know about the scientists who made significant discoveries. If your interviewee thinks that it is important, find out why.

 INTERNET Go online and use the search phrase "science quizzes" to find a website that has quizzes on various branches of science. Select at least one quiz, and take it. Report orally on your quiz results at your next class meeting.

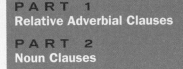

PART 1
Relative Adverbial Clauses

PART 2
Noun Clauses

Lesson 19

Marketing: Packaging Strategies

■ CONTENT VOCABULARY

Look up the words below that you do not know and enter them in your vocabulary journal. Write each word's part of speech, a definition, and an example sentence. Try to include them in your discussion and writing below.

to allot	a coupon	to launch	to reseal
to appeal to	to display	loyalty	to tamper with
a commodity	glass-blowing	perishable	a wrapper

■ THINK ABOUT IT

What products do you know that are well packaged? What are the characteristics of an effective package for any kind of product? Discuss your ideas with a classmate.

In your writing journal, write for five minutes about the questions below. When you are finished, share what you wrote with the class.

Of the items that you normally buy, which one has the most effective packaging? What do you like about the container? What kind of information do you think an effective package should include?

■ GRAMMAR IN CONTENT

CD2,TR7

A Read and listen to the passage below. The words in bold are relative adverbial clauses.

Old Friends and New Temptations

For manufacturers, packaging is the crucial final payoff to a marketing campaign. Sophisticated packaging is one of the chief ways people find the confidence to buy. It can also give a powerful image to products and commodities that are in themselves characterless. In many cases, the shopper has been prepared for the shopping experience by lush, colorful print advertisements, thirty-second television mini-dramas, radio jingles, and coupon promotions. But the package makes the final sales pitch, seals the commitment, and gets itself placed in the shopping cart. Advertising leads consumers into temptation. Packaging *is* the temptation. In many cases it is what makes the product possible.

You put the package into your cart, or not, usually without really having focused on the particular product or its many alternatives. But sometimes you do examine the package. You read the label carefully, looking at what the product promises, what it contains, what it warns. You might even look at the package itself and judge whether it will, for example, reseal to keep a product fresh. You might consider **how a cosmetic container will look on your dressing table,** or you might think about whether someone might have tampered with it or whether it can be easily recycled. The possibility of such scrutiny is one of the things that make each detail of the package so important.

With its thousands of images and messages, the supermarket is as visually dense, if not as beautiful, as a Gothic cathedral. It is as complex and as predatory as a tropical rain forest. It is more than a person can possibly take in during an ordinary half-hour shopping trip. No wonder a significant percentage of people who need to wear eyeglasses don't wear them when they're shopping, and some researchers have spoken of the trancelike state that pushing a cart through this environment induces. The paradox here is that the visual intensity that overwhelms shoppers is precisely the thing that makes the design of packages so crucial. Just because you're not looking at a package doesn't mean you don't see it. Most of the time, you see far more than a container and a label. You see a personality, an attitude toward life, perhaps even a set of beliefs.

The shopper's encounter with the product on the shelf is, however, only the beginning of the emotional life cycle of the package. The package is very important in the moment **when the shopper recognizes it either as an old friend or a new temptation.** Once the product is brought home, the package seems to disappear, as the quality or usefulness of the product it contains becomes paramount. But in fact, many packages are still selling even at home, enticing those who have bought them to take them out of the cupboard, the closet, or the refrigerator and consume their contents. Then once the product has been used up, and the package is empty, it becomes suddenly visible once more. This time, though, it is trash that must be discarded or recycled. This instant of disposal is the time **when people are most aware of packages.** It is a negative moment, like the end of a love affair, and what's left seems to be a horrid waste.

a payoff: a reward or final result

a jingle: a short song used for advertising purposes

predatory: dangerous, threatening

a trance: a state between being asleep and being awake; being semiconscious

a paradox: a contradictory statement or situation

paramount: of great importance or concern

Sample Sentences	Notes
Spring is the time **when some packaging changes to lighter colors.**	Adverbial clauses that specify a time, a location, or a reason usually follow one of the patterns below.
Marketers hope that their new products will be in places **where shoppers see them immediately.**	**Pattern 1:** head noun + relative adverb + rest of clause
	Generally, relative clauses of this type are restrictive, so there is no comma.
Shoppers may not be able to say the reason **why they choose a particular product** except that it looks attractive.	In formal usage, prepositional phrases are often used instead of relative adverbs: *Shoppers may not be able to say the reason **for which** they chose a product.*
I remember the time ~~when~~ I bought some perfume just because I liked the bottle. I can't remember the place ~~where~~ I bought it. Now I laugh about the reason ~~why~~ I bought it.	English speakers commonly delete some words in the next type of relative clause. **Pattern 2:** head noun + rest of clause
Do you know **when** that perfume first came on the market?	**Pattern 3:** relative adverb + rest of clause
Have you got any idea **where** I can get some more?	
Have you ever visited **the French factory** where that perfume is bottled?	Don't delete the head noun if it includes **important information.**
I've never thought about the way in which perfume is bottled.	The *wh-* word *how* does not function exactly like **when, where, why:** • **Pattern 1** does not apply: *how* can't modify the head noun *the way*
The way expensive perfumes are packaged adds to their value.	• **Pattern 2** applies: *the way ~~in which~~ we met / the way we met*
Since expensive perfumes still come in glass bottles, how they package it must be important to shoppers.	• **Pattern 3** applies: *~~the way in which~~ we met / how we met*

B Read over your journal entry, and <u>underline</u> at least one sentence that you can revise to include a relative adverbial clause. Write your revised sentence(s) below.

_____

_____

_____

C Edit the texts below so that there is a variety of relative adverbial clauses.

1. In former times glass containers were very precious, and only valuable commodities such as perfume were packaged in glass. The scarcity of glass was the reason ~~why~~ the 9 containers were so expensive. The island of Murano near Venice is the place where glassblowers practiced their craft.

2. The way that Europeans produced glass in those days was not their invention, but the invention of people in the eastern Mediterranean. The extensive experience of these people with glass production explains the reason why the blowpipe was invented there in Sidon, Phoenicia, about 100 BCE. This is the place where glassmaking had started sometime before 3000 BCE.

3. Glassblowing continued in Sidon until 1200 CE, and certainly, glass containers from there came to the attention of Europeans. This is the region where the Europeans fought during the Crusades in the eleventh to the thirteenth centuries. Their presence in the eastern Mediterranean clarifies the way that they came in contact with these valuable objects.

4. Once glassworkers began producing glass in Murano, the Italians maintained a monopoly on its production. Indeed, the glassworkers were not permitted to leave the island where they worked. For centuries they successfully guarded the secrets of the way that glass was blown. However, by the sixteenth century other glassblowers were practicing their craft in France, where the demand for bottles for wine was high.

D Using the clue in parentheses, complete each sentence with a relative adverbial clause.

TO: All distributors of *Luxor*
FROM: Stephanie Dunn, Marketing Manager
RE: Marketing Campaign for *Luxor*

You can expect to receive the first shipment of *Luxor* within the next two weeks. Please let us know (time)

when it arrives, so that we can put advertisements in your local newspaper. According to our agreement,
  (1)

you should put 5–6 bottles (location) _____
                                                                    (2)

so that window-shoppers will see that the perfume is actually in stock. (manner)

_____ is your decision since you have professional window-dressers on
                (3)

your staff. We have confidence that you will display *Luxor* as attractively as you have handled our other

perfumes. When customers purchase a bottle of *Luxor*, please ask them to fill out the enclosed survey

so that we can know (reason) _____ . That information will be of great
                                              (4)

help to our Product Development team. Finally, with regard to Ms. Nicole Babineaux's visit to your boutique,

we will inform you (time) _____ and expect you to publicize the event.
                              (5)

E Using relative adverbial clauses, write guidelines for displaying your new perfume.

1. The large display bottle must be _____ *where the light will shine directly on it.*

2. The two enclosed photo displays should be on countertops _____

   _____

3. Your employee who will hand out samples to customers ought to stand _____

   _____

4. The special decorative boxes for the large-sized bottles would look especially nice

   _____

5. The coupons for special gift sets of perfume can be _____

   _____

F Explain the reason for the type of packaging of the grocery items below.

1. Eggs are very fragile, and _____ *that is why each egg has to be protected by the carton.*

2. People enjoy soft drinks in many different locations and circumstances, and

   _____

3. It's hard to keep coffee or other ground foods fresh, so _____

   _____

4. Ramen noodles make a quick, easy snack, and _____

   _____

5. Toothpaste has a thick consistency, so _____

   _____

G Complete the sentences to explain the packaging for the items below.

1. Breakfast cereals usually come in a sealed plastic bag inside a cardboard box, and

   _____ *that's how they stay crisp.* _____

2. Most over-the-counter, or nonprescription, medicines have a safety seal around the lid

   because _____

3. Strawberries usually come in little pint cartons, and _____

   _____

4. Frozen vegetables are usually packaged in paper boxes because _____

   _____

H **PAIR WORK** Share information about the packaging and store location of various items in different countries. Include relative adverbial clauses whenever possible.

> In Cameroon, where I'm from, bread is sold on the street. We buy it **the way you do in bakeries**—without any plastic wrapper.

> It's the same in Albania, but you can find bread in a grocery store, too. It's usually **where the other baked goods are.**

PART TWO	Noun Clauses

■ GRAMMAR IN CONTENT

A Reread the text at the beginning of this lesson, and <u>underline</u> clauses that are introduced by *wh-* words other than *when, where, why,* and *how.*

Noun Clauses with *Wh-* Words

Sample Sentences	Notes
Producers have to consider **how much** the packaging adds to the price of the item. Managers should also check **how far** related items, such as flour and sugar, are from each other. Managers usually decide **whether** seasonal items should be displayed at the front of the store.	Like the relative adverbial clauses with *when, where, why,* and *how,* these *wh-* words introduce noun clauses: *how much/many* *how often* *how far* *how long* *how* + **Adjective** or **Adverb** *whether (or not)* *what* *which* *who*
How do they figure out **what** the customers find attractive about the products?	Only use a question mark at the end of the sentence if the main clause is in the form of a question. Noun clauses must be phrased as statements.
Whether the item appeals to teenage girls determines the colors of the packaging. Designers need to check **whether the colors on a package are appropriate in other cultures.**	These clauses function as: • **Subjects** • **Complements** • **Direct Objects** • **Objects of Prepositions**

B Revise each sentence, using a noun clause in place of the underlined noun phrase.

1. ~~The appearance of a container~~ *What a container looks like* ^ can catch a customer's eye.

2. Elegant packaging can contribute to the price of luxury items.

3. The appropriate packaging can affect the length of time that perishable items can stay on the shelf.

4. An eye-catching package may influence a shopper's decision on buying a new product.

5. When shoppers are undecided about the choice between products, the design of the label may be the deciding factor.

6. Designers also have to think about the recipients of gift boxes when they select colors and sizes.

7. Companies did research on customers' frequent use of certain food items like cheese and realized that resealable bags would make their products more convenient and, therefore, more attractive.

8. Snack food companies have taken advantage of Americans' diet-consciousness and reduced the number of cookies or crackers in some packages so that people wouldn't feel guilty about buying them.

9. When a company wants to launch a new product, they have to take into consideration customers' loyalty to a competing brand.

10. The promises of advertising and pretty labels play a role in people's expectations of a product.

mango is a source of natural sugars. Ideal for a boost of energy. A great snack.

C Complete each sentence with a noun clause using an adjective in the box below. Follow the example.

tamper-proof	colorful	protective	rigid/flexible
shatter-proof	~~recyclable~~	stackable	aseptic
lightweight	permeable	durable	fresh

1. Package designers need to think about _how well the packaging can be recycled._

2. Superior Egg Company has been pleased with _____

_____

3. Some items remain on the grocery shelves for months and months, so manufacturers have to think about _____

4. Some perishable items are flown to overseas markets; consequently, producers pay close attention to _____

5. Containers for medicines can be difficult for some people to open, but manufacturers have to be very careful about _____

6. Store managers are pleased with _____ because they have fewer broken jars and bottles to clean up in the store aisles.

7. Grocery stores allot each product or food item a particular amount of space, so the actual amount of any product on a shelf depends on _____

_____

8. Some fruit and vegetable products are sold in transparent containers because customers like to be sure of _____

CD2,TR8

D Listen to the press briefing by Marlene Bigelow, the spokesperson for Lambton Foods and for their product "FruityBites," and answer the comprehension questions using relative adverbial clauses or noun clauses.

1. What did parents complain about when the first snack came out?

   They complained about how much sugar the snack contained.

2. What was Lambton Foods unsure about?

   _____

3. Aside from a new recipe, what other change did Lambton Foods make?

   _____

4. What does Marlene Bigelow explain to the first reporter?

   _____

5. What does Sue Green ask about?

   _____

6. What information does Marlene Bigelow give about the plastic wrappers?

   _____

7. What is the last information that Bigelow gives the reporters?

   _____

■ **COMMUNICATE**

E **GROUP WORK** Create a dialog between a packaging designer and the manufacturer of an innovative toothbrush. They should discuss an eye-catching design for the new product. In your dialog use as many noun clauses as possible. When all of the groups are finished, each group can perform their dialog while the other teams listen and identify all of the noun clauses.

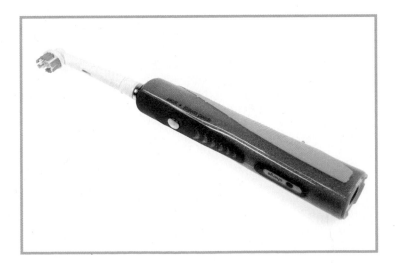

GRAMMAR AND VOCABULARY Write a composition on one of the topics below. Use as many words as possible from the Content Vocabulary on page 199, and (circle) them in your composition. Use sentences with relative adverbial clauses and noun clauses to express some of your ideas, and <u>underline</u> those sentences.

Topic 1: Describe the effective packaging of a particular item. Explain what the packaging looks like. Then, explain why the packaging is so appropriate to the product and to your lifestyle and/or culture.

Topic 2: "People in the U.S. should be more concerned about how much plastic packaging we use and how little recycling we do." Do you agree or disagree? Use concrete examples in your response.

PROJECT Interview at least one student on your campus about the packaging of popular products. Find out the following information, and present your findings orally at your next class meeting.

1. What American products are distinctive, or even famous, for the shape of their containers? (Ask your interviewee to describe the containers.)
2. Which American products have the most effective or attractive containers?
3. How important is the packaging in his/her decision to buy a new product?
4. What are five items in a grocery store that are typically not packaged in plastic?

 INTERNET Go online and use the search phrase "packaging competition" to find a website that shows winners in a recent competition for effective packaging. Such websites may represent a particular industry, such as "paperboard," or a certain company, for example, Dupont may sponsor an annual competition. Look at all of the winning packaging, and select one or two of the winners that you like. Be prepared to describe the product and its packaging and to tell your classmates why you find it effective or attractive.

PART 1
Anaphoric References

PART 2
Prepositions: *Against, Among, Between, Through, Toward*

Lesson 20

Health Sciences: Transcultural Nursing

■ CONTENT VOCABULARY

Look up the words and phrases below that you do not know and enter them in your vocabulary journal. Write each item's part of speech, a definition, and an example sentence. Try to include them in your discussion and writing below.

an assessment	physical therapy	solely	to treat
an intensive care unit	a recovery	straightforward	vital signs
the next of kin	a remedy	to take one's pulse	welfare

■ THINK ABOUT IT

Doctors and nurses treat patients from various cultures. What are some potential misunderstandings that could happen as a result of these cultural differences? Discuss your ideas with a classmate.

In your writing journal, write for five minutes about the questions below. When you have finished, share your experiences with your classmates.

Have you ever gone to the doctor's office or to the student clinic on your campus? What did you think about or worry about when you realized that you needed to see a doctor? What was strange or difficult for you when you were in the clinic or speaking with the nurse or the doctor? What procedures were different from those that you're accustomed to?

PART ONE   Anaphoric References

■ GRAMMAR IN CONTENT

A Read and listen to the passage below. The words in bold are some examples of anaphoric references.

Misunderstandings Among Nurses and Patients

Perhaps one of the most frustrating experiences in nursing is being unable to get patients to do what one wants **them** to do even when it is for **their** own good. What appears to be a patient's outright resistance to the medical and nursing regimen designed solely for **his** well-being and, hopefully, for **his** recovery can generate in a nurse any number of negative reactions: a sense of failure, helplessness, irritation, or even anger. However rigorously **she** may have disciplined **herself** not to reveal emotional responses **of this nature, they** are usually communicated to **her** patient in one or several of the ways in which people unconsciously transmit messages. **Such** messages, more meaningful to patients than is generally recognized, do not ameliorate the situation; rather, **they** tend to evoke such counter responses as anxiety, withdrawal, or alienation. The resulting impairment of the therapeutic process is often compounded by negative assessments of the noncompliant patient. **He** is labeled "uncooperative," "difficult," "stubborn," "perverse," or "a problem." Once **this** occurs, the kind of relationship between nurse and patient that is so important to **the latter's** welfare and to **the former's** satisfaction is broken.

When, despite careful explanations and appeals to reason, a patient persistently refuses to take **his** medication or exercise, for example, or to stay in bed or keep to **his** diet, several methods are commonly used to alter **his** behavior. **He** may be scolded, given less attention, or even threatened with the withdrawal of privileges. Conferences may be held on how to "handle" **him,** or how to motivate **him,** or whether to arrange for psychiatric consultation. Sometimes **these** methods work, but the frequency with which **they** don't—and especially *why* **they** don't—should concern anyone interested in improving the quality of patient care.

The behavior of noncompliant patients, however deviant or seemingly inappropriate, is not a matter of mere capriciousness. There are reasons why **they** respond as they do, and, apart from reasons that are solely physiologic or organic, **explanations** may be found on other levels: psychologic, sociologic, and/or cultural.

---

to ameliorate: to ease, to lessen

capriciousness: erratic or impulsive behavior

an impairment: damage, obstacle

outright: direct

noncompliant: disobedient

a regimen: a plan of treatment

rigorous: strong, demanding

to scold: to tell somebody in an angry way that he or she did something wrong

Sample Sentences	Notes
Nurse Dern has been concerned about **a patient** on her ward. **The patient** has **complained** about **the food** every day. **Those complaints** seem unreasonable since all of the other women in the ward like **it**.	Use various types of anaphoric references to make your speech and writing clearer and to avoid repeating words. These words and phrases refer to a noun or a whole idea that was mentioned previously in your conversation or your text. The article *the* and demonstratives *this, that, these,* and *those* are common referents. Pronouns and possessive determiners also function this way.
The doctor ordered a special diet on Monday. **Since then,** the patient hasn't been eating. The patient's behavior worries her because most patients like **such a** diet. To Ms. Dern, **such** behavior means something is wrong.	Some adverbs refer to times and places that were specified previously: *then, here, there, earlier, before then/this/that, since then/this/that.* Use *such* with nouns to signal that the noun or idea was mentioned earlier: *such a* + singular noun *such* + noncount noun/plural noun
Doctors often order diets **of this type** so that patients can regain their strength.	Other phrases also signal a previous reference: *of this type, in this style, of the same nature.*
Nurse Dern consulted Dr. Grant and Dr. Owen about her patient. **The former** suggested tests on the patient's digestive system. **The latter** preferred to wait and see.	Use special adjectives functioning as noun substitutes (*the former/the latter*) to point back to earlier information referring to the sequence as well as the antecedent.
The **physicians** finally referred **the medical case** to a specialist.	Use synonyms of nouns to avoid too much repetition and too many pronouns or to make the reference clearer for your listener or reader.

B Read over your journal entry, and <u>underline</u> at least one sentence that you can revise to include an anaphoric reference. Write your revised sentence(s) below.

_____

_____

_____

C (Circle) the anaphoric references in the texts below and then underline and draw an arrow to the word or phrase that it refers to.

1. During the regular weekly meeting, Nurse Peter King described Dr. Upton's treatment plan for a young patient with severe allergies. (She) had been admitted to the hospital on Friday and had been taking various medicines since then. Such allergies demand constant attention so that the proper drugs can be administered whenever needed.

2. Nurse practitioners often staff school clinics and small walk-in ambulatory care clinics. In the former, they treat schoolchildren who develop health problems during the school day. These problems aren't usually serious, but the nurses can send the youngsters home if necessary. In much the same way, such medical professionals treat people off the street at clinics that operate in many drugstores. Anyone with a serious condition or illness is referred to a doctor's care.

D Edit the text below, adding various types of anaphoric references including synonyms.

Good medical care depends on clear communication between patients and doctors or nurses. Unfortunately, clear communication doesn't always take place when patients in the United States can't speak English well. According to the U.S. Census, about 20% of the U.S. population does not speak English at home. In the last 10–15 years, hospitals and clinics have begun to tackle the problem of poor communication between patients and doctors and nurses. Now more than 40 states have laws about language access for medical care. The laws about language access are not always enforced because it can be expensive to enforce the laws. Also, hospitals and clinics often have difficulty locating translators for languages that are less commonly spoken, such as Hmong or Mongolian.

In response to the expense of enforcing the law and the difficulty locating translators, doctors, nurses, and hospital administrators are encouraging an increase in the number of interpreter-certification programs. Graduates of interpreter-certification programs can help doctors and nurses provide better medical care for patients and avoid costly mistakes.

E Listen to the conversation between two nurses and then answer the questions.

CD2,TR10

1. What attention has Mr. Bratt received from his nurse?

   _____

2. Which liquids are going to make him feel better sooner?

   _____

3. When did his complaints begin?

   _____

F Now listen to a follow-up conversation between one of the nurses and Mr. Bratt. Answer the questions when you have finished listening to the recording.

CD2,TR11

1. Who is "the latter" in this conversation?

   _____

2. What would be rude for Mr. Bratt?

   _____

3. Mr. Bratt says that in Sweden people don't act "that way." What does he mean?

   _____

■ **COMMUNICATE**

G **PAIR WORK** Tell the story of Mr. Kerry, who had to see a doctor while he was on a business trip abroad and had some unexpected experiences. Take turns telling the story, with each partner adding one sentence at a time. In each sentence you should include an anaphoric reference.

Mr. Kerry had been coughing and sneezing for three days and finally went to see a doctor in Mexico City.

His hotel recommended a nearby doctor, and Kerry took a taxi to that doctor's office.

When you finish your story, tell your classmates about Mr. Kerry's surprising trip to the doctor.

■ GRAMMAR IN CONTENT

A Reread the text at the beginning of this lesson, and (circle) examples of any of the prepositions listed in the chart. Which of the meanings below does the preposition have?

Prepositions: *Against, Among, Between, Through, Toward*

Sample Sentences	Notes
The nurses' station is **between** Radiology and the doctors' offices on the third floor. Go **through** the children's ward **toward** the elevators. Then, when you get to the emergency exit, turn left and you'll see the station **between** the women's restroom and the lounge. You'll find Dr. Huston's office **among** the other doctors' offices on the fourth floor. Don't lean **against** the emergency door—the alarm might go off.	Use these prepositions for location and destination: *against:* touching the side surface of *among:* in an unspecified position in the middle of three or more items (which are not uniquely specified) *between:* in the middle of two items *through:* moving along a passage; beyond *toward:* going in the direction of a destination (which is not necessarily the final destination)
Nurse Adams has protested **against** the rule about family visits after 7 P.M. His colleagues are **against** Adams because they know that such visits comfort patients. The nurses determine the work schedule **among** themselves. Nurses are on duty from 7 A.M. to 5 P.M., but visitors are only allowed **between** 2:00 and 4:00. **Between** meals the patients can't have any snacks. In double rooms, patients have to share a bathroom **between** themselves.	Other meanings for these prepositions: *against:* in opposition to; have no solidarity or sympathy for *among:* concerning more than two people *between:* a. specifying a beginning and end point b. intervals for events or objects that repeat c. concerning two people

At least one nurse is on duty **(all) through/throughout** the night.

The lights went out **(all) through/throughout** the hospital until the generators started up.

The nurse was able to communicate with Mr. Ortiz **through** an interpreter. He needed to understand that **through** physical therapy he could improve his strength and balance.

through:
a. duration
b. pervasive quality; all over
c. by means of
d. enduring; tolerating

For a. and b., you can also use *all through* or *throughout.*

B **Complete each sentence, using a preposition from the chart.**

1. Mr. Davidson, a heart patient, wanted to return to work two months after surgery. His nurse, Ms. Granger, advised _____*against*_____ such an action.

2. According to his doctor, Mr. Davidson could recover more quickly _____ physical therapy.

3. Whenever it's time for Mr. Davidson's medicine, the hospital pharmacist looks _____ the bottles of medicine in the drug cabinet to fill the prescription for him.

4. Mr. Davidson is still so weak that Nurse Granger has to help him out of bed. As he walks along, he leans _____ the nurse.

5. Mr. Davidson's doctor makes his morning rounds some time _____ 7:30 and 8:30.

6. The doctor still wants someone to monitor Mr. Davidson's vital signs _____ the night.

7. _____ all the nursing staff, Mr. Davidson trusts Nurse Granger the most.

8. When Nurse Granger heard an urgent page for her last night, she rushed _____ Mr. Davidson's room.

C **Explain the differences in meaning between the sentences below. Follow the example.**

1. To get to the visitor's lounge on the third floor, go

   a. through the red double doors. _____ *enter the doors* _____

   b. by the red double doors. _____ *go past the doors, but don't enter them* _____

2. Nurse Johnson was paged as he was wheeling a patient

   a. toward the Radiology Department. _____

   b. to the Radiology Department. _____

3. Nurse Johnson left the wheelchair in a space

   a. between the others. _____

   b. among the others. _____

4. When Nurse Johnson came back to get the wheelchair, it was

   a. against the wall. _____

   b. by the wall. _____

5. By midnight it was quiet

   a. all through the Intensive Care Unit. _____

   b. in the ICU. _____

6. Next of kin may visit patients in the Intensive Care Unit

   a. from 10:00 A.M. to 2 P.M. daily. _____

   b. between 10 and 2 daily. _____

7. Many patients can recover their strength

   a. through regular physical therapy. _____

   b. during regular physical therapy. _____

8. Family members may decide on a loved one's treatment plan

   a. between themselves. _____

   b. among themselves. _____

9. Patients should stay in their rooms

   a. between therapy sessions. _____

   b. after therapy sessions. _____

10. Once they had read the new policies about visiting hours, several nurses argued

   a. against them. _____

   b. for them. _____

A (Circle) the correct word or phrase to complete the idea of the sentence.

1. The conversation (between / among) Mrs. Liu's doctors took a long time yesterday, but both of them finally explained their plan of treatment to her.

2. Dr. Freeman walked (toward / through) the recovery room with Mrs. Liu so that she could see the special equipment that they needed after her surgery.

3. She trusted both Dr. Freeman and her nurses, but Mrs. Liu liked (the former / the latter) better because she had been kind enough to explain the equipment in the recovery room.

4. Mrs. Liu didn't understand (the way how / the way) some of the doctors spoke, but she could understand Dr. Freeman very well.

5. During her recovery one of the nurses asked Mrs. Liu every morning what (would she like / she would like) for lunch and dinner.

6. Now Mrs. Liu wonders (how long / how much) she will have to stay in the hospital.

7. Tomorrow Mrs. Liu will finally meet (Dr. Phyllis Klein, who / Dr. Phyllis Klein who) will supervise her physical therapy.

8. Dr. Klein is well-respected in her field according to Mrs. Liu's (favorite nurse, who / favorite nurse who) has taken care of many of Dr. Klein's patients.

9. Mrs. Liu's other doctors also praised Dr. Klein's work, (what / which) also reassured Mrs. Liu.

10. Many bouquets of flowers were sent (to Mrs. Liu / Mrs. Liu) during her recovery.

B If you paraphrase the sentences below with the verb in the passive voice, should the agent of the action be included? Write "Yes" if the paraphrase should include a *by* phrase; write "No" if the *by* phrase should be omitted.

_____ 1. Someone invented the air pump in the 1600s.

_____ 2. The study of alchemy influenced Isaac Newton for decades.

_____ 3. People in the eastern Mediterranean region developed glassmaking sometime before 3000 BCE; in addition, glassblowers from the same area invented the blowpipe around 100 BCE.

_____ 4. Plantation owners bought slaves from the Guinea Coast for their knowledge of rice cultivation.

_____ 5. The appropriate packaging can protect fragile or perishable items very well.

_____ 6. Engineers have updated designs for wheelchairs to take advantage of new lightweight materials.

C Write the verb in parentheses in the correct tense and voice.

1. A formal gift (expect) _____ to (wrap) _____ attractively.

2. Consumers sometimes admit (influence) _____ by the packaging of a product when they have a choice among several brands.

3. (select) _____ the winner of an award for effective packaging is the goal of leaders in that industry.

4. Some consumers are guilty of (let) _____ the packaging of a product affect their shopping.

5. For many years food items (require) _____ to have labels that (inform) _____ consumers about the ingredients.

6. Never buy a packaged food item that seems (tamper with) _____

7. Shoppers (should / warn) _____ _____ that the food had been contaminated, but they weren't.

8. People still remember when they (used to / buy) _____ food that had very little packaging.

LEARNER LOG Check (✔) Yes or *I Need More Practice.*

Lesson	I Can Use . . .	Yes	I Need More Practice
16	Verbs in the Passive Voice and Passives Taking Two Objects		
17	Gerunds and Infinitives in the Passive Voice; Passive Voice in Complex Sentences		
18	Restrictive and Nonrestrictive Relative Clauses; Reduced and Special Nonrestrictive Relative Clauses		
19	Relative Adverbial Clauses and Noun Clauses		
20	Anaphoric References and the Prepositions: *Against, Among, Between, Through, Toward*		

Physics: Golf and Tennis Balls

■ CONTENT VOCABULARY

Look up the words below that you do not know and enter them in your vocabulary journal. Write each word's part of speech, a definition, and an example sentence. Try to include them in your discussion and writing below.

to absorb	protocol	a reading	to spin
to generate	quantitative	to rebound	to wind
impact	a range	to release	to wobble

■ THINK ABOUT IT

Think about sports in which players hit, kick, or throw a ball. What forces determine how the ball flies, bounces, and rolls? Discuss your ideas with a classmate.

In your writing journal, write for 5–10 minutes about the questions below. When you are finished, share what you wrote with the class.

Have you ever played any sports that involve a ball? Of those sports, which ones did you find the most difficult? Why? How did you feel as you were trying to improve your skills in those sports?

■ **GRAMMAR IN CONTENT**

A **Read and listen to the passage below. The words in bold are participles that function as adjectives.**

CD2,TR41

Bounceability

An important property of the balls used in different types of ball games is the amount of energy they retain after bouncing off a surface such as golf club or tennis racket. In everyday speech people talk about the "bounce of the ball." A professional golf player can sometimes be observed to check the bounce of his ball by bouncing it on a smooth surface before starting a golf game. Scientists measure the "bounceability" of a ball by means of a quantity defined as the *coefficient of restitution.*

The term *restitution* comes from two Latin roots: "re" meaning again and "stature," to make, to stand (hence the word *statue*). To make restitution then literally means to restore an object or a situation to its original condition. We all know from experience how the return height of a **bouncing** ball decays with **repeated** bounces as shown in Figure 1. The fact that the ball fails to reach its original release height is a failure of the system to achieve restitution of the original height. The coefficient of restitution is a quantitative measure of the loss in height at each bounce. When released from the same height, a ball made of material with a low coefficient of restitution would not bounce back to the height achieved by a ball with a higher coefficient of restitution.

The term *coefficient* came into use in science when scientists were measuring many properties of materials and listing these **measured** properties before theories were known. The word was coined by joining "co," which means together, and "efficient," which originally meant capable of doing something. *Efficient* came from the Latin root words *ex*, meaning "out," and *facere*, meaning "to make." Thus, if we knew the coefficient of restitution, we would know how things worked together to make the ball bounce (See Figure 1.). Scientists exploring the properties of different materials would make balls of all sorts of different materials and measure the bounce of each ball. They would then plot the coefficient of restitution against the substance in the ball. For example, when the early manufacturers of golf balls experimented with how tightly they wound the elastic thread around the central core, they found that the tighter they wound the thread, the higher the coefficient of restitution of the **bouncing** ball. These better **bouncing** balls are called *high compression balls.*

We will meet the coefficient of restitution in any game where the ball is hit with a bat or a racket or when the ball bounces off a wall or other hard surfaces (See Figure 2.). When we bounce an ordinary rubber ball off a surface, we learn through experience that if we wish to catch the ball at the same height at which we release the ball from our own hand, we must give a ball a little bit of extra energy as we throw it down on the surface. This means we release the ball from our hand traveling at the speed it would have gathered if it had been released from a greater height. Then the first bounce will reach the position of our hand.

a) Figure 1

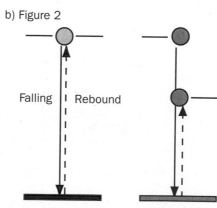

The coefficient of restitution (a) equals the square root of the rebound height (h_2) divided by the original height (h_1).

Symbolically:

$$a = \sqrt{\frac{h_2}{h_1}}$$

b) Figure 2

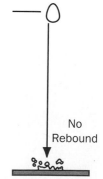

Falling   Rebound

No Rebound

Perfectly Elastic
e.g., Steel on Steel

Partially Inelastic
e.g., Rubber Ball

Completely Inelastic
e.g., Egg

Sample Sentences	Notes
The type of grass on a golf course can have an effect on how far a **rolling** ball will go.	An English participle can function not only as a verb form but also as an adjective.
Our newspaper ran a photo of the **smiling** winner of the local golf match.	Choose the *-ing* form of the participle if the noun that it modifies is the agent of the action or the cause of an emotion:
After the golfers asked the **whispering** spectators to keep quiet, the **surprised** onlookers left.	a rolling ball = the ball is rolling a surprising result = the result surprises you
Professional golfers throw out their **used** balls because they are **deformed**.	Use a participle if the accompanying noun is the receiver of the action or the experiencer of the emotion:
Such **deformed** balls don't fly straight when they're hit.	an **injured** person = a person who was injured a **disappointed** person = a person who felt disappointment
Physicists have studied the properties of **tightly wound** golf balls.	These participles may also be modified • by adverbs *(an often told story, a hard-working student, a never-ending problem)*
Modern golf balls have 336 **symmetrically placed** holes, or dimples.	• by nouns *(a prize-winning team, the heart-warming story, a moth-eaten sweater)*
Professional golfers are not allowed to use balls with **self-correcting** action.	

Verbs of Emotion Frequently Used as Adjectives

alarm	bewilder	disturb	frighten	overwhelm
amaze	bore	embarrass	insult	puzzle
annoy	comfort	encourage	interest	shock
astonish	convince	excite	mislead	tire

B Read over your journal entry, and <u>underline</u> at least one sentence that you can revise to include a participle that functions as an adjective. Write your revised sentence(s) below.

_____

_____

_____

_____

C Revise each of the sentences below to include at least one participial adjective.

1. A golf ball that is moving has energy.

   A moving golf ball has energy.

2. If a golf ball hits another ball, it transfers energy, and in science, energy that is transferred does "work."

   _____

   _____

3. *Work* is a term that is confusing because it doesn't mean the same thing in science as it does in other contexts.

   _____

   _____

4. Science teachers need to explain terminology that is specialized to students who are puzzled so that they understand scientific concepts more easily.

   _____

5. For some students, terminology that is bewildering makes science too difficult.

   _____

6. Scientific concepts are clear for some students, but for others the mental picture of a golf ball that is rolling or a tennis ball that is spinning can help a lot.

   _____

7. A photo of a golf ball that has been deformed can also convince students of the effect of the high-speed impact of a golf club on the ball.

   _____

   _____

D (Circle) the correct form of the participle in the sentences below. In some cases, both choices may be correct. If both participles can be used, explain the difference in meaning in each sentence.

1. Most people think that a rubber band is very elastic or stretchable, but it's an

   ((amazing) / amazed) fact that rubber is not very elastic in scientific terms.

2. (Bouncing / Bounced) metal balls have a higher rebound than rubber balls because

   metal balls do not absorb energy and thus have a greater coefficient of restitution.

3. The word "elastic" is a (misleading / misled) scientific term for many students

   because they don't realize it refers to energy rather than to shape.

4. Thus, a scientist who describes a material with the technical term *elastic* means that the material demonstrates greater (conserving / conserved) energy than a material with low elasticity.

5. Professors may give (fascinating / fascinated) demonstrations of this concept so that their (boring / bored) students become more (interesting / interested) in lab class.

6. An (interesting / interested) professor can make any subject come alive.

7. If a professor uses golf balls and other examples from sports, (struggling / struggled) students may gain confidence in their ability to understand physics.

8. An (inspiring / inspired) student may decide to major in physics or chemistry and make science a career.

E Circle the correct interpretation of each sentence.

1. During class the bored lab assistant gave the students feedback on their assignments.
   a. The lab assistant looked like she was sleepy or didn't care about class.
   b. We felt sleepy because of the lab assistant's way of giving feedback.

2. The fascinating student asked the professor to explain the example in the textbook.
   a. Everyone in class wanted to know and listen to the student.
   b. The student wanted to know more and more about the example.

3. The students became quiet when they saw the disturbed look on Professor Wheeler's face.
   a. The students realized that Professor Wheeler was upset about something.
   b. The students felt upset when they saw the expression on Professor Wheeler's face.

4. An alarmed campus police officer rushed into their lab class.
   a. The police officer felt anxious and afraid when she entered the classroom.
   b. The students in the classroom felt anxious and afraid when she entered.

5. The encouraged student did much better on his second take-home exam.
   a. The student helped to motivate his classmates to do better.
   b. The student felt motivation to do better in his class.

6. An increasing number of women are studying physics and chemistry in the United States.
   a. The number of women is growing.
   b. Something caused the number of women students to grow.

F Rephrase the participial adjectives in the sentences with relative clauses containing verbs or predicate adjectives.

1. The lab assistant was sure that the students could handle the clearly defined experiment for that week.

   The lab assistant was sure that the students could handle the experiment, which was/had been clearly defined for that week.

2. It has always been against university policy to conduct life-threatening experiments in lab classes.

3. Some of the students could not read the hand-written feedback on their lab reports.

4. Although physics graduate students have to attend classes, research-related tasks take up most of their time.

5. Most graduate assistants consider their poorly paid jobs a necessity if they want to become a professor later on.

6. If grad students are especially lucky, they might have the opportunity to work on a profit generating project for the university.

7. Doctoral students may even have their own university-sponsored research project.

■ **COMMUNICATE**

G **PAIR WORK** Work together to create a story about a situation that was embarrassing, depressing, shocking, or amusing.

■ GRAMMAR IN CONTENT

A Reread the text at the beginning of this lesson, and <u>underline</u> all of the phrases that include a subordinate conjunction such as *when* or *although* followed by a participial phrase. Compare your answers with a partner.

Participles in Reduced Adverbial Clauses

Sample Sentences	Notes
Most golfers use one or two balls **while playing a course.**	Like relative clauses, the following types of adverbial clauses can be reduced: time, conditional, and concessive.
Although appearing spherical, a used golf ball becomes deformed.	Omit the subject and revise the verb to a participial form:
A golf ball won't fly straight **if deformed.**	subordinate conjunction + *-ing* phrase (= active verb) subordinate conjunction + *-ed/-en* phrase (= passive verb)
When hit, a deformed ball won't "fly true" as golfers say.	
Until hearing this information, many players try to save money and use the same ball too many times.	NOTE: Always check that the subject of the main verb is the grammatical subject of the participial verb in the adverbial phrase.
The player decided to use a new ball, after **having made** several poor hits.	Express a time contrast to the verb in the main clause by using a <u>perfect participle</u>: *-ing* (= active) participle: *having called*
Although **having been told** that she needed to use a different club, the player hit the new ball with a driving iron.	*-ed* (= passive) participle: *having been called*
The player tried his shot again, **convinced that he could do better.**	**Subordinate conjunctions** can be omitted for these types of adverbial phrases:
Having hit the ball correctly, the player expected to see it fly straight down the fairway. (Because he had hit . . . / After he had hit . . .)	• Time • Causal (This type is not included above!) • Conditional • Concessive
Hit well, a golf ball should have a backspin. (If it is hit well . . . /After it is hit well . . .)	In this case, the participial phrase may be interpreted in various ways according to the context of the sentence. If the connection of ideas in your text is very important, do not omit the conjunction.
	Separate the participial phrase from the main clause with a comma.

B **Reduce an adverbial clause in each sentence below.**

1. When they are bounced against a surface, all balls have a measurable coefficient of restitution.

   When bounced against a surface, all balls have a measurable coefficient of restitution.

2. Athletes have to spend a lot of extra time practicing if they use a new ball with a different coefficient.

   _____

3. Tennis players know how balls bounce on the different surfaces because they have trained on clay courts and on grass.

   _____

4. Athletes may prefer to play on artificial turf when they consider the condition of the grass in a particular stadium.

   _____

5. When they refer to characteristics of a surface that affect how a ball bounces and rolls, scientists use the term *resistance*.

   _____

6. Although they appear more aesthetic than utilitarian, the dimples on a golf ball actually help reduce air resistance.

   _____

C **Listen to the conversation between Larry, a teaching assistant in a physics lab, and Gina, an undergraduate. Answer a question about each part of their conversation.**

CD2,TR42

1. When should Gina work on the database? *While she's waiting to take the next temperature reading, Gina should work on the database.*

2. Doesn't the equipment record the data itself?

   _____

3. Under what circumstance will the TA tell Professor Kerry that Gina was the only person who was recording the data?

   _____

4. When did Larry decide on Gina's role in the experiment?

   _____

5. What is an important step in becoming a successful scientist?

   _____

6. When did Larry visualize himself in his own lab?

   _____

Spin causes more air to flow over the top of the ball, which is a longer path, therefore it must move more quickly, which causes lift.

Direction of motion of the ball

D **Rewrite each sentence so that the subjects of the main clause and adverbial phrases are the same.**

1. When striking, a golf ball should have a backspin as it flies down the fairway.

   When struck, a golf ball should have a backspin as it flies down the fairway.

2. If served properly, a tennis player hits the ball over the net with a topspin.

   _____

3. Good tennis players put a spin on the ball when served.

   _____

4. According to the Magnus effect, the pressure of the air molecules forces a golf ball downward when rotating with a topspin.

   _____

5. A beginning golf player may not strike the ball well, although hit straight.

   _____

6. Understanding the advantage of the Magnus effect, a golf ball will go much farther.

   _____

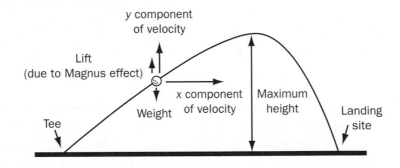

E **Paraphrase some ideas from each text with a sentence that includes an adverbial clause. Use reduced clauses, omitting any unnecessary conjunctions.**

1. Ned practices his golf swing regularly. His goal is to hit balls farther and with backspin. He is taking lessons right now to improve both skills.

    While taking golf lessons, Ned has been focusing on his swing. / Hoping to hit balls farther, Ned practices his golf swing regularly. / Although practicing his swing regularly, Ned is taking lessons to improve his skills.

2. Rachel has been a long-distance runner for several years and usually runs around the track at her university. At the beginning of summer vacation, she jogged on the sidewalks in her hometown, but her knees started to hurt. Her coach told her that the hard surface of the sidewalks had caused her injury.

    _____

    _____

3. Coaches and experts in sports medicine worry about the surfaces that athletes run and jump on. Without the proper shoes for their sport, athletes can damage their knees and feet when the energy that they exert against the track "bounces back" into their bodies. Sprinters and long jump athletes take advantage of the quick rebound from the track, but long distance runners need a lower coefficient of restitution to avoid injury.

    _____

    _____

4. Like balls, badminton birds, or shuttlecocks, can also spin, but the action is influenced by their construction. The old-fashioned type has 16 feathers, and the newer, cheaper shuttlecocks have a plastic skirt. Skilled players can cause shuttle cocks to rotate counterclockwise, but the ones with skirts rotate at half the speed of the feathered ones.

    _____

    _____

5. The center of gravity in a ball can be moved if the ball is damaged. Once that happens, the ball won't fly true or roll straight. Instead it wobbles. Sometimes baseball pitchers secretly "doctor" a ball, in other words put a foreign substance on the ball, so that it moves unpredictably, which makes it hard for the batter to hit.

    _____

    _____

Find and correct the four errors in the informal e-mail message below.

Professor Kerry-

Just to let you know that we finished Phase 1 of the experiment this afternoon. As anticipating, the temperature readings were all in the expected range. Although the students complained that they were boring, they actually did a great job. The most amazed thing is that several of them came to me later and wanted to do extra work.

Because using some different equipment for Phase 2, I'll have to close the lab for a few hours tomorrow morning. It's a good thing that we're a little ahead of schedule.

As soon as we're ready, I'll beep you-
Larry

■ **C O M M U N I C A T E**

G **PAIR WORK** Work together to prepare instructions for the steps in a process. Use as many adverbial and adjectival participles as possible in your list of steps. When you present your instructions to the class, one of you can demonstrate, or pantomime, as the other gives the instructions.

You start with a square sheet of paper when **making** an origami crane . . .
The **finished** product can be puffed up by blowing through a hole in the bottom.

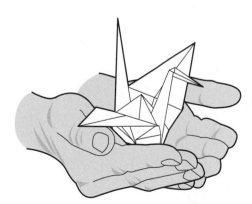

GRAMMAR AND VOCABULARY Write a composition on one of the topics below. Use as many words as possible from the Content Vocabulary on page 221. Use sentences with adjectival participles and participles in reduced adverb clauses to express some of your ideas.

Topic 1: Explain the correct way to handle the ball in a sport that you enjoy playing. How do you hit, bounce, or throw it properly? How does the ball move when players handle it correctly? What do beginning players need to practice so that the ball moves efficiently?

Topic 2: All students have favorite courses and favorite teachers. In your opinion, can an interesting teacher make you like a field that you never liked before? After taking a motivating class, do you want to take more courses in that field? Can any field be fascinating and exciting with the right teacher? Give concrete examples.

PROJECT Interview at least four students on your campus about taking science courses. Find out the following information from each student, and make a brief oral report on the results of your interviews at your next class meeting.

a. the student's major
b. the science classes that the student took in high school and has taken in college
c. if the student is interested in science and why
d. what kind of classes the student finds boring

 INTERNET Go online to find simplified explanations of how various machines and devices work. Use the search term "how things work." Choose something about science or electronics, and write a summary of the explanation. Present the information in your own words, using some reduced adverbial clauses.

PART 1
Complements of Sensory Verbs

PART 2
Other Verbs with Participial
Complements

Lesson (22)

Film Studies:
Documentaries

■ CONTENT VOCABULARY

Look up the words and phrases below that you do not know and enter them in your vocabulary journal. Write each word's part of speech, a definition, and an example sentence. Try to include them in your discussion and writing below.

corrupt	footage	prestigious	subject matter
to elicit	to perceive	a sequel	to survive
to excavate	to portray	the status quo	visual

■ THINK ABOUT IT

The photos on the next page surprised and delighted people in the 1880s. Before film, people had not been able to closely examine how horses galloped. What photos or films have you seen that revealed something completely new in your understanding of the world? Discuss your ideas with a classmate.

In your writing journal, write for 5–10 minutes about the questions below. When you are finished, share what you wrote with the class.

What kind of documentary films or TV programs do you enjoy watching? What do you like to see in such films and programs?

■ GRAMMAR IN CONTENT

CD2,TR43

A Read and listen to the passage below. The words in bold are clauses with participial complements.

Seeing Is Believing

During the last decade, documentaries have done very well at the box office. Films such as *Bowling for Columbine* and *March of the Penguins* have earned millions of dollars and have garnered prestigious awards in the film industry. Titles of other popular documentaries from the big screen or from TV may come to mind, but the majority of such films rarely match the drawing power of Hollywood-style movies. That is not to say, however, that documentary films lack power or influence.

A photo-sequence by the filmmaker Eadweard Muybridge.

Before filmmaking even began, photographs of historic events and of nature could capture the attention and imagination of the public. Through photographs, people could see what their eyes were not able to otherwise perceive. A famous example is the galloping horse of Eadweard Muybridge. By the 1880s, he was able to project photos of the horse on a screen so quickly that **viewers perceived the horse galloping.** Of course, on each frame a **viewer could only see the horse step or lift its feet.** Since those days, some documentary-makers have explored our natural world in much more detail and have caught animals hunting, protecting their territory, and taking care of their young on film.

In the 1920s, American filmmaker Robert Flaherty made the first two documentary films: *Nanook of the North* and *Moana.* Each of these films explored the lives of people in remote areas of the world. While in northeastern Canada exploring for minerals, Flaherty had come in contact with Eskimos and made friends. On film, **Nanook and other Eskimos were observed fishing, paddling their kayaks, hunting seals through the ice, and building igloos.** In the second film, Flaherty brought the world of Moana and his Polynesian family to American audiences, who **watched these islanders preparing for Moana's initiation rites.** Although these documentaries lacked story lines and portrayed real people quite different from American moviegoers, the films were very well-received.

As filmmakers in North America and Europe explored this form of visual expression, many found a new purpose for their efforts: recording their subjects to elicit reactions or actions among the viewers. From this point of view, the audience should leave the movie house thinking about their own actions or attitudes. For example, after seeing *Super Size Me,* many people have reconsidered the amount of fast food that they should eat. That 98-minute film did more to change attitudes about eating fast food than all the warnings of doctors and nutritionists!

Informative and educational, documentaries should, therefore, do more than interest and entertain us. Some of them are intended to reflect the lives of real people or other living things on our planet so that audience members can extend their horizons and develop an understanding or sympathy for foreign or exotic things. Other films function as a "call to arms," in other words, a visual stimulus to change the status quo.

the box office: the place to buy tickets at a theater or stadium; the total income from ticket sales

a story line: the plot or story

to garner: to get, to win

Sample Sentences	Notes
In a film about Africa we could hear **lions roaring** close to the camp, but we didn't hear **any other animals make a noise.**	Although sensory verbs usually function as stative verbs, you can express either limited or continuing actions in their complements.
We heard **one of the hunters shoot his rifle** to scare away some hyenas. I recorded **him shooting** at least three times.	Use a **bare infinitive complement** to express a completed action: **sensory verb + direct object + bare infinitive (phrase)**
I didn't expect to see **one hyena lying** under some bushes the next morning.	Use **a complement with a present participle** to express an action in progress: **sensory verb + direct object + -*ing* participial phrase**
Did you spot/photograph **the other hyena hiding** in the brush?	In both cases, the direct object of the sensory verb is the agent of the action in the complement.
After the film I overheard **one moviegoer comment** on the violence to her friend.	NOTE: Do not use *perceive, photograph, smell,* and *spot* with a bare infinitive complement.
In the film *C'mon Geese,* **the pilot** is overheard **saying** "C'mon geese!" because he wants them to follow his small plane. At the end of the film, **the geese** are seen **following his plane** and are heard **honking naturally** as they are in flight.	If **the direct object of the main clause** is the focus of attention, use a passive verb construction before the complement. • Use *hear, notice, observe, overhear, photograph, record, see, spot* in such passive constructions. • Most passive sentences of this type have a participial complement.

Common Sensory Verbs

feel/sense	notice	overhear	photograph	see	spot
hear	observe	perceive	record	smell	watch

B Read over your journal entry, and <u>underline</u> at least one sentence that you can revise to include a clause with a sensory verb followed by a complement. Write your revised sentence(s) below.

_____

_____

_____

_____

C Write two sentences to describe what you expect to see or hear in each scene below.

1. (in the Amazon rain forest/see)

   a. _____ *I hope to watch colorful birds hiding among the branches.* _____

   b. _____ *I expect to see a crocodile catch its prey in the water.* _____

2. (on the ocean floor/see)

   a. _____

   b. _____

3. (during a political campaign/hear)

   a. _____

   b. _____

4. (on a trip through the Sahara Desert/observe)

   a. _____

   b. _____

5. (in the control tower of a major international airport/hear)

   a. _____

   b. _____

D Now imagine that you are part of a camera team on location. What do you expect to smell or feel in each of these situations?

1. (in a tidal pool on the coast of Australia in the summer/feel)

   a. _____

   b. _____

2. (in various coffee shops in the U.S./smell)

   a. _____

   b. _____

3. (in a busy subway station/feel)

   a. _____

   b. _____

4. (at a carnival or other outdoor festival/smell)

   a. _____

   b. _____

E The sentences below tell about a scene from a film. Use your imagination to describe something else that can be seen or heard. Follow the example.

1. A well-known documentary director succeeded in interviewing one of the opponents of educational reform in the United States.

   The woman is heard criticizing the importance of test scores for elementary

   school students.

2. One director shot two hours of film of young girls who hope to be Olympic gymnasts.

   _____

   _____

3. While a director was investigating police corruption, she got footage of two police officers on their beat.

   _____

   _____

4. A director in Milan, Italy, who is interested in the effect of the fashion world on young models, accompanied one young woman during the preparations for an important fashion show.

   _____

   _____

5. A local director was fascinated by the graffiti artists in his city.

   _____

   _____

6. A director has been collecting interviews with master shipbuilders, including a local man who builds canoes.

   _____

   _____

7. Another director wants to convince people that skydiving is a great sport, so she filmed a skydiving instructor.

   _____

   _____

F **PAIR WORK** Choose one of the topics below and brainstorm the kinds of scenes that a good documentary on this topic should include. In this documentary, you want to change people's attitudes. Describe at least five possible scenes that you want in your documentary and then share those ideas with your classmates.

- the benefits of doing yoga
- the social integration of people with disabilities
- the serious problem of bullies in schools
- the danger of driving while you talk on a cell phone
- the need to graduate from high school

Let's make a movie about bullies. I know a lot of people could relate to that. How should we start it?

The audience should see a bully starting a fight with another kid. Suddenly, we hear the bell ringing . . .

PART TWO	Other Verbs with Participial Complements

■ GRAMMAR IN CONTENT

A Reread the text at the beginning of this lesson, and <u>underline</u> *catch, discover, find,* and *leave* as main verbs. Do any of the sentences with these verbs have a participial complement? Share your answers with a partner.

Other Verbs with Participial Complements

Sample Sentences	Notes
Undercover camera operators have often **caught** corrupt officials taking bribes.	Use a present participle in the complement (after the direct object) of the following verbs: *catch, discover, find, uncover, leave.*
You don't normally **come across** a police officer accepting bribes, so hidden cameras are often the only way to film the scene.	The verbs **catch, find, discover,** and **uncover** all refer to a physical, not an intellectual, discovery when they are used in this construction. The prepositional verbs **come across** and **come upon** also have this meaning and the same type of complement.
It's difficult to **uncover** public officials taking bribes.	
In films of little known cultures, the film crew may **discover** people living in primitive conditions. They might also **find** people behaving much better than "civilized" people.	
In order to tape the day-long ceremony, the sound engineer **left** the recorder running until the last guest had left.	

Sample Sentences	Notes
Do you **remember** the bride's father giving the groom three cows?	*Recall* and *remember* can also have a participial complement like the verbs above.
Some documentaries show the lives of homeless people in urban areas. These people **are found** living under bridges or sleeping in subway stations.	Use a passive construction if the direct object is the focus of attention. In this case, do not use either **come across** or **come upon**.

B Give suggestions for staying safe and healthy if you are shooting a film on location in an exotic or dangerous setting. Use the main verb *leave.*

1. At night, how can you avoid diseases that are carried by mosquitoes?

    You can leave the mosquito netting hanging down over your bed.

2. At night, how can you keep wild animals from entering your camp?

    _____

3. At night, how can you keep bears from entering your camp to look for food?

    _____

4. During the day, how can you make a quick escape in your vehicle if a lion attacks?

    _____

5. At night, what can alert you in case an earthquake begins so that you can escape?

    _____

6. At night, what can you do in a cold climate so that your water pipes don't freeze?

    _____

7. At night, how can you keep a snake or spider from sleeping in your shoe?

    _____

C Predict three things that your camera will find or catch at each of the locations below.

1. (at a bus station)

It'll find people rushing past each other, people standing in line to buy tickets, and people boarding buses.

2. (at the beach on a hot sunny day)

3. (on the banks of a river)

4. (at a political rally)

5. (at a traditional open-air market)

6. (at a rock concert)

7. (at a boxing match)

D Listen to parts of a conversation between members of a film crew on location in New York's Central Park. Then, answer the questions, expressing your answers using the participial constructions in this lesson.

CD2,TR44

1. Where did Fred put his camera?

2. What were the two strangers doing?

3. What were the strangers doing when Lou saw them?

_____

4. What did the strangers say when Lou noticed them?

_____

5. What did Lou hear while Fred was gone?

_____

6. Why was Fred happy that a cop was near?

_____

7. How did Fred feel as he was waiting for the cop to come closer?

_____

E Correct the five errors in the informal e-mail message below.

Derek,

We just finished up the filming. The Kingsford family was really terrific as they tried to survive in the lifestyle of the 1600s! Do you remember Joe Kingsford say that his family could handle it? He suffered more than any of his kids! On film you can actually hear he is crying at the end of a tough week during the harvest season. At the very same time you can see his kids sleep in their clothes – they're all dead tired.

His wife Sarah had the hardest time – she had never even gone camping before. You should see her face as the pigs are smelled walking around outside her front door. What a sight! We also caught her clean a chicken. She hadn't ever seen chicken feathers before.

The hard part for you is going to be the editing. There are so many amazing scenes to choose from. We'll have everything for you on Monday.

Regards,
Pat

■ **C O M M U N I C A T E**

F **GROUP WORK** Plan a documentary about your school or program. Remember that documentaries usually aren't scripted, so you need to brainstorm the kinds of scenes that an audience should see and hear to understand what it's like to be a student in your school or program. When your group is finished, share your ideas with the other groups.

GRAMMAR AND VOCABULARY Write a composition on one of the topics below. Use as many words as possible from the Content Vocabulary on page 233. Use sentences with sensory verbs and other verbs that take participial complements to express some of your ideas.

Topic 1: Documentary makers regularly discover people doing interesting activities or undertaking amazing projects. They also catch animals behaving in fascinating ways. However, documentaries are seen by fewer people and make smaller profits than feature films, like those made in Hollywood. In your opinion, what is the reason for the difference in popularity between the two types of movies? Give concrete examples.

Topic 2: Documentaries or factual programs about animals are very popular on American TV. Moviegoers around the world enjoy watching animals going about their daily lives or behaving in surprising ways. Why are viewers particularly interested in seeing and hearing wildlife living in various habitats and interacting with each other?

PROJECT Interview at least one student on your campus about documentaries. Find out the following information, and make a brief oral report on the interview at your next class meeting.

    a. What kinds of documentaries or factual programs does the student watch?
    b. Which documentaries or factual TV programs does the student recommend?
    c. What are some of the popular documentaries of the last 10 years that the student can remember?

 INTERNET Go online and use the search term "reviews of documentary films." Read the reviews or descriptions of some films that have interesting titles, and decide which movie you would like to watch. Prepare a short oral report for your class on your choice and the reasons for your choice.

PART 1
Reported Speech in Context

PART 2
Rules for and Exceptions to
Backshifts in Reported Speech

Lesson (23)

Computer Science: Artificial Intelligence

■ CONTENT VOCABULARY

Look up the words and phrases below that you do not know and enter them in your vocabulary journal. Write each word's part of speech, a definition, and an example sentence. Try to include them in your discussion and writing below.

to argue	to claim	to highlight	to indicate
to assume	to confirm	humanoid	a sensor
autonomous	a driverless vehicle	to imply	to state

■ THINK ABOUT IT

Look at the photo of the machine on the next page. How do you think such machines work?

In your writing journal, write for five minutes about the questions below. When you are finished, share your ideas with the class.

In your opinion, how will robots help us in our daily lives in the next 10 years? Who will benefit the most from robots?

■ GRAMMAR IN CONTENT

CD2, TR45

A Read and listen to the passage below. The sentences in bold in the first part of the text include a *that* clause.

Who's in the Driver's Seat?

March, 2004

A remarkable race of driverless robots took place in the desert between Los Angeles and Las Vegas. The 143-mile race was the idea of DARPA, the Defense Advanced Research Projects Agency, which is interested in developing autonomous vehicles for military purposes. **They imagined that some computer scientists and software hobbyists would take the challenge to develop such vehicles,** especially with the incentive of a $1 million prize. **DARPA thought that 20 teams might participate in the "Great Challenge,"** but instead 106 teams submitted applications for the competition.

At their orientation meeting, the participants heard the requirements of the race. **They found out that they wouldn't see the route until 2 hours before the race. DARPA had already decided that only 10% of the course should be on paved roads.** Consequently, the challenge involved creating a robot to travel over desert terrain with volcanic rocks, train tracks, and rivers. **In addition, the DARPA officials stated that the vehicles had to avoid contact with other robots.** These were the basic rules. **The officials also emphasized that there were no constraints on the robots' size, shape, or source of power.**

Robot developers learned many lessons when the "winner" of the Great Challenge only made it 7 miles and most robots didn't even go 1 mile. **Researchers now know that robotic vision caused the failure of many of those vehicles. They have learned that radar, lasers, stereovision, and GPS are crucial to a robot's vision but also that effective software has to analyze the ground ahead of the robot accurately.** When that finally happens, robots will be able to maneuver more effectively and go faster.

March, 2006

Oleg: Did you see the program about the second Great Robot Race on NOVA last night?

Tish: No. How did I miss it? I have been waiting to see it since I heard that they were making a TV show about it.

Oleg: It was incredible. They said several robots actually finished the race this time. We saw the top five vehicles cross the finish line.

Tish: Who came in first?

Oleg: Do you remember the one called "Sandstorm"? It's the one built by Carnegie Mellon University.

Tish: Sure. What about it?

Oleg: They explained that it got stuck the last time. They even showed the video of it with the tires burning! They said it was one of the favorites this time, so they spent a lot of time on the Carnegie Mellon team.

Tish: So, what happened? Did they win?

Oleg: No, a guy from Stanford and his team came in first. They said that this guy'd worked at Carnegie Mellon before. I guess that the team at CMU was pretty disappointed with the results.

Tish: I'll bet that there was a big celebration at the Stanford lab after that.

Oleg: You bet! They said that the winning team would get $2 million.

---

paved: a hard surface that makes transport easier

terrain: land; the surface of the land

a constraint: a limit or restriction

GPS: Global Positioning System

Reported Speech in Context

Sample Sentences	Notes
Professor Chavez: "Computers will be able to think like humans by 2025." ↓ Professor Chavez **said that** computers **would be able to think** like humans by 2025. ↓ Professor Chavez **asserted that** computers **would be able to** think like humans by 2025. Professor Chavez **said he was planning** a project with a driverless vehicle. Professor Chavez **guaranteed that** all of his graduate students **could participate** in the project.	The reporting verbs **say, tell, state, write** are neutral in meaning. Use other reporting verbs to express the intention of the speaker or writer. Such verbs add more meaning to statements with reported speech. See the list of some other verbs below. English speakers often omit **that** with the most frequently used reporting verbs, for example **say** and **tell.** Include **that** in formal contexts, especially with reporting verbs that express the speaker's intention.
Professor Dern: "Future humanoid robots **will probably rely on** special 'stepper motors' for rather small adjustments in movement. We're not sure yet if other types of specialized motors can be adapted to these robotic needs." ↓ **In her lecture,** Professor Dern assumed that future humanoid robots would <u>depend on</u> special "stepper motors" for small adjustments in motion. Then, she <u>questioned whether</u> other types of (specialized) motors could be adapted to robotic needs.	Use **connecting words and phrases** to make the information in reported speech as clear as possible to the listener or reader. Often words are (omitted) or <u>changed</u> in reported speech, but the meaning must remain the same.

Reporting Verbs

admit	demand	guarantee	recommend
announce	doubt	guess	stress
complain	explain	hint	swear

B Read over your journal entry, and <u>underline</u> at least one sentence that you can revise to include reported speech using a *that* clause. Write your revised sentence(s) below.

_____

_____

_____

_____

C Look at the notes a journalist wrote after interviewing Hans Morasev, a well-known robotics expert. Write a short report about the interview. Use reported speech and the verbs in the box below to complete the paragraph.

| highlight | ~~confirm~~ | assert | deny | imply |

Interview notes for Hans Morasev – June 3rd
- ✓ work on artificial intelligence in robots progressing slowly
- ✓ by 2010 robots should have cognitive abilities like reptiles
- ✓ robots able to perform like insects now
- ✓ doesn't think that humans will lose control over robots
- ✓ computers would be programmed to do the same things as the human brain

Morasev confirmed that work on artificial intelligence using robots was progressing slowly.

_____

_____

_____

_____

D Read the following excerpt from a transcript of an interview between a reporter and Dr. Elbaz, an archaeologist. Summarize the report using reported speech.

Chang: Good afternoon, Dr. Elbaz. This is Chang Zihong of the *New York Gazette*. What's the latest news on the robot's progress in Egypt?

Dr. Elbaz: We're all pleased with the robot's first day of work. As you know, it entered the first shaft of the Great Pyramid of Giza this morning at 6 A.M.

Chang: According to early reports, the robot got stuck down in the shaft. Is that really true?

Dr. Elbaz: No. I'm happy to report that it traveled slowly but continuously till it reached the bottom of the shaft.

Chang introduced himself as a reporter from the New York Gazette and inquired what the latest news was on the robot's progress in Egypt.

_____

_____

E Read the following newspaper article. When you are finished, complete the short summary in the space provided.

Boston- Lingua-Bots has announced the first sales of their innovative new robotic cleaning system named "BotButler." According to company spokesman B. Brummer, BotButler can understand 50 voice commands, including "load the dishwasher," "dust the furniture," and "scrub the floor." This humanoid robot stands 4 feet tall and weighs only 50 pounds. It is available online for $1,250 plus shipping and handling. Brummer stated, "BotButler is clearly superior to the first generation of cleaning bots like the Dyson vacuum cleaner and offers the latest robot technology."

The article reported that a company in Boston had announced the sales of a household robot.

_____

_____

_____

_____

■ **COMMUNICATE**

F **PAIR WORK** On a separate sheet of paper, write your "specifications" for a new robot. The specifications can describe one of the robots shown or they can describe a robot of your own creation. Share your ideas with a partner. Make sure you understand your partner's specifications. Then, tell the class about your partner's design, using reported speech.

■ GRAMMAR IN CONTENT

A Reread the text at the beginning of the lesson, and <u>underline</u> the sentences that include reported speech or reported ideas. Which of the sentences have backshifting in the *that* clause? Review the rules of backshifting in the chart below if necessary.

Rules for and Exceptions to Backshifts in Reported Speech

Sample Sentences	Notes
Dr. Clark: "Artificial brains aren't very sophisticated yet, but we have made some progress. By next year our robots will perform much more complex tasks." ↓ Dr. Clark **explained** that artificial brains **weren't** very sophisticated yet and **asserted** that they **had made** some progress. She **predicted** that by next year their robots **would perform** much more complex tasks.	Follow the rule of backshifts when the reporting verb is in the past tense: 1. Shift the tense of the main verb(s) in the *that* clause back "one step" in time. 2. Change modals to corresponding past forms: can → could may → might will → would must → had to
One professor **stated** that the technology **is** also available to manufacturers of industrial robots.	It isn't necessary to use backshifts in *that* clauses when the statement expresses: • an action or situation that is true and not temporary • information that people consider a general truth • an action or situation that was communicated to the speaker very shortly before the current conversation
Before the age of artificial intelligence, no one **denied** that man **is** the most intelligent being on Earth.	
Dr. Thurmond's students just **informed** her that their project **went** perfectly earlier that afternoon.	
Later, Kelly told Dr. Thurmond that the project **took** about 5 hours to finish.	English-speakers often ignore the backshift rule if: • it requires a verb in **past perfect** • the information and time context are clear without a backshift • it causes a change in meaning in modal verbs of probability
Kelly also mentioned that her team **prepared all of the materials and equipment the day before** to make it go smoothly.	
Kelly pointed out that they **may not have solved** all the problems in their project.	

B Read each situation below. Why wasn't the rule of backshifting followed? Write an explanation in the space provided. Follow the example.

1. Pat has just arrived at the computer lab late. She asked her lab partner for their latest assignment. Steve told her that they have to check the movement of the robotic arm.

   Steve probably found out right before Pat arrived that they have to check the robotic arm. There's no need to backshift because it happened so recently.

2. In response to the NASA disaster, one commentator wrote that people aren't robots and that they make mistakes.

   _____

   _____

3. Scientists have struggled to make humanoid robots walk upright because the researchers found that maintaining balance is not an easy feat.

   _____

   _____

4. Competitors in the "Great Robot Race" acknowledged that they spent a lot of time on upgrading the sensors in the vehicles before the race.

   _____

   _____

5. Near the end of the Great Robot Race, the MIT team didn't hear the final update. Someone among the spectators told them that the Stanford vehicle took the lead at milepost 139.

   _____

   _____

6. Dr. Morasev confidently predicts that robots will be able to reason in our lifetimes. He has written that computers can already perform many tasks more accurately than humans.

   _____

   _____

7. The NASA engineers and computer scientists were extremely relieved when they saw that the Mars rover landed safely on the surface and began moving forward.

   _____

   _____

8. For centuries people believed that our ability to think and communicate defines us as humans. Now, however, computers are rapidly developing those same skills.

   _____

   _____

C Listen to each statement and (circle) the letter of the sentence that correctly restates the information with reported speech. It's possible that more than one paraphrase is correct. In such cases, (circle) the letter of both sentences.

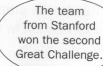

The team from Stanford won the second Great Challenge.

1. a. He said that the team from Stanford won the second Great Challenge.
   b. He said that the team from Stanford had won the second Great Challenge.

2. a. He said that hospitals use robots to transport medical supplies and deliver meals.
   b. He said that hospitals used robots to transport medical supplies and deliver meals.

3. a. He says robots can vacuum rugs without hitting furniture.
   b. He says robots could vacuum rugs without hitting furniture.

4. a. She said that many movie robots had become famous.
   b. She said that many movie robots have become famous.

5. a. She stated scientists are working on robots in the shapes of animals.
   b. She stated scientists were working on robots in the shapes of animals.

6. a. He stated that after our disappointing results, we must think about the future of intelligent robots.
   b. He stated that after their disappointing results, they had to think about the future of intelligent robots.

7. a. They say that in a few years driverless vehicles will move more quickly over rough terrain.
   b. They say that in a few years driverless vehicles would move more quickly over rough terrain.

8. a. He said that some people use the word "bot" as a nickname for robots.
   b. He said that some people used the word "bot" as a nickname for robots.

9. a. Experts say that robots may change human civilization.
   b. Experts say that robots might change human civilization.

D Find and correct the four errors in the following e-mail message.

Hey!

I'm so sick of working on our bot. Dr. T. says we had to find the solution to the sensor malfunction by Friday. I don't think that we would figure it out for at least another week. I'm so tired that I can't see straight!! But Dr. T. said, that we can kiss our spring break good-bye if we don't get some results soon.

Can you believe it? Our plane tickets to Orlando are non-refundable, right? Can you double-check the website? I think it says that tickets were non-refundable AND that no changes can be made.

Later-
Carl

E Look at the dialog on page 244. In the spaces provided report on four statements made by Tish and/or Oleg. Follow the example.

1. _Tish said that she has been waiting to see the program since she first heard about it._

2. _____

3. _____

4. _____

5. _____

■ COMMUNICATE

F **GROUP WORK** In a group, talk about robots that you have seen in films. What were the robots' special abilities? What role did they play in the plot? When you are finished, summarize your discussion for the class.

Several people in our group said that they love the movie *Star Wars*.

Robots played a big role in that movie. Maria pointed out that R2D2 saved his robot friend C-3PO several times.

GRAMMAR AND VOCABULARY Write a composition on one of the topics below. Use as many words as possible from the Content Vocabulary on page 243. Use sentences with reported speech and ideas with *that* clauses to express some of your ideas.

Topic 1: Many people adapt easily to technological change; however, others fear our growing dependence on computers and artificial intelligence in every aspect of our lives. Explain the opinions and attitudes of someone you know who criticizes this dependence. What has that person told you or expressed to you about these issues?

Topic 2: Every year new models of automobiles include more sensors and more sophisticated computers. In previous years, what did car companies claim that their cars could do? What did they announce that the new models would do? What kind of innovations do you predict the companies will produce in their vehicles in the next 15 years?

PROJECT Interview a student on your campus about robots. Find out the student's opinion regarding the following:

    a. What can robots do? Where do robots work right now?
    b. How much should we depend on robots in the future?
    c. Will robots be a danger to humans in the future?

Tell your classmates the results of your interview.

 INTERNET Go to the website www.thetech.org/robotics. Select one of the many video clips on this site. Watch the video and then prepare to report on three things that the speaker said. Be sure that you tell the name of the person and the exact title and website of the video when you present your information.

PART 1
Reported Speech: Paraphrases
with Infinitives and Gerunds

PART 2
Reported Speech and Thought:
Passive Forms

Lesson 24

Art History: Symbols and Allegories

■ CONTENT VOCABULARY

Look up the words below that you do not know and enter them in your vocabulary journal.
Write each word's part of speech, a definition, and an example sentence. Try to include them
in your discussion and writing below.

aesthetically	to commission	to disregard	perspective
affluence	to connote	an exhibit	a pigment
ambiguous	to depict	to grasp	transience

■ THINK ABOUT IT

Look at the painting on the next page and discuss its meaning with a partner. Do you like it?
Do you understand it? Do any flowers have a special meaning or symbolism in your culture?
Discuss your ideas with a classmate.

In your writing journal, write for five minutes about the questions below. When you are
finished, share your ideas with the class.

What would you tell a foreign visitor about the art from your country or culture? How can
foreign visitors understand what they see in a painting or other piece of art?

■ GRAMMAR IN CONTENT

CD2,TR47

A Read and listen to the passage below. The words in bold in the text are infinitive or gerund phrases used for reporting speech.

Art History and Cultural Context

To the modern eye, European paintings of tulips and other flowers of the sixteenth and seventeenth centuries may seem like pretty pictures of springtime blossoms; however, many of those flowers had a deeper significance to the viewers of those days. For example, tulips were known to symbolize a cautionary story of extravagance and foolishness to the Dutch.

Tulips arrived in Europe from Turkey in the 1500s and became popular among the rich, who could afford to have gardens. In the Middle East, especially Persia, the tulip symbolized love, but in the context of Protestant Holland the tulip gained quite different connotations. As wealthy Dutchmen developed more and more tulip varieties, the flower came to symbolize affluence. Tulip prices rose, and by the 1620s the Dutch obsession with tulips had led to an incredibly speculative market for tulip bulbs. It is said that the average annual wage in Holland at that time was 200–400 guilders, and a single *Semper augustus* tulip (with red flames on white petals) could cost 1,000 guilders. Many middle-class Dutchmen entered the tulip market, hoping to make a fortune. As the market rose, religious leaders **warned their congregations not to risk their financial and spiritual lives on a mere flower.** When the market crashed, the tulip also became a symbol of human foolishness and vanity.

Tulips, Lilies, Irises and Roses
by Anthony Claesz (1592–1635).

Those who resisted the temptation of the tulip trade often **asked artists to create paintings of flowers** that were valued so highly at the time. During the 1500s and 1600s, the Dutch and other Europeans believed that nature taught valuable lessons about God and creation. Religious leaders **recommended reading nature as a book** filled with lessons about and from God. Therefore, naturalistic paintings of flowers could be considered not only as beautifully realistic arrangements of vivid colors and shapes, but also as a collection of lessons or reminders. Obviously, a vase of cut flowers can signify the transience of life regardless of the flower varieties in the arrangement. In those days, lilies represented purity or justice to the Dutch, and violets were known to connote sweetness and modesty.

As products of their own time and culture, painters express their ideas and emotions with images that their viewers are able to grasp and appreciate. In seventeenth-century Holland, artists created still life paintings for the enjoyment and moral education of people in their own society. Art historians **advise learning about Dutch attitudes and beliefs** if modern viewers truly wish to understand those paintings. Similarly, artists from Islamic, Buddhist, Confucian, or other religious traditions have created images based on their beliefs, histories, literature, and natural surroundings. The same holds true for artists from any other time or background. It has been said that art is a universal language, but the message can't be completely clear until we learn to interpret artists' images appropriately.

a cautionary story: a story with a warning

Protestant: in this context, any European Christian not belonging to the Roman Catholic Church

a speculative market: business deals in which there is a chance of great profit or loss

a congregation: people who regularly worship at a particular church or synagogue

vanity: excessive pride

naturalistic: realistic, close to nature

Sample Sentences	Notes
Museum guard: "Check your bags in the coat room." The museum guard **told** the visitors **to check** their bags in the coat room.	Use infinitive complements to report: • Imperatives: *say, tell, order, command* • Invitations: *ask* + **object** + **infinitive** • Requests: *ask* + **object** + **infinitive** • Asking permission: *ask* + **infinitive**
Sean: "Would you like to come to the exhibit on Islamic art, Na Rae?" Sean **asked** Na Rae **to go** to the art exhibit.	Use *order* and *command* for imperatives to emphasize the authority of the speaker. Use one of these basic patterns:
Na Rae: "Sean, can you save me a seat?" Na Rae **asked** Sean **to save** her a seat.	• *tell* + **object** + **infinitive** • *say* + **infinitive**
Na Rae: "Sean, can I bring my cousin?" Na Rae **asked to bring** her cousin.	
Na Rae: "Pick up my cousin after work." Na Rae **said to pick up** her cousin.	
"You had better take careful notes on the lecture." Harry warned **that I should take** notes. Harry warned **me to take** careful notes.	When reporting speech, English speakers often select a main verb that expresses how they interpret the information or the speaker's intention. Use an infinitive (or in some cases a gerund) complement to paraphrase the direct speech instead of a *that* clause for variety in your English.
"Don't forget to bring the museum catalog to class." Susie reminded me **that I was supposed to bring** the catalog to class. Susie **reminded me to bring** the catalog to class.	The following verbs take an infinitive complement: *agree, claim, command, demand, order, promise, refuse, remind, say, tell, warn*.
"I swear that I didn't photograph the painting." Will **denied that he had photographed** the painting. Will **denied having photographed** the painting.	The following verbs may take a gerund complement: *advise, admit, confess, deny, mention, propose, recommend, suggest*.

B Read over your journal entry, and <u>underline</u> at least one sentence that you can revise to include a gerund or infinitive phrase used for reporting speech. Write your revised sentence(s) below.

_____

_____

_____

_____

C Match the quotes to the verbs that describe your interpretation of Carla's words. Carla is speaking to Brent, her partner on a multimedia art project.

_f_	1.	"Don't worry, I'll do it."	a.	confess
___	2.	"I wouldn't do it like that if I were you."	b.	request
___	3.	"I insist on doing it!!"	c.	agree
___	4.	"No way am I going to do it like that."	d.	warn
___	5.	"How about doing it this way?"	e.	claim
___	6.	"Sorry, I did it the other way."	f.	~~promise~~
___	7.	"Sure. No problem."	g.	demand
___	8.	"You should do it the other way."	h.	admit
___	9.	"I didn't do it the right way."	i.	refuse
___	10.	"I did it better than you."	j.	recommend

D Change the quoted comments below to reported speech using a main verb that expresses your interpretation of the speaker's message. Use one of the verbs in the box below.

advise	confess	ask	mention	~~recommend~~
warn	claim	demand	remind	promise

1. **Dr. Azzam:** It would be a good idea for all of you to read about how Asian artists represented longevity and the transience of life.
   Monique: Dr. Azzam, would you mind giving us the page numbers of that section in our textbook?

   Dr. Azzam recommended reading about how Asian artists symbolized longevity and the transience of life. Then, Monique asked him to give them the page numbers of that section in their textbook.

2. **Dr. Azzam:** I am going to include European and Asian flower symbols on the next test.
   Monique: Dr. Azzam, I don't really know where to find information about symbols.
   Dr. Azzam: You should be able to get that information in the readings on reserve in the library.

   _____

   _____

   _____

3. **Monique:** I don't really have time to go to the library.
   Dr. Azzam: Don't forget that you need to do the homework reading if you want to pass.
   Monique: OK, Dr. Azzam. I'll do it this weekend.

   _____

   _____

   _____

4. **Dr. Azzam:** In our next class, I'll cover mythological figures in Islamic, Asian, and European art, so all of you should have read Chapter 7 by then.

   _____

   _____

   _____

E On a separate sheet of paper, restate Professor MacDougall's instructions according to the notes below.

Due: next Friday – deliver to Art Department by 3:00 BUT if there's
a problem, 5:00 is the final deadline; no email attachments
Topic: comparison of a symbol in Islamic and Asian art -examples =
animals (cats, dragon) flowers
Length: 12-15 pages – double space, Times New Roman or similar font
Bibliography required - not just internet resources

F Use a variety of forms of reported speech to summarize the short conversations that took place in Professor Cruz's art history class.

1. **Dr. Cruz:** Take a look at the flowers on this Japanese scroll. Can everyone see them?

   She said to take a look at the flowers on the Japanese scroll and asked if everyone
   could see them.

2. **Johanna:** Can you explain the meaning of the chrysanthemum on the scroll again?
   Dr. Cruz: Certainly. In Japanese art, this flower signifies sun and life.

   _____

   _____

3. **Dr. Cruz:** Johanna, please don't forget to study the meanings of these flowers.
Johanna: I'll study them again tonight.
Dr. Cruz: Don't just memorize them. Learn them in the context of a particular piece of art. You'll remember them better that way.

_____

_____

4. **Dr. Cruz:** Who knows the meaning of the chrysanthemum in Chinese art? Philippe?
Philippe: Sorry, Professor Cruz, I haven't read about the flower symbols yet.
Dr. Cruz: I'm disappointed in these responses. You need to spend more time on these assignments.

_____

_____

5. **Marina:** Could we have a review session on the symbols? It would be a big help.
Dr. Cruz: We can't spend more class time on these symbols. Next week we have to move on to allegorical figures.

_____

_____

6. **Dr. Cruz:** I'd be willing to have an extra review class if there's interest. Would any of you come?
Philippe: Absolutely.
Johanna: Great.
Marina: I'll be there.

_____

_____

■ COMMUNICATE

G **PAIR WORK** Role-play a problem between two students who are working together on a class presentation. Choose two of the types of interactions listed below to include in your mini-drama:

- denial
- refusal
- confession
- warning
- demand

Then, perform your role-play for another pair, who will then summarize it for the class.

Did you remember to bring last week's notes so that I can copy them?

I never said that I would bring the notes. I thought _you_ were going to bring the notes.

■ GRAMMAR IN CONTENT

A Reread the text on page 254 and <u>underline</u> sentences with main verbs that express speaking or thinking. Do not underline sentences that already have words in boldface. Then, analyze the structure of the main verb and compare your analysis with a partner's.

Reported Speech and Thought: Passive Forms

Sample Sentences	Notes
It is said that Dutch tulips are even more beautiful today than they were in the 1600s.	Use a passive main verb for reporting speech or thoughts when the context is formal and the source of the information is not unknown or unimportant:
It has been suggested that the flowers in Dutch paintings don't all have symbolic meanings.	*It* + passive verb + *that* + reported information
It is reported that some tulip bulbs were worth their weight in gold; thus, it was much cheaper to commission a famous artist to paint a picture of tulips than to own the bulbs.	As in many English sentences, the new (and important) information comes at the end of the sentence. Using the word *it* as the grammatical subject is one way to allow the important information to come last.
It could be argued that American floral paintings were influenced more by Asian styles than by the Dutch.	
Birds and animals **are also known to have** different connotations; for example, the crane signifies longevity in Japanese art and vigilance in European art.	Use an infinitive complement with the verbs below when: • the main verb is in passive form • the agent or subject of the infinitive is also the subject of the main verb
	Subject + passive verb + infinitive complement
The unicorn, the mythical animal with one horn, **was understood to have been** a symbol of courtly love in medieval Europe.	
Impressionists **are said to have painted** their famous flower pictures without any thought of symbolism.	A perfective infinitive is used to reflect the past time of the action expressed in the infinitive.
People say (that) dragons connote good luck in Chinese art but may represent the devil in European art.	Since English speakers prefer active verbs, a less formal oral alternative form would begin with a phrase such as *People say (that)*.

Verbs Commonly Used in Passive Voice for Reported Speech and Thought

allege	believe	recognize	rumor	think
argue	doubt	report	say	understand
assume	hypothesize	reveal	suggest	

B Change the sentences below to reported speech or thought, disregarding the source of the idea. Use the passive voice, begin each sentence with *It*, and choose the main verb according to the level of certainty of the information.

1. According to experts, animals in European cave art from the Paleolithic Age (32,000 to 11,000 years ago) may have lived in that area.

    It has been suggested that animals in European cave art lived in that area.

2. Researchers are fairly sure that the art also includes imaginary animals like unicorns.

    _____

3. There has been some discussion as to whether ambiguous symbols in the caves also represent animals.

    _____

4. According to one theory in the 1950s, the large number of paintings of horses and bison must have meant that these animals represented the duality of male and female.

    _____

5. According to anthropologists, the red pigment found in Paleolithic cave art has been found in art from the same period around the world.

    _____

6. According to one article, cave artists often redrew pictures on top of the old ones in order to guarantee that the animals returned the next year.

    _____

7. One researcher wondered if cave artists used red pigment in the paintings because it is aesthetically pleasing.

    _____

Guernica symbolizes the chaos and terror of the Spanish Civil War.

C **Edit one of the sentences in each of the texts below, focusing on the information rather than the source of the information. Select main verbs that express the level of certainty of the information.**

1. In addition to images, colors have various connotations. In all cultures people have words for at least three colors: black, white, and red. ~~The assumption of researchers is~~ *Humans are thought to have* ~~that all humans have~~ an emotional reaction to red since it is the color of blood. It may represent life, or as the color of sunrise and sunset it may connote the East or the West.

2. Images of imaginary or mythological creatures can be found in art throughout the world. Although a creature may be frightening to people in one culture, it may be very positive in another cultural context. For example, people interpret the bat as a sign of happiness in China whereas in the European tradition it is connected with darkness and black magic.

3. Groups of images and figures in some works of art may be allegories, or representations of abstract ideas. For instance, artists have often depicted "the four seasons" with four different flowers or other types of plants. Likewise, viewers realized that human or mythological figures represented the four seasons when they were shown doing seasonal tasks.

4. Pablo Picasso's black and white painting *Guernica* (1937) is a modern allegory protesting war. One can see that the work expresses Picasso's outrage at the Nazi's destruction of this Spanish town in 1937. As in a nightmare, the scene contains many images of panic and claustrophobia.

Chinese ceramic teapot,
Kangxi Period (1662–1722).

CD2,TR48

D **Listen to a news conference about the investigation of the theft of a valuable piece of Chinese porcelain. Then, write a short news article about the theft. Use your answers to the questions and the main verbs in the box below to guide your writing.**

doubt	allege	~~say~~	understand
rumor	believe	argue	suggest

1. According to experts, how many Chinese teapots of this type are in U.S. museums?

   This teapot is said to be the only one of its kind in the U.S.

2. What rumors have they heard about porcelain pieces from the Qing period?

   _____

3. What allegations have been made about a collector in California?

   _____

4. What do curators agree on?

   _____

5. What is there a controversy about?

   _____

6. What have museum employees discussed since the theft?

   _____

E **Find and correct the four errors in the e-mail message below.**

Dear Mom and Dad,

You'll be happy to know that our teacher went with us today to the campus art museum. It seems pretty amazing to me that a university has its own museum. This museum is said that it owns several very valuable small paintings that they rarely show for security reasons.

Our instructor asked to go today because they just opened a special exhibit of Native American art from different parts of the U.S. Our instructor suggested to look at the exhibit together so that we could talk about the pieces. It was a great idea. The exhibit was fantastic, but sometimes I had no idea what the pieces really meant. According to Mr. Carson, it can be argue that only Native Americans can truly appreciate the spiritual meaning of their art. Anyway, it was a great afternoon.

Love,
Ken

■ COMMUNICATE

F **GROUP WORK** **Select four of the abstract ideas or themes below and discuss modern symbols in the context of any visual medium, including film. For example, what are some modern symbols of affluence?**

- affluence
- human foolishness
- timeless beauty
- power or strength

- success
- love
- wastefulness
- hope

- friendship
- personal identity
- war and peace
- cultural traditions

When you are finished, report to your class on the results of your discussion.

GRAMMAR AND VOCABULARY Write a composition on one of the topics below. Use as many words as possible from the Content Vocabulary on page 253. Use sentences with reported speech and thought to express some of your ideas.

Topic 1: Recall and recreate a conversation that you had with someone who spent too much money on a hobby or a fad. (A fad is a product line or activity that is extremely popular but only for a short time.) What did you recommend doing? How much did the person admit spending on the hobby or fad? What did you remind the person to do? What did that person agree to do?

Topic 2: Select a symbol that evokes a strong response from people in your country or culture. Describe the image or object, and then explain what it is believed to show or what is it said to represent. Be as specific as possible.

PROJECT Interview at least one student on your campus about visiting art museums and galleries. Find out the following information, and give a brief oral report on the information in your next class meeting.

    a. Where does your interviewee recommend going to see good art in your city or area?

    b. How often does your interviewee actually go to local galleries or museums?

    c. When your interviewee travels in the U.S. or abroad, does he or she go to art museums or galleries? Why or why not?

    d. What does your interviewee know about art in your culture?

 INTERNET Go online and use the search term "vanitas symbols in paintings." Look at two or three paintings, including a modern painting, on different websites, and make a list of different symbols that you find. Be prepared to give your interpretation of a few symbols in the paintings.

Public Health: Vaccines and Immunization

■ CONTENT VOCABULARY

Look up the words and phrases below that you do not know and enter them in your vocabulary journal. Write each word's part of speech, a definition, and an example sentence. Try to include them in your discussion and writing below.

an antiseptic	a dose	a pandemic	to swell
a campaign/drive	infectious	a quarantine	a syringe
to dispose of	a medical practice	to sterilize	a vial

■ THINK ABOUT IT

What do you know about diphtheria, polio, and hepatitis? What causes somebody to become ill with one of these diseases, and how can it be prevented? Discuss your ideas with a classmate.

In your writing journal, write for 5–10 minutes about the questions below. When you are finished, share what you wrote with the class.

What kinds of vaccinations have you had in your life? Approximately how old were you when you were vaccinated? Why did your parents think that those vaccinations were important? Have you had any vaccinations in the last few years? If so, why?

■ GRAMMAR IN CONTENT

A Read and listen to the passage below. The sentences in bold in the text include *that* clauses with subjunctive verb forms.

CD2,TR49

TO: Members of the Vaccination Team
FROM: Karin O'Malley, District Supervisor
RE: Upcoming Vaccination Campaigns

We have received confirmation from local public health officials that our immunization drive will receive widespread publicity in the weeks before your arrival. **Some weeks ago I urged that the local clinic in each region begin a word-of-mouth campaign.** Our public health colleagues will also have posters and leaflets printed so that nurses can distribute them in the clinics and in schools. As with all of our vaccination campaigns, we cannot make the people participate in the vaccinations, but we hope that they will want to bring their children to the clinics. **Also, it is crucial that local town officials be informed of our visits so that there is no unnecessary red tape.** We have learned on other vaccination drives that we have to get all local VIPs to see our program as something positive instead of as a criticism of their local health care.

It is imperative that each member of the team supervise the local health workers and not assume that the workers know the safest way to give injections. Have one member of the team serve as the equipment manager. That person should dispose of the syringes and bottles of vaccine personally. **I highly recommend that the equipment manager check your stock of puncture-resistant boxes.** On one occasion, another team discovered that their inventory of equipment did not contain a sufficient number of boxes for the number of immunizations that they actually administered. **Remember, it is preferable that a health worker be offended by our caution and supervision** than for that person to have a needle-prick injury.

You face a special challenge in keeping the vaccines cold enough. According to the manufacturer's instructions, the vaccine vials must be kept at 2–8 degrees C. Once the vials have been unloaded at the airport, **it is essential that one of you monitor the cold packs.** Local daytime temperatures range from 25–30 degrees C right now, so there is a real risk to the vaccine if you are not careful.

Finally, the local clinics have agreed to let you stay in the staff dormitories. This arrangement should help you to stay on schedule. We anticipate that people will respond better to our campaign this year. Consequently, **it's quite important that you be close to the clinics** so that you can maximize the number of immunizations at each site. Also, we will have the vaccine delivered to you at some of the sites, so you need to be on hand to receive it.

Best wishes.

---

word-of-mouth: an informal person-to-person means of communication

a leaflet: a flier of information for free distribution to the public

red tape: bureaucratic paperwork and restrictions

a VIP: a Very Important Person

to administer: to give, to dispense

to be on hand: to be available, to be on-site

Sample Sentences	**Notes**
Dr. Larson insists that her nurse **dispose** of any used syringe immediately.	Express potential control or influence over another person's actions after these verbs:
	suggest, propose weak control
Schools in my town have always required that parents **show** their children's vaccination records before the children can start school.	*recommend* *ask, request* *insist, urge* *demand, require* strong control
Why did the nurse suggest that I **lie down** before she gave me an injection?	Use a *that* clause with verbs in this group. Follow special rules for the *that* clause:
I asked that my doctor **not give** me the shot in my left arm since I'm left-handed.	• Use only the base form of the verb, even for the main verb *be*. • Use *not* without an auxiliary to express negation before the verb.
Do doctors recommend that patients **be vaccinated** against tetanus every 5 years?	• Do not use modals. • Use the base form for passive constructions.
It's advisable that you **not go** to areas where you might catch yellow fever.	As a result of these rules, the verb in the *that* clause does not express singular/plural subject-verb agreement (or time).
Is it really necessary that all children **be vaccinated** against chicken pox?	Follow the same rule for subjunctive complements with certain main-clause adjectives. Like the verbs above, these adjectives express a desire to control or influence the actions in the *that* clause.
It wasn't really urgent that the child **receive** a flu shot, but it seemed like a good idea.	
It may be desirable that everyone on campus **get** a flu shot this year.	*advisable* weaker *desirable, preferable* *important* *necessary, imperative* *urgent, essential, crucial, vital* stronger

B Read over your journal entry, and <u>underline</u> at least one sentence that you can revise to include a verb or adjective listed above plus a *that* clause with a subjunctive verb form. Write your revised sentence(s) below.

_____

_____

_____

_____

C Paraphrase each directly quoted sentence using one of the main verbs requiring a subjunctive *that* clause.

~~ask~~	insist	recommend	require	urge
demand	propose	request	suggest	

1. **School Nurse:** "Please stand in line and don't be impatient. OK, Jeff, can you please roll up your sleeve?"

   The school nurse asked that the children stand in line and not be impatient.

   Then, she requested that Jeff roll up his sleeve.

2. **School Principal:** "Mr. Grant, you have to bring Tyree's immunization record to our office. You should consult your family doctor about Tyree's records."

   _____

   _____

3. **Nurse:** "Dr. Tang, it would be a lot easier if everyone with the flu sits in one section of the waiting room."

   Dr. Tang: "All right. Dr. Jackson, you need to separate the flu patients from the others."

   Dr. Jackson: "Right away."

   _____

   _____

4. **Emergency Room Client:** "Nurse, you need to examine my daughter right away."

   Nurse: "Sir, please don't be worried."

   _____

   _____

D Match the speakers and their messages. Then write a sentence that identifies the speaker and expresses his or her message with the appropriate main verb and a subjunctive *that* clause. Follow the example.

X. Director, World Health Organization (WHO)
2. Aid worker for WHO
3. Director, U.S. Centers for Disease Control (CDC)
4. CDC agent
5. Head of Security, Chicago's O'Hare Airport
6. Delta Airways flight attendant
7. Director of your school's student clinic
8. Nurse in your school clinic

X. Avian flu vaccine should be available more cheaply in the Third World.
b. Every student should leave campus.
c. Residents of Houston should be quarantined to avoid catching the bird flu.
d. Every student should get a flu shot.
e. Anybody with suspicious symptoms should be examined at the airport.
f. Everyone in the neighborhood should test the water for contamination.
g. The last vaccine vial should be used for the children in the village.
h. The passenger in 15D should be re-seated in an area away from the others.

1. *The director of WHO has urged that avian flu vaccine be available more cheaply in the Third World.*

2. _____

3. _____

4. _____

5. _____

6. _____

7. _____

8. _____

E Determine the relative importance of the vaccination procedures below. Use an appropriate adjective and subjunctive *that* clause to express your opinion about the degree of importance. Follow the example, and note that some procedures may be of more or less the same importance.

✔	put antiseptic on injection site
_____	use cotton swab with antiseptic
_____	know patient's family medical history
_____	don't use syringe more than once
_____	dispose of syringe in safety box
_____	inform patients about possible reactions
_____	don't leave vaccine in warm place
_____	store vaccine appropriately
_____	use sterile equipment
_____	share information about low risks of vaccines

1. _____ It's crucial that a health worker put an antiseptic on the injection site. _____

2. _____

3. _____

4. _____

5. _____

6. _____

7. _____

8. _____

9. _____

10. _____

■ **COMMUNICATE**

F **WRITE** Imagine that doctors have confirmed that two students on your campus have the measles. What should the school do so that no one else catches this contagious disease? List five or six recommendations using subjunctive verbs, and then share your ideas with the class.

■ GRAMMAR IN CONTENT

A Reread the memo at the beginning of this lesson, and <u>underline</u> all of the clauses with the main verbs *cause, make, have, let, get,* or *help*. Compare your answers with a partner.

Causative Verbs	
Sample Sentences	**Notes**
Don't **let** the syringe **touch** anything!	Use *cause, get, make, have, let,* and *help* with **infinitive complements** to express causation. In this construction, the direct object is an agent or doer of the action expressed by the infinitive.
A flu shot may **cause** your **upper arm to be** sore for a few days. How did you **get** Billy **to stop** crying after his immunizations this afternoon? I should **get** my daughter **vaccinated** before school starts.	*Cause* and *get* take a **direct object** followed by an **infinitive phrase**. With *get,* the main subject encounters difficulty and must convince or force the subject of the infinitive. When using a **passive complement** with *get,* omit *to* and the passive auxiliary *be.* In such sentences, the agent of the action is often unstated or implied.
The U.S. Food and Drug Administration **makes drug manufacturers do** extensive testing on vaccines. **Health authorities** can **make citizens** with a dangerous infectious disease **stay** in restricted areas.	*Make, have,* and *let* take a **direct object** followed by a **bare infinitive phrase**. With *make,* the **main subject** has some kind of power over the **subject** of the **infinitive**. Coercion or the potential use of force is implied.
The doctor **had me roll up** my sleeve before she gave me the shot. Dr. Hearn **has children weighed** before he sees them.	With *have,* the **main subject** has some kind of authority or power over the **direct object** of the verb. Use passive complements with *have* following the same rules as with *get.* Use **passive complements** for *have* and *get* when the participle is preceded by a **direct object**.
Could you **help** the **nurse (to) give** some shots?	*Help* takes a **direct object** followed by an **infinitive phrase** or a **bare infinitive**.

B (Circle) the causative verb appropriate to the context and give the reason for your choice. Both options may be appropriate in some contexts.

1. An experienced health worker ((had)/ made) the mother hold her son for his injection.

    REASON: _A health worker doesn't have the power to force a mother to hold her son._ _She can ask, but she can't make her do it._

2. One of the nurses (had / made) the unruly children stand in line.

    REASON: _____

3. Dr. Dayton usually (has / makes) his nurses prepare 100 doses of vaccine at a time.

    REASON: _____

4. One mother (had / made) her oldest child watch several other children so that she could sleep for a little while.

    REASON: _____

5. Has Dr. Dayton ever (had / made) the people in line wait while he eats lunch?

    REASON: _____

6. Parents don't (have / make) their children keep quiet while they are waiting in line.

    REASON: _____

7. The health organization (has / makes) the staff keep strict records of the vaccines because they need to have up-to-date information on their inventory of medicines.

    REASON: _____

8. The team supervisor (has / makes) the local workers dispose of used syringes according to strict guidelines.

    REASON: _____

C Paraphrase each of the sentences with one of the causative verbs in this lesson. Follow the example.

1. My last flu shot brought about swelling in my arm.

   My last flu shot caused my arm to swell./My last flu shot made my arm swell.

2. Nurse Flint didn't allow the student nurse to give any injections.

3. Nurse Villalobos told little Vicki to swallow the sugar cube with the polio vaccine.

4. After many attempts, Dr. Quiller finally persuaded little Nick to sit quietly for his shot.

5. When it's time for their flu shots, Mrs. Upton usually forces her son to go first so that he doesn't get too scared.

6. Has your doctor ever told you to sign a form before you got a shot?

7. The injection couldn't have resulted in the swelling because my arm was sore before I went to the doctor's.

8. Dr. Thomason asked her nurse to call Clark Jones because she was worried about a possible allergic reaction.

9. Nurse Higgins sometimes gives children a piece of candy after a shot because it causes them to feel better.

10. Nurse Higgins finally convinced the people in the waiting room to stop complaining after she told them that the doctor had left for an emergency.

11. Dr. Franklin has always paid the DisposMed Company to pick up the medical waste from his medical practice daily.

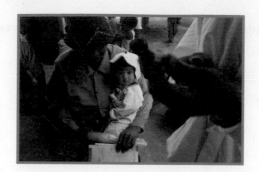

D <u>Underline</u> the five sentences that can be edited to include a passive complement for the main verb *have* or *get*. Make the changes, and explain why the change is appropriate. The first sentence has been underlined and corrected for you.

<u>WHO may have field workers vaccinate hundreds of people in one day.</u> First, some health workers get all of the people to sign their health forms. When that formality is finished, the team usually wants to have everyone sit down in the shade. While the crowd is sitting, someone gets the field supervisor to make an announcement about their procedures and instructions. At this point, they have a local person translate the instructions to the crowd. When the team is ready, they get some people to carry elderly patients into the clinic first. Meanwhile, local nurses get the little children to play together in a shady area.

At the end of the day, the field supervisor has someone put the vaccines back in the coolers and sterilize the equipment for the next day. The next day the staff will have someone explain the procedures again before they start.

1. _____WHO may have hundreds of people vaccinated in one day._____

   REASON: _There are two direct objects, and the agent of "vaccinate" is obvious._

2. _____

   REASON: _____

3. _____

   REASON: _____

4. _____

   REASON: _____

5. _____

   REASON: _____

E Listen to the health team as they plan to set up their immunization clinic. Tell the actions of the people in parentheses in sentences with causal verbs.

CD2,TR50

1. (Maria, Jim) _Maria had Jim carry the five coolers into the clinic._

2. (Maria, Larry) _____

3. (Maria, Barbara) _____

4. (Larry, Jim) _____

5. (Barbara, Jim) _____

6. (Jim, Larry, Maria) _____

F Find and correct the four errors in the e-mail message below.

Hi Judy-

Your e-mail made me to laugh so hard. Your stories about life as a WHO nurse bring tears – sometimes of laughter and sometimes of sadness. How do you keep your sense of humor?

I still can't believe that some little kids die of diseases that kids here never even catch. You should have one of your co-workers taken a few photos of you and some of those kids. Then, you could send them to some nonprofit organizations and maybe get some more money for medicines. (I'd suggest that you do not send one of those to your mother. She would be so upset. She would worry about you even more than she does now!)

By the way, be sure that you keep e-mailing her, too. It's pretty important that she receives an e-mail from you regularly. If not, she calls me and asks what's going on.

Cheers!
Lynell

■ COMMUNICATE

G **PAIR WORK** Public health officials are very concerned about the possible outbreak of a flu pandemic. In such circumstances what power and authority do health officials have? What can they have us do to prevent a pandemic? What can they make us do in case a pandemic breaks out? Brainstorm answers to these questions with your partner and then share them with your classmates.

Officials would probably have us store food and other supplies, don't you think?

I would hope so. They might even make schools close.

GRAMMAR AND VOCABULARY Write a composition on one of the topics below. Use as many words as possible from the Content Vocabulary on page 265. Use sentences with subjunctive complements and causative verbs to express some of your ideas.

Topic 1: What do you recommend that school authorities do if many students at your school got an infectious disease? What should they have the students and their families do? What is essential that every student do? Give your proposals and recommendations.

Topic 2: When an outbreak of any serious infectious disease occurs, the risk to people in other parts of the world is much greater than it used to be. The ease of international travel and the interaction of people from around the globe make the spread of disease more likely. What can we do to prevent a pandemic? What should the authorities make citizens do? What is advisable and crucial in the first days and weeks? What can the authorities insist that every traveler do?

PROJECT Interview at least two students on your campus about childhood diseases. Find out the following information, and give a brief oral report on the responses at your next class meeting.

    a. Which childhood diseases (measles, mumps, chickenpox) did your interviewee have?
    b. What did your interviewees' parents insist that they do?
    c. What did your interviewees' parents have them eat?

 INTERNET Go online to the website http://wwwn.cdc.gov/travel/contentVaccinations.aspx. Choose one part of the world and check the immunizations that the U.S. Centers for Disease Control recommend for travelers. Report on the recommendations in class, and be ready to describe briefly any disease that may be a threat to travelers in that area.

A Change each of the quotes to reported speech in sentence a. Then, paraphrase the quote with a complement following the main verb provided in sentence b.

1. "Bob, you have to practice serving the ball."

   a. Bob's tennis coach warned him *that he had to practice serving the ball.*

   b. Bob's coach insisted *he practice serving the ball.*

2. "Your foot touches the line every time you serve."

   a. His coach stated _____

   b. His coach has observed _____

3. "I videotaped you when you were playing doubles with Nick."

   a. The coach told Bob _____

   b. The coach taped Bob _____

4. "I was able to see clearly how you put a top spin on many of your balls."

   a. The coach commented _____

   b. On the videotape, the coach caught Bob _____

5. "I'll try harder to control the spin that I put on the balls."

   a. Bob said _____

   b. Bob promised _____

6. "You should practice at least 3 hours every day."

   a. The coach warned him _____

   b. According to the coach, it is essential _____

7. "Nick, can you show Bob how you serve the ball?"

   a. The coach asked Nick _____

   b. The coach had Nick _____

B (Circle) the correct form of the adjective.

1. We listened to a (fascinating / fascinated) lecture on documentaries produced in various countries.

2. The lecturer showed some (amazing / amazed) scenes from films made on location in remote areas of the world.

3. I'll always remember the (amazing / amazed) expressions on peoples' faces when they saw themselves on these films. They couldn't believe their eyes!

4. In one (frightening / frightened) scene, some children were being chased by a wild dog.

5. Luckily, an adult shouted quite loudly at the dog, and the (scaring / scared) dog ran away.

6. In another scene, an (exciting / excited) person ran to the filmmakers and led them to a small hut where a baby had just been born.

7. Some of the people inside the hut were (annoying / annoyed) because they didn't think that the outsiders should be there.

8. The (interesting / interested) filmmakers wanted to continue filming but decided it would be better to leave.

LEARNER LOG Check (✔) *Yes* or *I Need More Practice.*

Lesson	I Can Use . . .	Yes	I Need More Practice
21	Participles as Adjectives; Participles in Reduced Adverbial Clauses		
22	Complements of Sensory Verbs; Other Verbs with Participial Complements		
23	Reported Speech and Exceptions to Backshifts in Reported Speech		
24	Reported Speech in Paraphrases with Infinitives and Gerunds; Reported Speech with Passive Forms		
25	Subjunctive Complements and Causative Verbs		

PART 1
It Clefts

PART 2
It in Subject Position with
Adjective Complements

Lesson (26)

Biology: Stress and the Immune System

■ CONTENT VOCABULARY

Look up the words and phrases below that you do not know and enter them in your vocabulary journal. Write each word's part of speech, a definition, and an example sentence. Try to include them in your discussion and writing below.

an antibody	to debilitate	physiological	to suppress
to compromise	a gland	to resist against	to thrive on
to cope with	an immune system	to stimulate	whereas

■ THINK ABOUT IT

Do you know what organs are involved in our bodies' immune systems? Take a look at the illustration on the next page and talk about the function of the organs with a partner. Why are our immune systems important? What can compromise human immune systems? Discuss your ideas with a classmate.

In your writing journal, write for 5–10 minutes about the questions below. When you are finished, share what you wrote with the class.

How does your body react to stress? What stresses you out, and how do you feel when you are in a stressful situation? Does stress ever motivate you?

■ GRAMMAR IN CONTENT

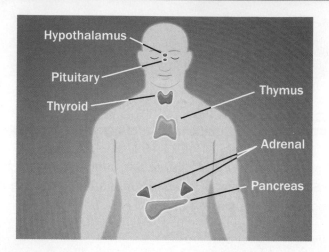

CD2,TR51

A **Read and listen to the passage below. The sentences in bold in the text are sentences with *it* clefts.**

Stress Can Help or Hurt You

While some people seem to thrive on stress, others of us are less productive and even get sick when we are under stress. Both kinds of reactions come from the sophisticated functioning of our immune systems. **It is this system that helps our bodies resist disease, infections, and toxic substances. However, it is also this system that can weaken or debilitate us so that we have lower resistance to the common cold or even cancer.**

Although most people have some inherited immunity against bacteria and viral infections, several glands provide us with additional resistance to disease. T cells, for example, are produced by the thymus gland, which is behind the breastbone. B cells from bone marrow are another important component of the immune system. Together these cells form a potent defense for the body. It has been shown that T cells fight off bacteria, some viral infections, fungi, and cells from transplanted organs, whereas B cells produce antibodies, which are able to fight against foreign substances.

In addition to those two specialized cells, the human immune system relies heavily on the hypothalamic-pituitary-adrenal system. The hypothalamus, located above the roof of the mouth, not only connects to the pituitary gland at the base of the brain but also interacts with most other areas of the brain. **It is from the hypothalamus that the body monitors the concentrations of hormones in the blood.** Certain concentrations of hormones from the pituitary gland can start the body's defense reactions, increase resistance, and speed recovery from infection or injury. For example, the hormone epinephrine, or adrenaline, raises the heart rate and blood pressure and helps to increase the effect of other hormones that are released during a stressful or dangerous situation. However, it is interesting to note that the same hormones that defend the body from attack can also suppress the immune system when they are released in extreme amounts. As a result, the T and B cells may be damaged, for instance, and the body's resistance will be reduced.

Researchers in the field of psychoneuroimmunology seek to understand the sensitive relationship between our immune system and sources of stress in our lives. Some studies have shown that stress can actually enhance our immune systems. **It is not the stress but its nature or duration that determines its negative effect on the immune system.** In other words, an intensely stressful situation or a stressful situation that lasts for a long time will probably have a negative impact on the immune system. It takes more than the typical stresses and strains of modern life for most healthy people to suffer long-term problems.

---

sophisticated: complicated, complex

a fungus; fungi (pl.): a type of organism. Mushrooms are an example of fungi.

a hormone: a substance created by one organ that affects another organ physiologically

bone marrow: the tissue in bones that produces red blood cells

Sample Sentences	Notes
It is our weekly deadline **that** stresses me out. **It's** my boss **who** thrives on stress.	Use *it* clefts to stress or correct one piece of information in the sentence.
Could it be your hectic lifestyle **that** you need to change?	Put the emphasized noun or noun phrase after *it* + *BE*, and explain the noun phrase further with a relative clause: *It* + *is/was* + Noun Phrase + *who/that/Ø* ...
He said that **it was** the coffee **that** made him so nervous.	Follow these restrictions for *it* clefts: • use only the simple tenses of *BE* • use only *who, that,* or *Ø* in the relative clause
It may have been because of the new deadline **that** he was feeling so stressed. **Was it** during the exam **that** he got so nervous? **It was** because he worked under such stress **that** he got sick.	Emphasize or clarify information in structures other than noun phrases in the same way: *It* + *is/was* + Prepositional Phrase + *that* ... *It* + *is/was* + Clause + *that* ...
It's **drinking too much coffee—not** staying up late—that really affects me. It was **because he worked under such stress** that he got sick, **not** because he caught his son's cold. **It isn't the stress but my co-workers** that make me unhappy.	Clarify or correct information by: • giving **the accurate information** and introducing the wrong information with *not*. Use a comma before *not*, or enclose the negative phrase within two dashes. • negating **the mistaken information** and introducing the accurate information with *but.*
In 1932, Walter Cannon, a Harvard University physiologist, introduced stress vocabulary to the scientific world. ↓ **It was Walter Cannon** who introduced stress vocabulary to the scientific world.	You can emphasize your ideas in two ways: • with unusual word order • with a relative clause at the end of the sentence where new or important information is explained These sentences are effective because they are unusual. Use *it* clefts sparingly when writing.

B **Read over your journal entry, and <u>underline</u> at least one sentence that you can revise to include an *it* cleft. Write your revised sentence(s) below.**

_____

_____

_____

C Complete the sentences below; then, use an *it* cleft to emphasize the information that you added to each sentence.

1. Stress sometimes affects _____my stomach_____. (part of your body)

   _____It's my stomach that stress sometimes affects._____

2. I don't enjoy _____ (activity), and sometimes it really stresses me out.

   _____

3. I feel the most stress _____. (location of an activity)

   _____

4. This class sometimes stresses me out _____. (reason)

   _____

5. I get almost sick from stress _____. (time/duration)

   _____

6. I feel a lot of stress _____. (time clause)

   _____

7. I think _____ (person) is very stressed out right now.

   _____

D Correct the students' statements on the next page using the study notes below.

Name of Gland	Location	Function
pituitary	attached to floor of brain by thin stalk	growth of bone & muscle; stimulates other glands; affects general metabolism
thyroid	2 lobes; along side of trachea	regulates metabolic rate
parathyroid	4 glands; on thyroid lobes near the trachea	metabolism of calcium & phosphorus → bones
pancreas	near liver	produces insulin → carbohydrate, fat & protein metabolism
adrenal	near kidneys	produces steroids & epinephrine (increases blood sugar)

1. **Instructor:** Kim, where are the parathyroid glands located?
   Kim: The parathyroid glands are located alongside the trachea.
   Instructor: Juan?

   Juan: _It's the thyroid, not the parathyroid, that is located alongside the trachea._

2. **Instructor:** What does epinephrine affect?
   Justin: Epinephrine affects carbohydrate metabolism.
   Instructor: Akiko?

   Akiko: _____

3. **Instructor:** Which gland produces insulin?
   Marcus: The adrenal gland does.
   Instructor: Benjamin?

   Benjamin: _____

4. **Instructor:** How many lobes does the thyroid consist of?
   Alicia: The thyroid consists of 4 lobes.
   Instructor: Mona?

   Mona: _____

5. **Instructor:** OK, Evan, what does the thyroid regulate?
   Evan: It regulates blood pressure.
   Instructor: Orlando, is that correct?

   Orlando: No, _____

6. **Instructor:** According to your reading, what does the parathyroid regulate?
   Fatima: From what I remember, the parathyroid regulates the metabolism of
   calcium and iron.
   Instructor: Gil, do you agree with that?

   Gil: No, _____

7. **Instructor:** Sandra, where is the parathyroid located in relation to the thyroid?
   Sandra: The parathyroid is located inside the thyroid gland.
   Instructor: Does everyone agree with that?

   Tran: No, _____

8. **Instructor:** Last question. Why is the pancreas important?
   Irena: The pancreas is important for stimulating other glands.
   Instructor: Sorry, Irena. Who can tell her the reason that the pancreas is important?

   Lamar: _____

E (Circle) information in each sentence that you want to emphasize. Use the circled word, phrase, or clause in an *it* cleft structure.

1. Stress can affect (people with asthma,) not those with hay fever.

   It's people with asthma that stress can affect, not those with hay fever.

2. According to research, stress affects the severity of an asthma attack, not the onset of an attack.

   _____

3. Many stress sufferers develop hives.

   _____

4. Stress can cause heart damage because stress-anxiety reactions raise blood pressure.

   _____

5. Researchers point to stress-induced hormone production as another cause of damage to the arteries.

   _____

6. Blood pressure is also related to caffeine consumption.

   _____

7. Some people suffer from stomach ulcers, not from heart problems, when they are under severe stress.

   _____

8. The stomach produces too much acid, and that leads to an irritated stomach lining.

   _____

9. You feel dizzy, have shortness of breath, and your heart pounds when you have an attack of anxiety hyperventilation.

   _____

10. Long-term stress affects the physical health of many people.

   _____

F Identify information that you want to emphasize in each text below. <u>Underline</u> the information, and rewrite the sentence with an *it*-cleft structure.

1. Some of the reactions that people have to stress may also be caused by other factors. <u>Some coffee drinkers experience a rise in blood pressure or more acid in their stomachs due to caffeine.</u> Other people, for example, may have heart trouble because their cholesterol level is too high.

   It's due to caffeine that some coffee drinkers experience a rise in blood pressure or . . .

2. Humans and most animals have an automatic physiological response to danger that stimulates the body functions into hyperactivity. People refer to the "fight or flight" response when they describe the changes that occur in our bodies. Although it helps us to react to danger, this "red alert" condition only lasts a short time.

   _____

3. The body works efficiently to get more oxygen in the blood. For instance, breathing becomes quicker. Then, the heart pumps the blood more rapidly as the blood pressure rises. Extra red blood cells come from the spleen in order to absorb more oxygen.

   _____

4. The body needs glucose in addition to oxygen for energy. The liver changes sugar, which is stored there as glycogen, into glucose. The glucose enters the bloodstream and flows throughout the body for quick energy.

   _____

5. As the blood and glucose circulate, our bodies' senses change in intensity. Our hearing becomes more acute. Our vision becomes more sensitive because our pupils dilate. On the other hand, our brains decrease the feeling of pain.

   _____

■ COMMUNICATE

G **PAIR WORK** With a partner, talk about things that stress you out. Emphasize differences between yourself and your partner by using *it* clefts.

Giving a presentation makes me really uptight and nervous. I'd rather write a paper.

For me it's the exact opposite. **It's not talking in class but writing** that stresses me out.

■ GRAMMAR IN CONTENT

A Reread the text at the beginning of this lesson, and <u>underline</u> any clause with *it* in subject position, except for the boldfaced *it*-cleft sentences.

Review: *It* in Subject Position with Adjective Complements

Sample Sentences	Notes
It's obvious that stress can harm you. **It** must have been annoying that people were talking during the exam. **It** was silly of you to oversleep on the day of your job interview. **It** wasn't easy for us to relax before the exam.	*It* often takes the position of grammatical subjects in English because: • English speakers prefer long or "heavy" grammatical subjects at the end of a sentence • new information typically appears at the end of a sentence Use *it* in subject position in sentences with different types of adjective complements.
It is sad that so many people suffer from stress-related health problems. **Is it really true that** a little stress is a good thing?	Adjectives with *that* clauses include adjectives of emotion and adjectives of truth.
It was wrong of you to procrastinate. ↓ You were wrong to procrastinate. It hasn't been easy for Kim to finish **the project**. ↓ **The project** hasn't been easy for Kim to finish. It's irritating to work with **Judy. Karen** is annoying to work with, too.	Adjective that describes a person's behavior + (*of* + PERSON) + infinitive phrase. As an alternative, use the PERSON as the subject of the sentence and omit *it*. Adjective that describes an experience + (*for* + PERSON) + infinitive phrase. As an alternative, use the **direct object** or **object of the preposition** in the infinitive phrase as the subject and omit *it*. Adjectives that describe an experience include *convenient, difficult, disappointing, easy, embarrassing, fun, (im)possible, interesting,* and *surprising.* See Appendix 2 for a list of adjectives that describe emotion, truth, behavior, and experience.

B Use *it* in subject position to paraphrase the sentences below.

1. Rob was careless to leave the headlights on because now the car battery is dead.

   It was careless of Rob to leave the headlights on because now the battery is dead.

2. The mid-term test results were embarrassing for us to look at.

   _____

3. Two exams in one week are not easy to study for.

   _____

4. Patricia may have been unwise to take 16 credits this semester.

   _____

5. Twins or triplets are probably pretty hard for even the best parents to handle.

   _____

6. My roommate was very generous to offer Evan a place to stay, but we don't have much space in our room.

   _____

7. The project deadline has been alarming for us to think about ever since our boss assigned it.

   _____

8. Wasn't Terry crazy to invite his whole soccer team for dinner this Saturday?

   _____

9. Why is Terry's wife wrong to worry about Saturday's dinner?

   _____

10. Why are the guests going to inconvenience her?

   _____

C What's the difference in meaning between the sentences? In some cases there may be no difference in meaning.

1. a. It was awkward that Terry invited his team for dinner.
   b. It was awkward of Terry to invite his team for dinner.

   DIFFERENCE: _In a. the situation is awkward. In b. Terry's behavior is awkward_
   or it's his fault that the situation is awkward.

2. a. It wasn't fair that Jim's boss gave him another project this week.
   b. It wasn't fair to give him another project this week.

   DIFFERENCE: _____

   _____

3. a. It's not possible that Jim can deal with any more work.
   b. It's not possible for Jim to deal with any more work.

   DIFFERENCE: _____

   _____

4. a. It may have been disappointing to Jim that his boss was so inconsiderate.
   b. It may have been disappointing of Jim's boss to be so inconsiderate.

   DIFFERENCE: _____

   _____

5. a. It seems very inconvenient that so many projects are due this week.
   b. It seems very inconvenient of Jim's boss to make so many projects due this week.

   DIFFERENCE: _____

   _____

6. a. It is silly that Jim's boss assigned him to two important projects.
   b. It was silly of Jim's boss to assign him to two important projects.

   DIFFERENCE: _____

   _____

7. a. It seems surprising that Jim hasn't complained about his workload.
   b. It seems surprising of Jim not to complain about his workload.

   DIFFERENCE: _____

   _____

D Comment on the behavior of the person in each situation below. Select an adjective from the box for your comment. Use each adjective only once.

crazy	~~unwise~~	foolish	inconsiderate	careless
generous	silly	foolhardy	perceptive	wrong

1. Ray didn't study for his final in biology until the night before the exam.

   It was unwise of Ray to wait until the last minute to study for his exam.

2. Lynn drank so much coffee that she couldn't sleep well before her exam the next day.

   _____

3. Lucy volunteered to help her roommate Cathy with a project for biology so that Cathy could finish it on time.

   _____

4. After a long weekend, Charlie drove back to campus through a big snowstorm even though his exam wasn't until the next afternoon.

   _____

5. Drew lost part of his team's biology project as he biked to campus.

   _____

6. Students in the library all around Barbara were chatting while she was trying to study for her biochemistry mid-term.

   _____

7. Professor Lopez realized that the students in his physiology class hadn't had enough time to prepare for the mid-term, so he postponed the exam for two days.

   _____

8. Sally was short on time, so she decided to give her three-minute speech in Public Speaking class without any preparation.

   _____

■ **COMMUNICATE**

E **WRITE** Make a list of guidelines or tips for preventing stress. Present your ideas to your classmates.

It's wise to get some exercise when you're feeling stressed.

GRAMMAR AND VOCABULARY Write a composition on one of the topics below. Use as many words as possible from the Content Vocabulary on page 279. Use sentences with *it* clefts and adjective complements to express some of your ideas.

Topic 1: We admire people for various reasons: their skills, their accomplishments, their personalities. It may be the way in which they have handled a difficult or stressful situation that makes us admire them. Describe someone that you admire for this reason. Use as much detail as possible.

Topic 2: Some people thrive on stress. It's energizing, not debilitating, for them. Would your friends or family members describe you in this way? Is it true or untrue that you respond favorably when you work or interact in a stressful environment? Explain and give concrete examples.

PROJECT Interview at least one student on your campus about his or her attitude toward counseling. Find out the following information, and give a brief oral report on your findings at your next class meeting.

1. Does your interviewee think that it is important for students at your school to have access to counseling services?
2. What is your interviewee's attitude about going to a counselor?
3. According to your interviewee, what's the most important counseling option available to students at your school?
4. According to your interviewee, is it embarrassing to go to a counselor? Why, or why not?

 INTERNET Go to your school's website (or the website of a nearby school) and find out what kind of counseling is available for students who need some kind of help. Be ready to discuss (1) all of the counseling options that are available and (2) the counseling options that you think are the most important. In your opinion, should the counseling options be confidential; in other words, should the counselors protect the privacy of students who use the counseling options?

PART 1
Conditional Clauses: Past
Counterfactuals

PART 2
Conditional Clauses: Word Order

Lesson 27

Criminal Justice:
Identification Documents
and Technology

■ CONTENT VOCABULARY

Look up the words below that you do not know and enter them in your vocabulary journal.
Write each word's part of speech, a definition, and an example sentence. Try to include them
in your discussion and writing below.

to avert	to compromise	to counterfeit	rigorous
biometric data	to confiscate	fake	to verify
to breach	counterfactual	a fingerprint	widespread

■ THINK ABOUT IT

Look at the driver's license on the next page. What kind of information is usually included on a
driver's license? Does your driver's license have any information on a computer chip inside it?
Do people where you live use their driver's licenses as national IDs? Discuss your responses
with a classmate.

In your writing journal, write for five minutes about the questions below. When you are
finished, share what you wrote with the class.
What kind of ID do you carry with you every day? What kind of information is contained on
that ID? Is that information different from the information on a passport? If you had lost
your passport on your trip to another country, what would you have done?

■ GRAMMAR IN CONTENT

CD2,TR53

A Read and listen to the passage below. The sentences in bold in the text are sentences with *if* clauses that express an unreal, or counterfactual, condition in the past.

High-Tech ID

When Maureen Patterson and her business partner Brenda O'Neill used to head for the airport, they would check to be sure that their tickets and passports were readily available. Even though they only traveled to Montreal to meet with clients, the women knew that after 9/11, American passengers with passports generally re-entered the U.S. more easily than those with only their driver's licenses. They had learned the hard way: one time Ms. O'Neill had actually missed their return flight to Chicago because of the delays in her line at the security checkpoint. **If she had taken her passport along, she could probably have avoided that inconvenience.** Later, the laws were changed, making passports obligatory for U.S. air travelers to Canada. Now the women always travel with proper ID.

Since 9/11, officials have been searching for ways to ensure the security of U.S. identification documents. **If the 9/11 terrorists hadn't obtained fake IDs, they wouldn't have been able to enter the United States and the attack could have been averted.** At least that is the rationale for law enforcement and security officials at the state and federal levels who have been adapting various technologies to protect citizens' identities. **The appropriate government agencies wouldn't have developed new versions of drivers' licenses and passports so quickly if the technology hadn't existed in other forms before this need arose.**

In contrast to older forms of ID, new cards or documents have to be machine readable. Most driver's licenses, for example, have had bar codes or magnetic strips for some time. With either, the license meets the new, more rigorous standard for IDs. The computer chips that are embedded in these "smart cards" have to make contact with a scanning device to make the encoded information accessible. A more controversial method of adding "machine-readability" is to incorporate radio frequency ID (RFID) in a license or passport. This technology has been used for years in stickers that commuters have on their windshields to pass through highway tollbooths without stopping to pay. Since the sticker, or in this case a passport or license, can be read from a distance, the identification of vehicles or passengers can be confirmed speedily, and foot or vehicular traffic flows more smoothly. Had this technology been available in 2001, airport security officers could have spotted some problems with the biometric data in the IDs of the terrorists and would have used additional methods to verify their identities or their status.

Critics of the new ID technologies fear that anyone with such RFID cards or documents will be in greater danger of identity theft. If hackers manage to compromise the system, they could have access not only to a person's passport number and date of birth, but other private information as well.

a rationale: a reason, a justification

a bar code: a series of vertical lines on many products that can be read by a scanner

to embed: to place within, to enclose

to encode: to put information in a code or in a different set of symbols

Conditional Clauses: Past Counterfactuals

Sample Sentences	Notes
If I had forgotten my passport last week, **they never would have let** me on the airplane to Moscow.	Express actions or situations that never happened or were impossible in the past in conditional sentences.
If my passport had been stolen, I would have been forced to stay in Moscow longer.	**Main Clause** [= result clause]: SUBJECT + *would* + *have* + PAST PARTICIPLE
Of course, **if I had been** on an all-expense-paid vacation, **I would have enjoyed staying** in Moscow longer.	**Passive Main Clause:** SUBJECT + *would have been* + PAST PARTICIPLE
I wouldn't have felt comfortable **if I had left** my passport in my hotel room.	**Dependent *if* Clause** [= conditional clause]: *If* + SUBJECT + PAST PERFECT
If your passport had been stolen, would your embassy in Moscow have helped you?	**Passive *if* Clause:** *If* + SUBJECT + *had been* + PAST PARTICIPLE
Would you have locked your passport in the hotel safe **if you had been** in my shoes?	Begin a sentence with the *if* clause in most cases. Place the main clause at the beginning if: • the conditional clause is long and "heavy" or • the main clause contains a strong or interesting topic you want to stress or the *if* clause is an afterthought
Would you have had a hard time **if you had had to get** a new passport overseas?	Remember that the verb tenses in these sentences express a counterfactual condition in the past time.
If you had had to travel alone to Moscow, what **would you have done?**	When the *if* clause begins the sentence, separate it from the main clause with a comma.
I probably **could** have gotten some photos in Moscow if I had actually needed them.	*Would* is the most frequently used modal in past counterfactual conditional sentences. Use *could* or *might* to express: • a past opportunity or ability (= *could*) • a past possibility (= *might*)
If I hadn't put my passport inside my pocket, a pickpocket **might** have stolen it.	In both examples, the past action or situation in the result clause did not take place.

B Read over your journal entry, and <u>underline</u> at least one sentence that you can revise to include an *if* clause that expresses an unreal, or counterfactual, condition. Write your revised sentence(s) below.

_____

_____

_____

C **Complete the sentences below for DeShawn Williams, who imagines how her trip to China could have been ruined.**

1. If my roommate Angela and I had waited until the last minute to apply for passports, _____ *we wouldn't have received them in time.* _____

2. If we hadn't applied for a visa to China, _____

_____

3. If I had packed my passport in my suitcase, _____

_____

4. We wouldn't have gotten through the security checkpoint in Seattle _____

_____

5. If the Chinese immigration officials had confiscated my passport, _____

_____

6. We wouldn't have been able to fly from Shanghai to Beijing _____

_____

7. If Angela and I had switched passports by mistake, _____

_____

8. We would have been questioned for a long time on our return to Seattle _____

_____

D In each situation below, there was a problem of identification that prevented the crime from being solved. How could law enforcement officials have solved these crimes? Work in small groups to brainstorm solutions.

1. Unfortunately, the surveillance camera at the First National Bank wasn't operating when the bank was robbed.

   If the camera had been operating, they could have identified the robbers.

2. The crime scene investigators dusted Danson's Custom Jewelry Store for fingerprints, but none of the prints were usable.

3. The thief was able to use Bert's driver's license because he resembled Bert.

4. Intruders were able to breach security at TechSure Corporation because they forced the CEO to put her finger on the scanner near the office entrance.

5. Although the kidnappers had spent several days at their "safe house," the crime scene investigators could not find any DNA samples.

6. A spy was able to enter the United States in 2000 with a counterfeit passport because it was the old-fashioned kind without any encoded biometric information.

7. A thief broke into the high tech company two weeks before their retinal scanner was installed.

8. The kidnapper disguised his voice when he called the family to make his demands.

E Use the appropriate conditional verb forms in the conversation below. Be careful of the time of each action. Insert the subject whenever necessary.

1. **Ed Higgins:** Meredith, did you put the passports in our suitcase?

   Meredith Higgins: Why _____would I have done_____ (do) such a thing?

   Ed: I can't find them anywhere.

2. **Meredith:** I _____ (look) in the carry-on bag again if I

   _____ (be) you.

   Ed: I've looked in it five times.

   Meredith: Here, let me look.

3. **Meredith:** Did you look in the outside pockets?

   Ed: Of course I did.

   Meredith: Well, the passports are right here. If they _____

   (be) any closer, they _____ (bite) you!

   Ed: You know, that is really a ridiculous saying.

4. **Meredith:** Whatever. The main thing is that we have the passports.

   Ed: You're right.

   Meredith: If I _____ (be) you, I

   _____ (calm down). The security official might think that

   you are acting strangely.

5. **Ed:** That's the last thing that we need.

   Meredith: You know, if you _____ (help) me pack last night,

   you _____ (know) that the passports weren't in the suitcases.

   Ed: All right, all right. Can we drop this subject?

6. **Meredith:** Sure. I'm a little worried about getting through this security line.

   Ed: We still have 30 minutes. Don't worry.

   Meredith: It _____ (be) better if we

   _____ (leave) the house earlier. You know how the traffic can

   be this time of the day.

   Ed: Now you are worrying too much. Even if we _____ (be)

   20 feet back in line, we still _____ (have) enough time to get

   through security.

F **PAIR WORK** Imagine that you and your partner volunteered to check IDs for a concert that your student club sponsored. Now the other students are upset at you because many people entered who shouldn't have. Because the concert was on campus, the rules said "No one under 18" and "No alcohol permitted." Practice asking and answering questions about the problems that occurred.

> What **would** you **have done** if a professor **had brought** his 15-year-old son?

> I **would have told** them that nobody under 18 was allowed. Then I **would have told** the professor's son about another upcoming event he could attend.

PART TWO	Conditional Clauses: Word Order

■ GRAMMAR IN CONTENT

A Reread the text at the beginning of this lesson, and find another sentence that expresses a counterfactual situation. How is that sentence different from the boldfaced sentences in the text? Compare your answer with a partner.

Conditional Clauses: Word Order	
Sample Sentences	**Notes**
Had I known about the new ID regulations, I would have brought my passport. The security lines would have moved faster **had the travelers followed** the new rules.	In formal English, *if* can be omitted in certain cases. This rule applies to *if* clauses with: • *had* (in past counterfactual conditions) • *should* (meaning "happen to")
Should you find someone's ID, check for a phone number so that you can contact the person. Contact the embassy **should you need** more pages in your passport.	*If* is omitted less frequently in conditional clauses with *were* (in present hypothetical or counterfactual conditions). In this case, the conditional clause appears in the initial position.
Were passports unnecessary, travel would be considerably more convenient. **Were the radio frequency ID** absolutely secure, no one would worry about identity theft.	Change the word order at the beginning of the clause: *Had* *Should* ⎤ + SUBJECT *Were* ⎦

B **Rewrite each sentence by omitting the *if* clause and then putting the conditional clause at the beginning of the sentence.**

1. I would have applied for a passport sooner if I had known about the new rules.

    Had I known about the new rules, I would have applied for a passport sooner.

2. If the passport biometric coding were easy to decode, they wouldn't have decided to use it.

    _____

3. If you were to burn the tip of your right index finger, would that fingerprint be the same after your finger healed?

    _____

4. If they should smudge a fingerprint during the investigation, could crime scene investigators identify the fingerprint?

    _____

5. If a criminal had left any fingerprints at the scene of the crime, could a fingerprint expert have known that she was a smoker?

    _____

6. If someone should steal your biometric data, you might not be able to use it for the rest of your life.

    _____

C Make a conditional sentence that expresses how you will or would deal with the situation differently. Omit *if* in your sentence. Be aware of the timeframe in each situation.

1. When the police officer stopped my car and asked to see my driver's license, I realized that it had expired.

   Had I taken it out of my wallet recently, I would have remembered the expiration date.

2. When I go to the ATM, other people seem to watch me type my PIN number.

   _____

3. I was in such a hurry to pack that I put my passport and airline ticket in my suitcase with my travel books.

   _____

4. At the mall yesterday I didn't have a photo ID so I couldn't use my credit card at Dunbar's.

   _____

5. I can never remember my different passwords on different Internet sites.

   _____

6. I didn't realize that I needed passport photos for my visa, so I couldn't send the paperwork to the embassy until yesterday.

   _____

7. I haven't kept my passport up to date; therefore, I'll have to get a new, more expensive one before my trip.

   _____

8. I didn't have enough money to rent a car, so I had to use public transportation.

   _____

D Listen to each statement in the recording and (circle) the letter of the correct interpretation.

Mr. Richards, if you had brought all the necessary documents, you would have received your passport last week.

1. (a.) Mr. Richards submitted all the necessary documents.
   b. Mr. Richards didn't receive his passport last week.

2. a. Mr. Richards didn't need his passport right away.
   b. Mr. Richards didn't submit his passport application at the Post Office.

3. a. The photo was the wrong size.
   b. The photo is the wrong size.

4. a. They don't have all of the paperwork.
   b. They didn't have all of the paperwork.

5. a. He included his birth certificate.
   b. He didn't include his birth certificate.

6. a. They didn't send it by express mail.
   b. He included extra postage.

7. a. The ATM machine rejected her bank card.
   b. Miss Sanders typed in the correct PIN number.

8. a. The ATM machine recognized her card.
   b. She didn't type in the correct number the second time.

9. a. Her PIN number isn't valid.
   b. Her PIN number wasn't valid.

10. a. The ATM machine kept her card.
    b. She typed in the correct number.

E Find and correct the four errors in the e-mail message below.

Dad-

If I would have listened to you, I could have saved myself a lot of trouble. Yesterday morning I lost my passport downtown. It's a good thing that my advisor made a photocopy of it during orientation. I went to the office right away and told them about it. If they have not helped me, I don't know what I would have done. First, we had to call the police and make a report. Then, I had to call the consulate and tell them. If there weren't a consulate here I might have to fly to Washington to get a new passport. Luckily, I can pick up my new one in 5 days.

Don't tell Mom!
Jackie

PASSPORT

United States
of America

■ **COMMUNICATE**

F **GROUP WORK** Many people are critical of modern airports and the security procedures that passengers have to go through. Have you been to an airport recently? How could the airport have been set up better for passengers? If you haven't been to an airport recently, have you gone through a security check somewhere else? How could the security area have been set up better? Share your thoughts and experiences in a group discussion.

> When I arrived in Miami, the baggage and immigration were too close together. If they had located the immigration area farther from the baggage claim, it wouldn't have been so confusing.

GRAMMAR AND VOCABULARY Write a composition on one of the topics below. Use as many words as possible from the Content Vocabulary on page 291. Use sentences with conditional structures to express some of your ideas.

Topic 1: People often respond to extreme or dangerous situations by making changes in laws or procedures so that the danger can be avoided in the future. For example, if 9/11 hadn't happened, forms of ID wouldn't have changed so quickly in the United States. Describe another example of a change in a law or an attitude in the United States or another country that was a response to something dangerous or frightening that happened.

Topic 2: Describe an incident in which you or someone that you know had to show some ID. Why did that person have to show the ID? What would have happened if the person had not been able to show a form of ID? According to that person, could the situation have been handled more appropriately? How?

PROJECT Interview at least one student on your campus about IDs. Find out the following information:

1. What kind of ID does your interviewee carry every day?
2. How often has your interviewee had to show the ID recently? To whom?
3. Does your interviewee have a passport? Why or why not?
4. Would your interviewee mind being fingerprinted when he/she visits another country?

 INTERNET Go online and do a search using the key word "fingerprints." Find out about the history, use, and classification of fingerprints. You and your classmates may even want to take your own fingerprints (using ink pads) and then try to sort or classify them using the information you learned online.

PART 1
Conditionals: Conjunctions

PART 2
Conditional Sentences: Verbs +
That Clauses; Mixed Conditions

Lesson (28)

Astrobiology and Marine Sciences: Exploration

■ CONTENT VOCABULARY

Look up the words and phrases below that you do not know and enter them in your vocabulary journal. Write each word's part of speech, a definition, and an example sentence. Try to include them in your discussion and writing below.

in close quarters	extraterrestrial	a specimen
a creature	hypothetical	a submersible
an expedition	a space capsule	symbiotic

■ THINK ABOUT IT

Look at the photos on the next page of some creatures that live in the oceans. Have you seen any of them before? Could these creatures tell us about life forms in outer space? How might they give scientists insights into conditions that are suitable for life? Discuss your ideas with a classmate.

In your writing journal, write for five minutes about the questions below. When you are finished, share your opinions with the class.

In your opinion, does life exist beyond Earth? Should we try to find new life forms? What might happen if we did? Do you know what scientists are doing now to find extraterrestrial life?

■ GRAMMAR IN CONTENT

CD2,TR55

A Read and listen to the passage below. The words in bold in the text are clauses that are introduced by a conditional conjunction.

Exploring Our World and Beyond

Throughout human history we have explored. In ancient times, adventurers set sail **even if they feared** that they might drop off the end of the world. Others left home for months or years to satisfy their curiosity about other lands and people. Still others stared into the evening skies, saying to themselves, "**If only I could travel to the ends of the universe.**" Although these explorers were often motivated by curiosity and restlessness, others represented commercial interests that hoped to benefit from the precious metals, exotic furs, or agricultural products that foreign places and people might have to offer. Times have changed, but the attractions and benefits of exploration remain.

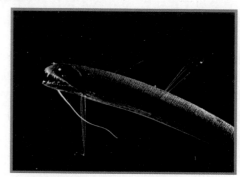

This other-worldly looking fish lives near the ocean floor.

Contemporary adventurers focus on the exploration of our universe and Earth's underwater world. As technology has enabled marine biologists to venture into extremely deep regions of the ocean, they have discovered incredible life forms. Similarly, geologists and oceanographers who have been searching the ocean floors for new sources of minerals, such as manganese, nickel, and gold, have discovered not only rich seafloor mining possibilities, but also unexpected life forms. For example, snails the size of baseballs were found near a submarine hot spring at a temperature of 280 degrees Celsius. If these researchers had not seen such life forms, no one would suspect that life could survive in such extreme conditions. Since then, biologists have been uncovering other unexpected conditions in which life can thrive, including extremes of temperature, salinity, pH, and atmospheric pressure.

Our search for life in space has benefited greatly from such findings. Astrobiology, a branch of biology that studies life forms we may encounter in outer space, has guided the search for extraterrestrial life. **Unless we actually find life in the universe or it finds us,** scientists have to be content with looking for secondary evidence that life exists or existed. In other words, they have to analyze debris from asteroids or comets and rock samples from our visits to the moon and Mars in order to check for evidence of life. Scientists may wish that they had other means of collecting data, but current technology limits our ability to go out and search for ourselves as we used to do. Computer models of the "Habitable Zone," a term that defines the set of conditions that support life on Earth, allow researchers to search beyond our solar system to identify other similar planets. These conditions include an atmosphere with oxygen, the stable presence of water, and gravity, among others. **Only if these conditions are met** do researchers believe that there is hope for finding another planet that supports life. Even though a number of similar planets are known to exist outside our solar system, scientists have already determined that none of them matches Earth's characteristics. Naturally, the search goes on.

a commercial interest: a group of businesspeople or companies that work together

salinity: the amount of salt in a liquid or solid

debris: the leftover pieces of something broken or destroyed

secondary: not original or direct

to thrive: to live or grow well

Sample Sentences	Notes
Life forms may be too simple to communicate with us **even if** we find them. **Even if** we wanted to communicate with beings in far away galaxies, our level of technology wouldn't allow us to do so. In the early years of space exploration, people were chosen to be astronauts **only if** they were men. **If only** we had been able to build a space station on Mars years ago, astronauts could have gathered more data about the planet. **If only** the Mars rovers were able to move over more of the surface of Mars!	Select one of the phrases below to modify the meaning of *if* in conditional clauses. • *Even if* emphasizes an unexpected or surprising connection or relationship. • *Only if* expresses a single or unique condition. Use negative fronting (see Lesson 15) when **only if** begins the sentence. • *If only* expresses regret. *If only* + clause can be used without a main clause to comment on an unfortunate action or situation.
They'll launch the satellite tonight **unless** there's a thunderstorm. (**Explanation:** They'll launch it only if it doesn't storm.) The astronauts will check the exterior cameras soon **unless** they haven't finished another task. (**Explanation:** They'll check the cameras only if they've finished their other work.) They can't continue checking the equipment **unless** they get some rest. (**Explanation:** They can continue only if they can rest.) The old equipment doesn't work properly **unless** they monitor it regularly. (**Explanation:** The equipment works properly only if they monitor it regularly.) Technicians didn't call for help **unless** the equipment shut down completely. (**Explanation:** Technicians called for help only if the equipment shut down completely.)	Introduce an exceptional or unique hypothetical condition with *unless*: • *Unless* implies a negative condition. Essentially, *unless* introduces a condition that is opposite to the condition introduced by **only if**. • When a clause with *unless* contains a negative, the paraphrase is affirmative with **only if**. • When an *unless*-clause is affirmative, the paraphrase with **only if** contains a negative. The changes in affirmative or negative form can occur in the main or the conditional clause. Check the meaning of the sentence to decide the appropriate position for the negation. Avoid using negation in both clauses for clearer communication of your ideas.

B Read over your journal entry, and <u>underline</u> at least one sentence that you can revise to include a clause introduced by one of the conditional conjunctions listed above. Write your revised sentence(s) below.

_____

_____

_____

C Edit the conjunctions in the sentences about historic explorers, adding *even* or *only* as appropriate. Follow the example.

1. A man of modest means, Columbus could afford to set sail for the New World ^only if Queen Isabella financed his voyage.

Christopher Columbus

2. If Charles Darwin hadn't developed his theory of evolution while sailing on the *Beagle,* he still would have been famous for his extensive collections of animal and plant life from this voyage.

3. Leif Erickson would have been credited with discovering America if enough Scandinavians had settled in the New World.

4. Captain James Cook would have been famous for his three voyages of discovery in the Pacific Ocean if the Cook Islands hadn't been named for him.

5. If you read about the arduous expedition of Meriwether Lewis and William Clark across the land of the Louisiana Purchase to the Pacific Ocean, can you understand the important contribution of the Native American woman Sacagawea.

6. The admiration and respect of South Americans for the German naturalist Alexander von Humboldt can be fully appreciated if you know how many things—from schools to an ocean current—have been named after him.

7. If the British team of Stanley and Livingston had never found the source of the Nile River, they would still be famous.

D Read each sentence and look at the two sentences that follow. Which one correctly paraphrases the first sentence? (Circle) the letter of the best choice.

1. Unless scientists find other intelligent life in the universe, people won't care too much about space exploration.
   a. People will care about space exploration only if scientists find other intelligent life in the universe.
   b. People won't care about space exploration only if scientists find other intelligent life in the universe.

2. If only we could prove that life exists on other planets.
   a. The speaker means that we can't prove that life exists there.
   b. The speaker expresses regret that we haven't been able to prove that life exists there.

3. Americans would be more enthusiastic about space exploration if only the *Challenger* hadn't exploded.
   a. The speaker emphasizes that the unfortunate *Challenger* explosion caused Americans to lose their enthusiasm for space exploration.
   b. The speaker means that the *Challenger* explosion caused Americans to lose their enthusiasm for space exploration.

4. The government will reduce its spending on space exploration unless citizens communicate their support of it.
   a. The government will reduce its spending only if citizens do not communicate their support of the space program.
   b. The government will reduce its spending only if citizens communicate their support of the space program.

5. Astrobiologists wouldn't have assumed that life forms live in extreme conditions unless they had seen such specimens on Earth.
   a. Astrobiologists have assumed that life forms can live in extreme conditions only because they have seen such specimens on Earth.
   b. Astrobiologists haven't assumed that life forms can live in extreme conditions only because they haven't seen such specimens on Earth.

6. Even if we find extraterrestrial life forms in the universe, they may not be complex life forms like us.
   a. The speaker implies that we can't expect to find complex life forms.
   b. The speaker implies that we have the remote possibility of finding complex life forms.

7. According to some scientists, we should search for extraterrestrial life only if we also want to be found by other life forms.
   a. We shouldn't search for extraterrestrial life unless we want to be found.
   b. We should search for extraterrestrial life because we want to be found.

E Using your own words and ideas, complete the conditional clause in each sentence below.

1. A person can't travel into space unless _she undergoes training as an astronaut._

2. In the old days, sea captains couldn't begin long exploratory voyages unless
_____

3. Columbus wouldn't have been able to set sail unless _____
_____

4. Even though Columbus set sail to find a new route to India, _____
_____

5. Even if Columbus had landed on Cuba instead of Hispaniola, _____
_____

6. Unless _____,

   an overland expedition was able to move only a few miles per day.

7. Unless _____,

   a caravan of vehicles would have difficulty crossing rough terrain.

8. Many European explorers wouldn't have reached their destinations in America unless
_____

9. There are many stories of Native Americans helping European explorers even though
_____

10. Even if _____,

   Europeans continued to explore the American West.

"Rare Earth" Hypothesis – Ward and Brownlee

our planet = unusual → little chance of other life forms in universe

a) our unique position in relation to sun	→ liquid H_2O is stable
b) stable relationship to great planets	→ their powerful gravity protects us from asteroids and comets, e.g. Jupiter
c) our large moon	→ decreases gravitational pull of Sun and Jupiter, so Earth has stable orbit & rotation
	→ stable seasons
d) our atmosphere	→ protects life from solar radiation
	→ keeps heat near Earth
e) our magnetic field	→ protects us from solar wind (=deflects wind)
f) plate tectonics	→ maintains carbon balance in atmosphere
	→ continues building mountains so that erosion doesn't result in completely flat land

F With a partner, explain some conditions necessary for life based on the notes from Astrobiology 101 shown above. Use *unless, only if,* or *even if.*

1. There is little chance of life as we know it unless there is a planet similar to Earth.

2. Only if a planet rotates in the same unique position in relation to a star will water be stable.

3. _____

_____

4. _____

_____

5. _____

_____

6. _____

_____

7. _____

_____

G PAIR WORK Discuss the type of exploration that would attract you to study a particular field. If you had the training and the financial backing for an exploratory trip, what kind of fieldwork would you undertake? What kind of new information about our world or universe would be the focus of your exploration?

> I would be interested in doing research on life forms at the South Pole, but only if I were part of a team. It'd be too dangerous by myself.

PART TWO	Conditional Sentences: Verbs + *That* Clauses; Mixed Conditions

■ GRAMMAR IN CONTENT

A Reread the text at the beginning of the lesson, and <u>underline</u> any other clauses that include conditional forms of verbs.

Conditional Sentences: Mixed Conditions and *That* Clauses

Sample Sentences	Notes
People with boring jobs might wish **that they had explored** other job options earlier in life. Children sometimes wish that a spaceship **would take** them on an adventure. Pretend that you **were living** in a lab deep under the ocean. What would you do to relax? Suppose that Alan Shepard **hadn't been chosen** as an astronaut. Who would have been the first American in space?	Use verbs of wishing or imagining to introduce *that* clauses that express counterfactual conditions. *Wish* introduces: • **present counterfactual** conditions • **past counterfactual** conditions • **future hypothetical** conditions *Imagine, pretend,* and *suppose* introduce: • **present counterfactual** conditions • **past counterfactual** conditions • **future hypothetical** conditions These three verbs are commonly used in the imperative form with this structure.
If we had already discovered a planet with life on it, **researchers would receive** more money for research. **If people hadn't told** so many unbelievable stories about extraterrestrials, **we might take** the evidence more seriously.	Use a combination of conditional verb forms to express the hypothetical or nonfactual impact of a past action on a present situation: *If* + PAST PERFECT, would / might / could + BASE FORM

B **Complete the part of the conversations below with a *that* clause and a question.**

1. **Barbara:** I'm really getting burned out. In fact, sometimes I regret getting a PhD in biology because I have to spend so much time in the lab.

   Shelley: Suppose _that you get training to be a wildlife biologist. Would you feel better about spending time outside doing research?_

2. **Cindy:** Dad, can we go back to the planetarium again next weekend?

   Eric: Let's wait till they have a different star show, honey. I'm glad that you liked it so much.

   Cindy: I hope someday that I can go into outer space.

   Eric: Pretend _____

   _____

3. **Justin:** Why in the world do you believe in UFOs and space aliens?

   Lenny: How can you not believe? There's a lot of evidence.

   Justin: Evidence? I won't believe it until I see some hard evidence.

   Lenny: Suppose _____

   _____

4. **Ms. Brinkley:** I understand that you need another $5 million for the seafloor mining operation. Why should we spend that kind of money on exploration that has little chance of becoming profitable?

   Dr. Forester: Our competitors are having considerable success with similar seafloor exploration. Imagine _____

   _____

   Ms. Brinkley: That kind of result would certainly impress me.

5. **Gina:** What could we do to get on TV? I think that it's our turn for "15 minutes of fame," don't you?

   Jackie: That's one of the silliest things that I have ever heard you say.

   Gina: No, I'm serious. What about extraterrestrials? There haven't been any stories about them in a while. OK, let's pretend _____

   _____

6. **Dr. Klinger:** OK, class, today we're going to talk more about the possibility of finding life elsewhere in the universe. You'll remember that life on Earth survives and even thrives in some unlikely environments. So let's suppose _____

   _____

C **Comment on your interest in participating in each of the exploratory missions below with a conditional sentence.**

The International Space Station

1. Astronauts who carry out experiments on the Space Station have to spend up to six months there.

   I wish that I could visit the Space Station, but I wouldn't want to stay there that long.

2. The submersible *Clelia* regularly transports three researchers and/or observers on short research missions in shallow water, during which they collect samples and photograph or videotape plant and animal life. On occasion, their missions include investigating archaeological sites and sunken ships.

   _____

   _____

3. In 1845, Sir John Franklin and his crew sailed in two ships from England to North America to find the Northwest Passage. (In those days, people thought that a waterway existed between the North Atlantic and the North Pacific.)

   _____

   _____

4. Since 2001, archaeologists have been exploring the area once occupied by the Fremont, a group of Native Americans who lived in a mountainous area in Utah. So far, they have discovered many simple structures and artifacts in remote areas.

   _____

   _____

5. Meteorologists regularly explore storm phenomena by flying into hurricanes or by following tornadoes in vehicles to collect data.

   _____

   _____

6. Since 1960, cavers of various nationalities have been exploring Krubera Cave in Abkhazia on the Black Sea. In 2004, a Moscow-based team made it to 1,775 meters below the surface, and Ukrainians reached 2,080 meters. There are still more areas to explore.

   _____

   _____

D **Listen to the interview with Dr. Isadora Vincenzi and answer the questions below.**

CD2, TR56

1. Who expected to see creatures living near a hydrothermal vent?

   _____

2. Did biologists discover the creatures?

   _____

3. Did staff members of the Woods Hole Oceanographic Institution see the creatures first?

   _____

4. Is Dr. Vincenzi a chemist?

   _____

5. When does Dr. Vincenzi do fieldwork near a black smoker?

   _____

6. Did Dr. Vincenzi discover the symbiotic relationship between two life forms?

   _____

7. Who else discovered this particular relationship?

   _____

■ **COMMUNICATE**

E **GROUP WORK** Brainstorm five questions that will elicit speculation about how our world or universe would or might be different. Base each question on a past situation or event, and imagine that it didn't actually take place or that it occurred differently. When you are finished, share your questions with the class.

> What if the Japanese had settled America before the Europeans? What would North America be like today?

GRAMMAR AND VOCABULARY Write a composition on one of the topics below. Use as many words as possible from the Content Vocabulary on page 303. Use sentences with conditional structures or conjunctions to express some of your ideas.

Topic 1: "Exploring" can mean discovering new ideas and ways of thinking. As you think about your education so far, what regrets and wishes do you have about the kinds of classes that you have and have not taken or opportunities that you have or have not taken advantage of? Explain and give concrete examples.

Topic 2: People who choose to explore often have to subject themselves to difficult conditions during their journeys. Sailing ships and caravans were certainly uncomfortable means of travel. Nowadays, explorers may have to spend long stretches of time in a space station, a submersible like *Alvin*, or another restrictive and potentially dangerous place. Under what circumstances would you consider undertaking such research and exploration?

PROJECT Interview at least one student on your campus about extraterrestrial life. Find out the following information, and make a brief oral report of your findings at your next class meeting.

1. Does the person you interviewed believe that there is extraterrestrial life?
2. How much effort should people put into finding extraterrestrial life?
3. What is the opinion of the person you interviewed regarding the current space program, including the Space Station?

 INTERNET Visit a website related to space exploration, or go directly to the website www.discoverynow.us and click on one of the audio selections. (These audio selections have also been played on the radio.) Prepare a short summary of the report, and comment on the information with a sentence using *wish, imagine,* or *suppose.*

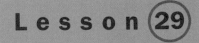
Sociology of Sports

■ CONTENT VOCABULARY

Look up the words and phrases below that you do not know and enter them in your vocabulary journal. Write each word's part of speech, a definition, and an example sentence. Try to include them in your discussion and writing below.

an assumption	to disprove	to hustle	to sacrifice
a cliché	folk wisdom	a rationale	a sphere
to compete	gender	to resort to	underlying

■ THINK ABOUT IT

Read over the sports clichés below and talk over their meanings with a partner. Be prepared to paraphrase them.

He has all the moves.
He's a natural hitter.
She turned the game around.

We stayed too long with our game plan.
They have a killer instinct.
It was a team effort.

In your writing journal, write for five minutes about the questions below. When you are finished, share your ideas with the class.

What do young people learn when they participate in sports during their school years? In your opinion, what are the positive and negative lessons that young people may learn from their physical education classes or from competing in sports?

■ GRAMMAR IN CONTENT

CD2,TR57

A Read and listen to the passage below. The words in bold in the text are complements of the preceding noun.

Truth or Just Clichés?

Because sport is a major phenomenon in modern society, one might speculate as to why it has only recently been approached as a legitimate area to study by social scientists. Perhaps one answer to this question lies in the assumption **that sport was primarily meant to be physical rather than social interaction and was thus devoid of interest to social scientists.** In an insightful essay entitled "The Interdependency of Sport and Culture," Gunther Lüschen points out that even the most simple physical activities, such as walking, are social in nature. In a like manner, the more complex physical activities that are classified as sport involve greater suffusion from the social and cultural milieus. Another explanation for the late entry of social scientists into the analysis of sport may be that the world of sport is often perceived in terms of illusion and fantasy, as a sphere apart from the "real world."

The 2006 Asian Games.

Eric Dunning, an expert on the sociological aspect of sports, has argued that sociologists who define play and sport in terms of fantasy, and who are thus ambivalent about seriously studying the topic, may be reflecting a Protestant Ethic orientation that considers the study of play, games, sport, and leisure as frivolous and unbecoming of a "serious scientist." In response to these sentiments, Dunning emphasizes that "sports and games are 'real' in the sense they are observable, whether directly through overt behavior of people or indirectly through the reports which players and spectators give of what they think and feel while playing and 'spectating.'"

There is an increasing realization **that sport permeates and articulates with many other social institutions.** Furthermore, sport is an important ingredient in people's lives. In the absence of scientific investigation, folk wisdom and assumptions have prevailed as "facts." These include ready-made words, statements, phrases, and slogans that trigger speech and behavior in a kind of stimulus-response fashion and thus bypass cognitive thought and reflection. Because sport has become so much a part of our everyday life, this segment of social life is especially vulnerable given the clichés and assumptions. Furthermore, as we noted previously, these assumptions are easily transferred as metaphors to other spheres of social life. In a sense, a double falsehood may be perpetrated if a falsehood as it applied to the sport world is transferred as "fact" to other spheres of behavior. Anton C. Zijderveld, a sociologist, argues that modern society is filled with conflicting norms and values, vagueness, and emotional and moral instability. Thus, our society is clichégenic in the sense that it promotes clichés that provide ready-made but artificial clarity, stability, and certainty.

In the world of sport these clichés are readily apparent; for example, one of the most frequently cited functions of sport is that it "builds character." This common assumption has been the theme of many speakers at athletic banquets. On closer investigation, we find that this "truth" is probably more accurately described as a half-truth. Another commonly held assumption is that athletic pursuits detract from academic concerns (resulting in the "dumb jock" stereotype). Research findings are also providing important qualifications to this assumption. The belief **that sport provides a model of racial equality and a means for many blacks to become professional athletes** is another unfounded assumption. Considerable data have been accumulated that, likewise, raise serious questions about this folk belief. Another commonly held stereotype is that female athletes are physical "Amazons" who tend to be more masculine than most females and are thus likely to suffer from a confusion of sex roles and self-concept. Once again, recent research has refuted these assumptions. Additional questions might be raised regarding the validity of other assumptions such as the following: Sport is a preparation for life; sports are a way to get ahead; the will to win is the will to work. Recent research has begun to raise questions about these assumptions. Scientific investigation moves beyond conjecture to test assumptions in a disciplined manner. New observations and findings about the world of sport frequently demonstrate that previously held perspectives of social reality were distorted.

frivolous: silly, not serious

unbecoming: inappropriate

an Amazon: a tall, aggressive woman; in mythology, Amazons were women warriors

Noun Complements

Sample Sentences	Notes
The belief **that effort and persistence will result in victory** motivates many young athletes. Do you have the impression **that the coach pushes the team too hard?** Everyone is talking about the news **that the women's soccer team beat the men's team.** How can their coach accept the excuse **that the team lost their momentum** in the second half? How can their coach accept the excuse **that the players gave** about their poor playing?	Explain the meaning of some abstract nouns with a complement clause (see the list below). Such clauses: • begin with *that* • are always directly after an abstract noun These clauses differ from relative clauses because they actually explain what the noun means: Their idea **that sport is a preparation for life** can't be proven. ↓ Their idea is **that sport is a preparation for life,** and this idea can't be proven.
Coach Rogerson's **recommendation that Pat play** defense more aggressively was the right one. The coach was angry about Pat's **demand that he be paid** more than the other players. As a result, Coach Rogerson has **given the order that Pat not play** for the next three games.	Use a subjunctive verb form in the complement (see Lesson 21) after nouns that are related to the verbs that require this kind of verb form, for example: *demand, order, recommendation.*

Abstract Nouns That Often Have a Noun Complement

assumption	excuse	news	recommendation
belief	fact	order	reply
claim	idea	possibility	report
demand	message	proposal	suggestion

B Read over your journal entry, and <u>underline</u> at least one sentence that you can revise to include a noun complement. Write your revised sentence(s) below.

_____

_____

_____

_____

C Write "X" by the sentence in each pair with a noun complement.

1. ___X___ a. Can you support the assumption that women are too weak to compete in boxing?

   _____ b. Can you support the assumption that the Boxing Federation expressed in the media?

2. _____ a. Have you read the report that women at universities still receive fewer athletic scholarships than men do?

   _____ b. Have you read the report that our university published about athletic scholarships for women?

3. _____ a. A report that the Athletics Department distributed will be unpopular.

   _____ b. A report that some men's sports will be cut is going to be unpopular.

4. _____ a. The claim that women weren't really interested in sports used to be a rationale for keeping women out of some sports.

   _____ b. The claim that people made about women's lack of interest in sports was a rationale for keeping women out of some sports.

5. _____ a. For centuries people had the impression that sports could be physically harmful to girls.

   _____ b. For centuries the impression that people had about women's sports was unquestioned.

6. _____ a. The idea that society had about "ladylike" sports hasn't disappeared yet.

   _____ b. The idea that girls should only play "ladylike" sports is still strong in some places.

7. _____ a. Those old-fashioned ideas sent a message that sports are not appropriate for girls.

   _____ b. Those old-fashioned ideas sent a message that is inappropriate in today's society.

Naoko Takahashi set a world record of 2:19:45 when she won the Berlin Marathon on September 30, 2001.

D Use the notes below from a lecture on American cultural values in sports and comment on the similarity or difference between your values and those in American sports.

Playing sports = learning to play the game of life

US cultural values:

1. personal character: be honest, be loyal to your team, be a leader, don't be selfish, sacrifice for the team, be a good sport

2. discipline: accept the rules and live by them, learn self-control

3. competition: always hustle, be persistent, losers lack motivation, winning isn't everything, teamwork means social responsibility

4. fitness: keep physically fit, "clean living," be mentally alert, continue education

1. _I don't believe the idea that an athlete should not be selfish is part of American culture._

2. _____

3. _____

4. _____

5. _____

6. _____

7. _____

E Complete each sentence with a noun complement on the topic of violence in sports.

1. Some people avoid large sporting events because they have the belief
   that they might get hurt if some of the fans get violent.

2. Some spectators leave before the end of a big soccer match because of the possibility

   _____

3. Organizers of championship games pay great attention to the claim

   _____ so they hire referees who have
   reputations as fair and impartial.

4. When police have to break up fights among fans, they aren't interested in hearing the

   excuse _____

5. Beer companies ask for proof of the assumption _____

6. The fact _____ makes many people avoid
   the area around a soccer stadium after an important game.

7. Coaches and referees break up fights among athletes as quickly as possible because

   of their belief _____

■ **COMMUNICATE**

F PAIR WORK Talk over the questions about sports for young people with your partner and then write your answers. Then, share the answers with your classmates.

1. What sports did you play in elementary school?
2. How much importance was placed on sports in elementary and high school?
3. Which sports did girls play, and which did boys play?
4. What underlying messages about sports did you receive through your teachers and parents?

■ GRAMMAR IN CONTENT

A Reread the first three paragraphs of the text on page 316, and <u>underline</u> each phrase that is a restatement of the preceding noun.

Appositives

Women competed in tennis and golf in Paris, ~~which was~~ the site of the 1900 Olympics. Martina Navratilova, ~~who was~~ the incredible tennis star, won her record ninth singles title at Wimbledon in 1990. Thousands of girls benefit from Title IX, ~~which is~~ the law that gave female students access to school-sponsored sports. Have you heard of Wilma Rudolph, ~~who was~~ the winner of three Olympic gold medals?	Like relative clauses, an appositive describes, restates, or elaborates the noun phrase it follows. However, the appositive is a shortened form of a relative clause in which *who is/was* or *which is/was* has been deleted.
The tennis player **Althea Gibson** was the first African American woman to win a title at Wimbledon. (restrictive) Any professional player wants to compete at Wimbledon, **the most famous tennis tournament in the world.** (nonrestrictive)	Appositives can be **restrictive** or **nonrestrictive**. No commas are used with a restrictive appositive. The nonrestrictive appositive provides nonessential information about the preceding noun phrase, so commas are used.
The first woman to run the Boston Marathon, **namely** Katherine Switzer, was disguised as a man. Now girls can participate in male-dominated sports, **such as soccer.** These sports, **especially contact sports**, used to be considered too rough for women.	Use an adverbial connector with the appositive: • to make it explicit • to express that the appositive is an example of the other noun phrase • to express the appositive in a particular or special example

Other Adverbials Used to Introduce Appositives

chiefly	for example	in particular	particularly
especially	for instance	notable	primarily
e.g. (= *for example*)	i.e. (= *that is*)		

B Underline the appositive phrases in the texts below. Then, add commas where necessary. Each text may have more than one appositive.

1. Beginning with Title IX <u>the law that opened educational activities to any student regardless of gender</u> female students gained the opportunity to participate in many more sports at school. In addition, they became eligible for athletic scholarships the ticket to higher education for many students.

2. Club sports the only opportunity open to female athletes before 1972 received no funding from schools. Female participants had to buy their own uniforms and play with used equipment the "hand-me-downs" from the men's teams.

Louisiana plays against Arizona during the Women's NCAA Mideast Regional Games in 2001.

3. Before Title IX, female teams had to pay their own way to sporting events. If they couldn't afford it, the team might resort to a bake sale a typical female strategy to raise money from friends and neighbors.

4. Distributing funds among various collegiate sports programs is the responsibility of the athletic director the administrator for all university team sports. Female coaches traditionally the coaches with the least influence on financial decisions on campus still have to fight for support for some of their sports. Title IX does not guarantee that an equal amount of money is spent on each sport or on each individual student athlete.

5. The primary athletic organization for colleges and universities the NCAA now sponsors championships for over 30 sports for female athletes. Basketball the number one competitive sport for women in the U.S. is increasingly popular among fans, and the NCAA "Final Four" for the women's teams always has high TV ratings.

CD2,TR58

C Listen to the speakers from the Gators basketball team and answer the questions about their conversation.

1. What assumption does Coach Lyons express?

   _____

2. What belief does Rina express?

   _____

3. What impression does Vanessa express?

   _____

4. What message does Coach Lyons express?

   _____

5. What recommendation did Coach Lyons express?

   _____

■ COMMUNICATE

D **GROUP WORK** Discuss the image of athletes in your cultures. Do star athletes serve as role models for young people? What lessons should young people learn from them? Talk about the image of female and male athletes in the media. Then, share your ideas and beliefs with your classmates.

GRAMMAR AND VOCABULARY Write a composition on one of the topics below. Use as many words as possible from the Content Vocabulary on page 315. Use sentences with noun complements and appositives to express some of your ideas.

Topic 1: Do people in your culture share the assumption that participating in sports is a crucial part of growing up? Use two or three sayings, proverbs, or clichés from your language to explain the beliefs, ideas, and messages about participation in sports.

Topic 2: Many Americans share the belief that young people should participate in sports to prepare them for "the game of life." Do you agree with the assumption that young people learn important values for their future when they participate in sports at school or in sports clubs? Give concrete examples to support your opinion.

PROJECT Interview at least two female students on your campus about their participation in sports. Ask about the following information, and make a brief oral report on the information in your next class meeting.

1. what sports each of them participated in during their school years
2. whether they participated on a varsity or a school team
3. whether they know any women students who have athletic scholarships
4. how much support women's teams have on your campus or in your area

 INTERNET Go online to sports websites, such as www.espn.com, www.sportsillustrated.cnn.com, or www.msn.foxsports.com, or check the website of your local newspaper for the sports report. Compare the photos of male and female athletes. Try to find photos of men and women who compete in the same sport. Do the photos demonstrate that the gender of the athlete is important for the style of photo on the website? Prepare a short oral report on your research.

Political Science: Political Parties

■ CONTENT VOCABULARY

Look up the words and phrases below that you do not know and enter them in your vocabulary journal. Write each word's part of speech, a definition, and an example sentence. Try to include them in your discussion and writing below.

an adherent	a campaign	to downgrade	to oust
to advocate	a catch-all	an elite	to overgeneralize
autonomous	a constituent	partisan politics	

■ THINK ABOUT IT

In the United States, people often avoid talking about politics and religion with people that they do not know very well. Do your family members or people that you know also avoid these topics under similar circumstances? Why, or why not? Discuss your ideas with a classmate.

In your writing journal, write for five minutes about the questions below. When you are finished, share your ideas with the class.

In your opinion, are young people in your country interested in politics? Who has more interest in politics—older people or younger people? Why?

■ GRAMMAR IN CONTENT

CD2,TR59

A Read and listen to the passage below. The words in bold in the text are logical connectors.

Who Do American Political Parties Really Represent?

In broad terms, political parties are organized in three ways: by geography, by economic interests, and by ideology. These divisions are by no means mutually exclusive; **to the contrary**, geography and economic interests often coincide, only to be divided by ideology.

For example, in the 1850s, the Democratic Party was dominated by the southern farmers who owned large cotton and tobacco plantations worked by slaves. To keep the loyalty of this key constituency, the Democratic Party supported slavery, which was an economic issue in the South but an ideological and moral issue in the North. Opposition to slavery on principle became the preserve of the Liberty Party (1840–48) and eventually of the Republican Party. For the Free Soil Party (1848–54), also, the issue of slavery was economic, but from a different viewpoint. The Free Soil Party did not challenge slavery in the South, **but** it did oppose the spread of slavery into western territories in order to prevent slave labor from competing with free white settlers.

For over a century, the Republican Party managed to capture the White House and a majority in Congress without carrying a single state of the former Confederate States of America.

Some parties have evolved on the state level, such as the Law and Order Party (1841–51) in Rhode Island, the Farmer-Labor Party (1918–44) in Minnesota, and the Liberal Party (1944–) in New York. These state parties succeeded in gaining power within a single state, but never spread elsewhere. They nevertheless had the potential of playing a national role by affecting the electoral college vote in presidential elections and by influencing policies of national parties seeking to capture the loyalty of their adherents.

It is tempting, and not entirely misleading, to see broad economic issues at the heart of the differences between the major parties, with Democrats broadly presenting themselves as representatives of working people and Republicans as representatives of the business sector. But that division ignores important sets of issues that are not economic in nature. Social issues have long played an important part in party loyalty. Such issues range from political rights for minorities to women's rights to abortion to government regulation of individual behavior, the use of drugs, for example. Social issues often cut across economic or class lines and across regional lines, serving to unite voters whose economic interests might be widely divergent or even antithetical. When these issues involve deeply held religious beliefs, as they often have, they can be compelling to some voters. Examples of religion playing a key role range from the anti-Catholic, anti-immigrant sentiments of the Know-Nothing Party (1849–57) to arguments over reciting prayers or including religious symbols in public buildings and public schools.

Given that such a wide variety of topics and issues become embroiled in the process of choosing a government, it is no wonder that the beliefs and actions of political parties fail to fit into neat, consistent categories of ideology, geography, or economics. They are, **rather,** part of the complex swirl of human affairs known as politics.

---

mutually exclusive: things that cannot occur at the same time or under the same conditions

the preserve: an exclusive area of influence or power

the electoral college: the group of elected representatives that officially elects the U.S. president

an adherent: a supporter

antithetical: directly opposite

a sentiment: a thought, viewpoint

given that: acknowledged, assumed

a swirl: a twisting motion or that figure created by such a motion

Sample Sentences	Notes
Some political parties don't have many members, **so** they can't get their ideas put into policy. (= *informal*) Some political parties have very few members; **therefore**, they have little chance of changing government policy. (= *more formal*)	Use various types of connectors to make your ideas clearer and your English more sophisticated. You should learn the differences among connectors grouped by meaning to express yourself more effectively. The differences can be in style and/or in meaning.
Political parties used to represent particular social classes or elites, **but** now major parties try to attract big segments of the population. American voters in one region often agree on economic issues, **yet** their religious values may separate them. **While** the British Labour Party started as a party supported by trade unions, nowadays many businesspeople support it. Many political scientists have predicted that political parties would die by now; **nonetheless**, parties in many countries continue to attract new supporters. Many political scientists predicted that political parties would die by now; **instead**, parties have adapted to new technologies and people's concern about social issues.	EXPRESSING CONTRAST: • Coordinating conjunction: *but* • Subordinating conjunctions: *while, whereas* (= more formal) • Logical connectors: *however, in contrast, nevertheless, on the other hand, nonetheless* CONTRADICTING AN EXPECTATION: • Coordinating conjunction: *yet* • Logical connectors: *rather, instead, to/on the contrary* Follow the rules of punctuation for each type of connector. See Lessons 12 and 13. Other *connectors* include therefore, thus, furthermore, and consequently.

B Read over your journal entry, and <u>underline</u> at least one sentence that you can revise to include a logical connector from the chart above. Write your revised sentence(s) below.

_____

_____

_____

C Edit the texts to add correct punctuation and capital letters. In some cases, there may be more than one possible solution.

1. Before World War II, political parties in Europe and the U.S. represented various segments of society such as the working class. ~~during~~ *During* and after the war, thousands of women joined the labor force yet the political importance of the working class decreased as more and more people became part of the middle class while women didn't earn high wages they contributed significantly to their family income.

2. After World War II most major political parties became "catch-all" parties according to Kirchheimer who coined this terminology catch-all parties try to appeal to the general population by becoming less ideological such parties downgrade issues and interests nevertheless these parties can usually be defined as leaning more to the right or to the left.

3. Despite their left-wing/right-wing division catch-all parties focus on shifting the voters in the center of the political spectrum to their side they tend to "sell" their issues and solutions to the voting public in contrast smaller special interest groups advocate specific views on a particular issue to the general population.

4. It is often difficult to explain the differences between catch-all parties because they often sell their image more strongly than their issues or solutions to social or economic problems party officials feel that such marketing strategies will lead to victory on election day on the contrary many voters especially young ones are alienated from politics by such strategies.

D Reread the text at the beginning of the lesson, and (circle) the other examples of connectors from this lesson. Then, answer the questions below on a separate piece of paper.

1. Do all of the examples in the text follow the punctuation rules for these connectors? What are the "mistakes"?

2. Which connector(s) did the author use most frequently?

3. Which connector(s) did you find in the middle of a clause? What kind of punctuation did the author use? Why?

4. Use a different connector to revise clauses connected with the coordinating conjunction *but*.

E Select the correct connector, and state the reason for your choice.

1. The way that reporters use the terms "red state" or "blue state" gives the impression that these names are well-established. The major TV networks only started using "red" for Republican and "blue" for Democratic consistently in 2000.

   (a.) however   b. on the contrary   c. either a or b

   Reason: *The second sentence expresses a correction of the first sentence, but it isn't a contradiction of expectation.*

2. Residents of major cities in agricultural regions may well support the philosophy of one American political party. Farm- and ranch-owners often consider their interests better represented by the other major party.

   a. while   b. whereas   c. either a or b

   Reason: _____

3. Virginia is traditionally a Republican state. A popular former governor was a Democrat.

   a. but   b. yet   c. either a or b

   Reason: _____

4. The major political parties count on continuing support from Americans who become members. To get their candidates elected, each party also has to attract independent voters during the campaign season.

   a. on the other hand   b. instead   c. either a or b

   Reason: _____

5. Before the age of catch-all parties, families tended to support the same party from generation to generation. Contemporary catch-all parties risk losing such loyal members because the parties don't seem to represent strong positions anymore.

   a. however   b. but   c. either a or b

   Reason: _____

6. Being independent appeals to many younger citizens. American college campuses still have clubs for students who strongly support the Republican Party or the Democratic Party.

   a. instead   b. nevertheless   c. either a or b

   Reason: _____

7. Many people think that there are only a few political parties in the United States because they usually hear only about Democrats and Republicans. American voters have a wide range of choices, from the Communist Party USA to the Green Party.

   a. on the contrary   b. but   c. either a or b

   Reason: _____

F Complete the sentences in the different conversations below with a clause, and add the correct punctuation.

Tyrell: No political party seems to speak to me. How can I get excited about participating in the political process?

Takashi: Maybe you don't care right now; nevertheless *,the decisions that politicians make can impact your future! ,it's your duty, isn't it?* Don't you worry about that?
(1)

Tyrell: Of course, I think about the future however

_____
(2)

Dave: What do you think of the political parties back in your home country?

Maria: To tell you the truth, I can't really see any difference among the largest ones. Last year the majority in our Parliament changed. The opposition party has been in power since then yet

_____
(3)

Omar: Maria, you're so negative. Haven't you been following the debates? The new majority leader has proposed an educational reform, and they are discussing new environmental laws whereas

_____
(4)

Maria: Yeah, they're always talking and discussing instead

_____
(5)

Susan: I don't know very much about the political parties in your country. Do university students pay much attention to politics?

Jeung Ae: Some students are very active in politics and often demonstrate in the streets about different issues on the other hand

_____
(6)

Susan: It sounds like you aren't very concerned about the effect of politicians and their policies on your life or on the future.

Jeung Ae: On the contrary, _____
(7)

G On a separate piece of paper, write a paragraph about the differences between the Libertarian Party and the Green Party.

Issue/Viewpoint	Libertarian Party (1971- present)	Green Party (1989-present)
primary emphasis	reduce the size and role of government	limit the powers of corporations
taxes	opposes all taxes	opposes unfair taxes
education	no compulsory education; no tax money for education	more tax money should go to schools in poor areas
foreign policy	cut defense spending; quit the United Nations	cut defense spending and give more money to social welfare
health care	no tax money for any social welfare program	national health insurance for all

Candidates from smaller, more issue-oriented political parties like the Libertarian and Green parties also participate in the U.S. political process. Whereas the Green Party seeks to limit the role of corporations in American life, the Libertarian Party advocates reducing the role of government.

■ **COMMUNICATE**

H **PAIR WORK** Make a list of the issues that are important to citizens in your community. Compare and contrast these ideas with a partner.

While some people oppose the public display of religious symbols, this is not an issue where I come from.

■ GRAMMAR IN CONTENT

A Reread the text at the beginning of this lesson, and <u>underline</u> five sentences that have just one clause with more than two verb forms in them.

Complex Sentences: Review	
Sample Sentences	**Notes**
Analysts advised that party leaders reveal the truth about their financial situation. ↓ *Analysts advised them to reveal . . .* *Analysts advised revealing the . . .* Some single-issue parties are quite popular in certain regions, yet they never win in a general election. ↓ *Despite being quite popular in certain regions, some single-issue parties . . .* There are many laws against accepting large sums of money for political campaigns. ↓ *Political campaigns are not supposed to accept large sums of money . . .* A political party that takes a firm stand on an issue may not have widespread support in the general population. ↓ *A political party taking a firm stand . . .*	In addition to using a variety of connectors between clauses, you can express your ideas by using different types of sentences, both simple and complex. Make your writing more complex and dynamic by incorporating various verb structures in your main clauses. Do this by: • using more gerund or infinitive complements • using more gerunds as objects of prepositions • expressing your attitudes and interpretations more effectively with modals • using more participial and reduced forms

B Revise the sentences below and on the next page so that they have only one clause.

1. In each House of Congress, the leaders of the major and minority parties may propose ~~that they suspend~~ *suspending* partisan politics during times of crisis.

2. The majority leader in the U.S. Senate functions as a senator from his or her home state; in addition, the majority leader takes responsibility for expressing the party's position on important issues.

3. Sometimes the minority leader in the Senate has to acknowledge that they don't have enough votes to block the passage of a law.

4. Despite the fact that the U.S. vice president acts as the presiding officer of the U.S. Senate, the vice president has little real power in the Senate.

5. In the House of Representatives the rules require that members of the majority party elect a leader who is called the Speaker of the House.

6. A speaker usually has a moderate political ideology and strong parliamentary skills; as a result, the speaker will be able to guide legislation through the House.

7. An effective Speaker of the House must often persuade members of Congress that they should support legislation that is preferred by the majority party.

CD2,TR60

C **Listen to each part of the interview of Senator Maura Koloski and answer each comprehension question using a single clause with a modal.**

1. How does Senator Koloski interpret the low attendance at her speech?

   Students may/might/could consider listening to a speech a waste of time.

2. What is Senator Koloski's alternative to making a speech to young people?

   _____

3. What part of her message does the senator predict that students will care about?

   _____

4. What does Senator Koloski assume that students worry about?

   _____

5. According to the senator, what is the duty of elected officials?

   _____

6. What position does the senator consider a necessity in order to control tuition costs?

   _____

■ COMMUNICATE

D **GROUP WORK** Think of an issue that can serve as the basis for a new political party. (For example, the environment is the main issue behind "Green" parties.) Then, brainstorm strategies that this party should use to attract young voters. Write a brief, dynamic memo with your strategies to the party leadership.

GRAMMAR AND VOCABULARY Write a composition on one of the topics below. Use as many words as possible from the Content Vocabulary on page 325. Use various types of complex sentences and connectors to express your ideas.

Topic 1: Contrast the attitudes toward politics and political parties of people of your generation with those of the older generation in your country or culture. Use concrete examples.

Topic 2: In his book *Politics,* the Greek philosopher Aristotle (384–322 BCE) wrote "Man is by nature a political animal." Do you agree or disagree? Give concrete examples to support your opinion.

PROJECT Interview at least one student on your campus about national political parties. Find out the following information, and make a brief oral report on your findings at your next class meeting.

1. What are the main parties?
2. What are the main differences between the parties?
3. What are the most important political issues for college students?
4. Who are the most effective political leaders today?

 INTERNET Go online to the website www.elections.ca to find out some information about political parties in Canada. On the website, under Information for You, select "Political Parties" / "List of Registered Political Parties and Parties Eligible for Registration." On this webpage, select one of the parties and read their website. Make a short oral report on one or two issues that the party presents on its website.

A Complete the conditional sentences, using the words in parentheses in the appropriate forms to complete the ideas in the sentences. Add *not* where necessary.

1. If Megan's immune system _____ (compromise) by her stressful lifestyle, she _____ (recover) from surgery more quickly last month.

2. Some people think that Megan _____ (recuperate) by now if she _____ (weaken) her immune system by sleeping too little and eating an unhealthy diet.

3. _____ (she/realize) the effect of her lifestyle on her health, obviously, she _____ (modify) her behavior to strengthen her body.

4. If she _____ (known) then what she _____ (know) now, she _____ (be) more careful.

5. Megan _____ (be able) to participate in her normal activities right now if she _____ (take care) of herself before.

6. Even if she _____ (change) her lifestyle, it _____ (take) some months to see the positive effects.

7. If only she _____ (listen) to the advice of her friends and family a long time ago!

8. Unless she _____ (make) up her mind to live a less stressful life, Megan's general health _____ (improve) very much.

B (Circle) the words that correctly complete the idea of the sentence.

1. Many astrobiologists share the belief (which / that) life forms in the universe may have similar properties to some creatures on Earth.

2. How many researchers support the recommendation that their submersible (return / returns) to the black hole to gather new data?

3. Marine biologists, (notably / i.e.) astrobiologists, have made a number of interesting claims about life forms in outer space based on their research on underwater creatures.

4. The (geologist John Edmond / geologist, John Edmond,) was one of the people who discovered the first hydrothermal vents deep on the ocean floor near the Galapagos Islands.

5. It was the variety of life forms at the black smoker (that / which) surprised John Edmond and the other geologists on the research team.

6. It wasn't the variety of the life forms (but / rather) the size of the life forms that impressed the geologists.

7. It was perceptive (for / of) the geologists to call marine biologists about their discovery immediately upon their return from the Galapagos Islands.

8. At the beginning of the research about black smokers it was risky (for / of) the biologists to spend too much time at such ocean depths.

9. Research on life forms around black smokers may seem to be relevant to life on planets with water; (on the other hand, / on the contrary,) the research demonstrates that life forms can flourish in conditions previously considered too hostile for life.

10. Astrobiologists have found other life forms in extremely hostile environments; (while, / nevertheless,) creatures near black smokers continue to be the focus of their research.

LEARNER LOG Check (✔) *Yes* or *I Need More Practice.*

Lesson	I Can Use . . .	Yes	I Need More Practice
26	*It* Clefts and *It* in Subject Position with Adjective Complements		
27	Past Counterfactuals and Inverted Word Order in Conditional Clauses		
28	Conditional Conjunctions, Conditional Verbs with *That* Clauses, and Mixed Times in Conditional Sentences		
29	Noun Complements and Appositives		
30	Logical Connectors and Complex Sentences		

Verbs Followed by Gerunds and Infinitives (See Lesson 10)

Verbs Followed by Gerunds				
admit	defend	finish	postpone	resent
anticipate	delay	give up	practice	resist
appreciate	deny	go on	put off	resume
avoid	detest	imagine	quit	risk
complete	discuss	involve	recall	stop
consider	dislike	keep	recollect	suggest
can't help	enjoy	miss	recommend	take up
can't see	escape	not mind	report	tolerate

Verbs Followed by Infinitives				
agree	claim	hesitate	offer	resolve
appear	consent	hope	plan	seem
ask	decide	intend	prepare	strive
be able	demand	learn	pretend	struggle
beg	deserve	manage	promise	tend
care	fail	mean	refuse	threaten
cause	have to	need	regret	

Verbs Followed by Either an Infinitive or Gerund				
afford	can't stand	dread	love	remember*
attempt*	cease	forget*	prefer	start
begin	commence	hate	propose	stop*
can't bear	continue	like	regret*	try*

*Infinitive and gerund objects differ in meaning.

Adjectives of Emotion

afraid	glad	proud	sad	thankful
angry	grateful	resentful	sorry	

Adjectives That Describe Behavior

arrogant	courageous	greedy	silly	wrong
brave	crazy	impetuous	stingy	
careful/careless	foolish	nice	sweet	
considerate/ inconsiderate	generous	perceptive	wise/unwise	

Adjectives Related to Truth and Understanding

apparent	clear	likely/unlikely	plain	true
certain	evident	obvious	possible/impossible	well-known

Adjectives That Describe or Evaluate an Experience

admirable	dangerous	embarrassing	interesting	shocking
amusing	deplorable	entertaining	odd	simple
annoying	difficult	fortunate/unfortunate	peculiar	surprising
awkward	disappointing	fun	remarkable	tough
commendable	disturbing	hard	risky	understandable
convenient/ inconvenient	easy	inconceivable	safe	upsetting

■ **Adjective** An adjective describes a noun. Example: *That's a **small** desk.*

■ **Adverb** An adverb describes the verb of a sentence or an adjective. Examples: *He is **very** smart. I run **quickly**.*

■ **Adverb of Frequency** An adverb of frequency tells how often an action happens. Example: *I **always** go to the library after class.*

■ **Affirmative** An affirmative means *yes*.

■ **Article** An article (*a, an,* and *the*) comes before a noun. Example: *I have **a** book and **an** eraser.*

■ **Base Form** The base form of a verb has no tense. It has no ending (*-s* or *-ed*). Examples: ***be, go, eat, take, write***

■ **Clause** A clause is a group of words that has a subject and a verb. Example: ***Harry likes** college.*

■ **Comparative Form** A comparative form of an adjective or adverb is used to compare two things. Example: *I am **taller** than you.*

■ **Consonant** The following letters are consonants: ***b, c, d, f, g, h, j, k, l, m, n, p, q, r, s, t, v, w, x, y, z.***

■ **Contraction** A contraction is made up of two words put together with an apostrophe. Example: ***She's** my friend.* (She is = she's)

■ **Count Noun** Count nouns are nouns that we can count. They have a singular and a plural form. Examples: ***book – books, nurse – nurses***

■ **Frequency Expressions** Frequency expressions answer *How often* questions. Examples: ***once a week, three times a week, every day***

■ **Imperative** An imperative sentence gives a command or instructions. An imperative sentence usually omits the word *you*. Example: ***Open** the door.*

■ **Information Questions** Questions that ask *what, when, who, how,* or *which*.

■ **Intransitive** Intransitive verbs do not have an object.

■ **Irregular Verbs** See Appendix 3.

■ **Linking Verb** A linking verb connects the subject of a sentence to a noun, adjective, or prepositional phrase.

■ **Modal** Some examples of modal verbs are ***can, could, should, will, would, must.***

■ **Negative** Means *no*.

■ **Noncount Noun** A noncount noun is a noun that we don't count. It has no plural form. Examples: ***water, money, rice***

■ **Noun** A noun is a word for a person, a place, or a thing. Nouns can be singular (only one) or plural (more than one).

■ **Object** The object of the sentence follows the verb. It receives the action of the verb. Example: *Kat wrote a **paragraph.***

■ **Object Pronoun** Use object pronouns (*me, you, him, her, it, us, them*) after the verb or preposition. Example: *Kat wore **it**.*

- **Phrasal Verb** A verb followed by a particle, such as *point out, think over,* and *turn in.*

- **Plural** Plural means more than one. A plural noun usually ends with *-s* or *-es.* Examples: *The book**s** are heavy. The bus**es** are not running.*

- **Possessive Form** The possessive form of a noun has an apostrophe: *the teacher's class, Jupiter's moons.* Possessive pronouns *(my, mine, our, ours, his, her, hers, their, theirs, its, your, yours)* do not use an apostrophe.

- **Preposition** A preposition is a short, connecting word. Examples: *about, above, across, after, around, as, at, away, before, behind, below, by, down, for, from, in, into, like, of, on, out, over, to, under, up, with*

- **Punctuation (. , ' ?)** Punctuation marks are used to make writing clear (for example: periods, commas, apostrophes, question marks).

- **Regular Verb** A regular verb forms its past tense with *-d* or *-ed.* Example: *He lived in Mexico.*

- **Sentence** A sentence is a group of words that contains a subject and a verb and expresses a complete thought.

- **Singular** Means one.

- **Stative Verb** Stative verbs have no action. They do not often take the progressive form. Examples: *love, like, think, own, understand, want*

- **Subject** The subject of the sentence tells who or what the sentence is about. Example: *The **water** does not taste good.*

- **Subject Pronoun** Use subject pronouns (*I, you, he, she, it, we, they*) in place of a subject noun. Example: ***They*** (= the books) are on the desk.

- **Tense** A verb has tense. Tense shows when the action of the sentence happened.

    Simple Present: *She occasionally **reads** before bed.*

    Present Progressive: *He **is thinking** about it now.*

    Simple Past: *I **talked** to him yesterday.*

- **Transitive** Transitive verbs have an object.

- **Verb** Verbs are words of action or state. Example: *I **go** to work every day. Joe **stays** at home.*

- **Verb of Perception** Verbs related to the senses, such as *look, see, watch, hear, listen, taste, smell,* and *feel.*

- **Yes/No Questions** Yes/No questions ask for a *yes* or *no* answer. Example: *Is she from Mexico? **Yes,** she is.*

APPENDIX 4 Common Irregular Verbs

The following chart gives the past and past participles of some common verbs. You must memorize these forms, because they are irregular.

Base Form	Past Tense	Past Participle
be	was, were	been
begin	began	begun
bite	bit	bitten
break	broke	broken
bring	brought	brought
build	built	built
buy	bought	bought
catch	caught	caught
choose	chose	chosen
come	came	come
cost	cost	cost
cut	cut	cut
do	did	done
draw	drew	drawn
drink	drank	drunk
eat	ate	eaten
feel	felt	felt
find	found	found
give	gave	given
go	went	gone
grow	grew	grown
hide	hid	hidden
have	had	had
hear	heard	heard
keep	kept	kept
know	knew	known
make	made	made
pay	paid	paid
read	read	read
say	said	said
see	saw	seen
speak	spoke	spoken
take	took	taken
teach	taught	taught
tell	told	told
think	thought	thought
write	wrote	written

Review: Lessons 1–5
(pages 49–50)

A.
1. The
2. has exceeded
3. had planted
4. the
5. germinated
6. have been harvesting/
   have harvested
7. Ø
8. appears
9. the
10. observed
11. Ø
12. Ø
13. grow
14. am going to develop
15. will send/am going to
    send
16. the
17. Ø
18. the
19. burned down
20. struck/had struck
21. are going to build
22. returns

B.
1. have posed
2. plant
3. cotton
4. the soybean
5. walk
6. had brought; grew
7. for us
8. the barn
9. will have completed
10. have considered

Review: Lessons 6–10
(pages 109–110)

A.
1. b
2. b
3. a
4. c
5. a
6. a
7. b
8. c
9. b
10. a

B.
1. ascertains
2. has decreased
3. must have been
4. could use
5. aren't supposed to
   follow
6. have had to submit
7. to review
8. approving
9. not having considered/
   not considering
10. not being able to begin

Review: Lessons 11–15
(pages 163–164)

A.
1. Thus,
2. While
3. Firstly,
4. Ultimately,
5. Similarly,
6. Both
7. Even though
8. Evidently,

B.
1. a
2. b
3. b
4. b
5. a
6. a
7. b
8. b

Review: Lessons 16–20
(pages 219–220)

A.
1. between
2. through
3. the former
4. the way
5. she would like
6. how long
7. Dr. Phyllis Klein, who
8. favorite nurse, who
9. which
10. to Mrs. Liu

B.
1. No
2. Yes
3. Yes
4. No
5. Yes
6. No

C.
1. is expected/to be
   wrapped
2. being influenced
3. to be selected
4. letting
5. have been required
6. to have been tampered
   with
7. should have been
   warned
8. used to buy

Review: Lessons 21–25 (pages 277–278)

A.
1. (a) that he had to practice serving the ball.
   (b) that he practice serving the ball.
2. (a) (that) she had noticed that his foot touched the line almost every time he served.
   (b) his foot touching the line almost every time he served.
3. (a) that she (had) videotaped him when he had been playing/ was playing doubles with Nick.
   (b) playing doubles with Nick.
4. (a) that she had been able/was able to see clearly how he put a top spin on many of his balls.
   (b) putting a top spin on many of his balls.
5. (a) that he would try harder to control the spin that he put on the balls.
   (b) to try harder to control the spin that he puts on the balls.
6. (a) that he should put in at least 3 hours of practice every day.
   (b) that he put in at least 3 hours of practice every day.
7. (a) if he could show Bob how he served the ball/to show Bob how he serves the ball.
   (b) show Bob how he serves the ball.

B.
1. fascinating
2. amazing
3. amazed
4. frightening
5. scared
6. excited
7. annoyed
8. interested

Review: Lessons 26–30 (pages 335–336)

A.
1. hadn't been compromised; would have recovered
2. could/might have recuperated; hadn't weakened
3. had she realized; would have modified
4. had known; knows; would have been
5. would be able; had taken care
6. changed; would take
7. had listened
8. makes; won't improve

B.
1. that
2. return
3. notably
4. geologist John Edmond
5. that
6. but
7. of
8. for
9. on the contrary,
10. nevertheless,

Words in blue are part of the Content Vocabulary section at the start of each lesson.
Words in black are words glossed with the readings in each lesson.
Words in **bold** are words from the Academic Word List.

Credits

Text Credits

"Survival in Virginia," from *Jamestown 1544–1699,* © 1980, Carl Bridenbaugh, pp. 34–35. By permission of Oxford University Press, Inc.

"If u thnk txt-spk is the deth o nglsh, thnk agin," Allen Grove, *Daily Press,* Feb. 4, 2007, pp. H1, H4.

Principles of Emergency Planning and Management by David Alexander, Oxford University Press, 2002, pp. 4–5. By permission of Oxford University Press, Inc.

"Education in the 'Real World'," from "What's Love Got to Do with It? Making Economics Relevant in Courses on Economic Development," by Janet M. Tanski, in *Putting the Invisible Hand to Work,* eds. KimMarie McGoldrick & Andrea L. Ziegert, U. of Michigan Press, 2002, pp. 254–55.

"The Gullah: Cultural Isolation and Preservation," from Josephine Beoku-Betts, "We Got Our Way of Cooking Things: Women, Food and Preservation of Cultural Identity," *Gender & Society,* Vol. 9, No. 5, October 1995, Clarity Press, Inc. 1998. Reprinted by Permission of SAGE Publications, Inc.

"Old Friends and New Temptations," from *The Total Package* by Thomas Hine, © 1995 by Thomas Hine. By permission of Little Brown & Company.

"Misunderstandings Among Nurses and Patients," by Frances C. MacGregor, from "Uncooperative Patients: Some Cultural Interpretations," January 1967, *The American Journal of Nursing,* Vol. 67, No. 1 (1967): 88–91.

"Bounceability," by Brian H. Kaye, *Golf Balls, Boomerangs and Asteroids,* pp. 8–9. 1996. Copyright Wiley-VCH Verlag GmbH & Co. KGaA. Reproduced with permission.

"Truth or Just Clichés?" from pp. 6–8 of *Social Aspects of Sport, 3rd ed.* by Eldon E. Snyder. Copyright © 1989 by Simon & Schuster. Reprinted by permission of Pearson Education, Inc.

"Who Do American Political Parties Really Represent?" from *Flash Focus: Political Parties,* 2005, Scholastic Library Publishing, pp. 4–5.

Illustrators

InContext Publishing Partners: p. 7 (bottom)

Precision Graphics: pp. 4, 7 (top), 10–11, 13, 21, 26–27, 29, 34, 37–39, 42, 46, 56, 61, 70, 76–78, 83, 88, 95, 100, 107, 117, 121, 126, 134, 152, 155, 160–161, 175, 192 (bottom), 197, 202, 217, 222, 229, 231, 241, 246–247, 250–251, 257, 263, 266, 275, 282, 301, 309, 319, 326, 331

David Preiss/Munro Campagna.com: pp. 14, 60, 168, 190–191, 192 (top), 280

Photo Credits

Page 2: © Stock Connection Blue/Alamy   Page 18: © Chip Somodevilla/Getty Images   Page 24: © Nick Hanna/Alamy   Page 32: © Sean Gallup/Getty Images   Page 51: © Steve Hamblin / Alamy/RF   Page 64: © wsr/Alamy   Page 67: © Photos.com/RF   Page 74: © imagebroker/Alamy   Page 83: © AP Photo/Bikas Da   Page 86: © AP Photo/Al Schell, Pool   Page 98: (All photos) © Photos.com/RF   Page 112: © JUPITERIMAGES/Comstock Images/Alamy/RF   Page 124: © PYMCA/Alamy   Page 126: © Scott Olson/Getty Images   Page 127: © Andrew Fox/Alamy   Page 132: © AP Photo/Don Ryan   Page 135: © AP Photo/Rich Pedroncelli   Page 144: © Jim West/Alamy   Page 152: © Bridget Webber/Stone/Getty Images   Page 161: © Shutterstock/RF   Page 166: © AP Photo/ Charlotte Observer, Layne Bailey   Page 180: (Left) © Photos. com/RF, (Right) © Tetra Images/Getty Images/RF   Page 200: © kolvenbach / Alamy/RF   Page 206: © wsr/Alamy   Page 207: © Shutterstock/RF   Page 210: © Peter Arnold, Inc. / Alamy   Page 224: © Andrew Barker/Shutterstock/RF   Page 234: © Eadweard Muybridge/Time Life Pictures/Getty Images   Page 236: © Steve Cukrov/Shutterstock/RF   Page 239: © Susan Meiselas / Magnum   Page 240: © James Quine / Alamy   Page 244: © AP Photo/Damian Dovarganes   Page 247: (Left) © Paul Nicklen/National Geographic/Getty Images (Right) © Vladimir Pcholkin/Taxi/Getty Images   Page 254: © Christie's Images/ The Bridgeman Art Library   Page 260: © Ralph Morse/Time Life Pictures/Getty Images   Page 261: © 2008 Estate of Pablo Picasso/Artists Rights Society (ARS), New York.   Page 262: © Oriental Museum, Durham University, UK/The Bridgeman Art Library   Page 266: © Chris Hondros/Getty Images   Page 268: © Michael Malyszko/Taxi/Getty Images   Page 274: © John Vink / Magnum   Page 292: © AP Photo/Louis Lanzano   Page 301: © ShutterStock/RF   Page 304: © Peter David/Taxi/Getty Images   Page 306: © Sebastiano del Piombo/The Bridgeman Art Library/Getty Images   Page 312: © Time Life Pictures/ NASA/Time Life Pictures/Getty Images   Page 313: © EMORY KRISTOF AND ALVIN CHANDLER/National Geographic   Page 316: © AP Photo/Hamid Jalaludin   Page 318: © AP Photo/str   Page 322: © AP Photo/Michael Conroy